the BANQUET'S WISDOM

A SHORT HISTORY OF THE THEOLOGIES OF THE LORD'S SUPPER

Wisdom says, *"Come and eat my bread, drink the wine I have drawn! Leave foolishness behind and you will live, go forward in the ways of perception."* (Proverbs 9:5–6)

GARY MACY

D1224545

Paulist Press ■ New York ■ Mahwah, N.J.

ACKNOWLEDGMENTS

The Publisher gratefully acknowledges use of the following materials: selections from *The Eucharist* (The Message of the Fathers, vol. 7), by Daniel J. Sheerin, © 1986 Michael Glazier, Wilmington; selections from *Huldrych Zwingli, Writings*, Volume 2, translated by H. Wayne Pipkin, Pickwick Publications, Allison Park, Pennsylvania; a reprint from *This Is My Body: Luther's Contention for the Real Presence in the Sacrament of the Altar*, by Herman Sasse, copyright © 1959 Augsburg Publishing House, used by permission of Augsburg Fortress; selections from *Canons and Decrees of the Council of Trent*, translated by H. Schroeder, B. Herder Book Co., St. Louis, Missouri, copyright © 1941.

Library of Congress Cataloging-in-Publication Data

Macy, Gary.
    The Banquet's wisdom : a short history of the theologies of the
Lord's supper / by Gary Macy.
        p.   cm.
    Includes index.
    ISBN 0-8091-3309-1
    1. Lord's supper—History.   I. Title.
BV823.M359   1992
234'.163'09—dc20   91-45240
                                                                  CIP

Published by Paulist Press
997 Macarthur Blvd.
Mahwah, N.J. 07430

Printed and bound in the United States of America

Contents

To my aunt and godmother,
Jo LaValle
who taught me much about living out the presence of the Lord

Preface

In a book of this sort, so little is truly original, and so much is the result of listening enraptured to so many good teachers, that I fear that the only parts of the book to which I can honestly take credit are the errors. I cannot enumerate the many outstanding scholars, living and dead, whose lives and works influenced this book but it would be ungrateful indeed not to mention those who tried their utmost to steer me straight once they saw that I was actually going to finish the book. First of all, I must thank Bernard Cooke, who patiently read through the drafts of this endeavor. His suggestions, and the timely appearance of his book, *The Distancing of God*, forced me to rethink and then rewrite both the chapters on the early church and the conclusion of the book. For more years than I care to remember, he has been my teacher, and for this I am blessed indeed. Joseph Powers, Walter Principe, Pierre-Marie Gy and Keith Egan also patiently slogged through different versions of the text and saved me from many embarrassments. I offer special thanks as well to my long-time colleague at the University of San Diego, Jack Lindquist, whose comments helped steer this cradle Catholic through the intricacies of the reformation. I also owe a debt of thanks to Jean French from Bard College who edited the final text in an act of sheer charity while we were colleagues at an NEH seminar.

The University of San Diego allowed me time off from teaching by awarding me a number of Faculty Research Grants, and Paulist Press, especially in the person of Lawrence Boadt, showed

Job-like patience while waiting for me to finish this book. To both of these institutions, my heartfelt thanks.

Finally, I would like to apologize to my wife, Saralynn, who patiently endured the impatience, anger, sloth, and self-pity which accompanied the different stages of this work.

Introduction

The eucharist, the Lord's supper, is a sign of Christian unity, and yet, since the time of the reformation, the celebration of the eucharist, and, more particularly, thought about the eucharist, remain the greatest barriers to that Christian unity. In the past few decades, attempts have been made to lessen the differences in the forms of celebration of the eucharist. A person unfamiliar with Christianity could, for instance, now attend Roman Catholic, Anglican, Lutheran, and several Reformed services and detect only minor differences between them. The barriers of theological understanding, however, stand more firmly. The Christian communities mentioned above remain in disunity, unable, or unwilling, to recognize the mutual legitimacy of their strikingly similar ceremonies.

To put thus simply the problem does not, unfortunately, make the problem a simple one. Four hundred years of bitterness, war, alienation, and political and social oppression have made all sides in the dispute defensive, protective, and, even in an age of ecumenism, wary of selling their hard-won heritage short. Ideas *are* that for which people die, and all too many people have died over the question of how the celebration of life over death ought to be understood. This is a sad and ironic history and should not be minimized or ignored in our attempts to heal the wounds of disunity.

Still, in the history of Christianity, four hundred years is a short time. For over fifteen hundred years, Christians were, for the most part, "in communion." (Eastern and western Christians certainly had their differences over the eucharist, on and off, during that long period, but rarely was it suggested that their worship at the Lord's supper was not true Christian worship.) The Christian people, as a whole, have a much longer history of unity than of

3

disunity. This simple historical observation raises some interesting questions. How did we as a community get from there to here? How did the earlier centuries manage to maintain the communion which seems so to elude us? This book will try to uncover some of the answers to these questions. Perhaps in rediscovering our former union, we Christians may find the grounds for overcoming our present disunion.

1

Whose History Is It?

History seems a deceptively simple enterprise. One simply relates what happened in the past. It happens every evening. Dan Rather relates the day's events and ends his recitation by assuring us (one way or another) that "that's the way it is." Few people seriously doubt that what they have just observed is "history in the making," or at least all the history made that day. Now surely, relating, say, the history of the eucharist should just be a simple matter of stringing together a series of ecclesiastical "that's the way it was" presentations, and you would have it. Except that you wouldn't have it. Not really.

Think back to last evening's news. Was what you saw on television really "the way it was"? Did your own day consist of the series of events described by Dan Rather? Probably not, and yet your own day was more "the way it was" for *you* than the events presented on the news. Was the news you saw "the way it was" for people in Siberia, or Sri Lanka, or Cape Town, or Chulucanas, Peru? Almost certainly not; news from these places usually holds no interest for American audiences. No, the news isn't literally "the way it was" for everyone at once; no one expects it to be. The news is always *someone's* news—news in which a particular group of people is interested.

Someone has to ask *something* about what's going on, and then *someone else* has to explain it. Notice that all these someones are in the present, not the past. Try a little experiment. Suppose for a moment that you were going to produce one news story for tomorrow evening. It can be any subject you want, but it has to be interesting. Your first job would be to pick a good story. Not everything can fit into even an hour-long show, and your story is only one of many. So, probably, you would leave out the fact that you and your spouse just had a baby after years of wanting one. Although the biggest event in your life, it wouldn't be that interesting to the American public in general. You would need to eliminate all sorts of important events and just pick one. That would be your first decision, and this decision would be influenced by what *you* thought was important, that is, what one very particular person in the present thought about something in the past.

The next thing you would do is get to work to uncover the past. This is harder than it seems, since the past is, well, past. All the people you interview, and all the documents you read, and all the video tape you watch would exist in the present. If they only existed in the past, you couldn't talk to them or read them, or watch it. All of the past which we have is in the present. Worse, present witnesses to the event are often biased. To counter this, you would have to talk to as many people as possible, check their stories, read background material, and, if possible, watch video tape of the event. Your second great decision would be to decide what was really going on here. Once again, you notice, *you* are deciding. This time, your decision will be very much influenced by your own interest in the event, and your own stand on the rights and wrongs of the affair. If, for instance, your story was about the abortion issue, your own feelings and beliefs on this issue would probably be more influential than you think in your evaluation of the evidence.

And then, after you interview twelve people, and read twenty documents, and watch two videos of the event, your producer would say, "OK, you've got ten minutes to fit that in between Russia and Afghanistan. Make it good!" How can you say everything you know about the event in a way that will capture "what really happened"? You will need to judge your audience well. What can you assume they already know? What will they need to know to understand what you are going to say? What will hold their interest? So you pick your best video footage, and most insightful comments, and your segment of the news airs for ten minutes. Exciting, huh?

Congratulations! Your brilliant analysis has won you an Emmy, and the offers from movies and TV are pouring in. Before you rush off to your new career, however, take a moment to ask yourself: Was your brilliant news story really what happened? Well, you would have to admit, astute as it was, it wasn't what happened. It didn't even tell all of what you knew about the event, and all of what you knew about the event was not all there was to know. Another person with other interests and other skills would have picked a different story, or even presented the same story in a very different way. (And probably not won an Emmy, of course!) To actually recreate the past, we would have to live it all over again for the first time, and we can't do that. We only have the present, and human beings who interpret that present to discover the past.

Now this means that, far from being an impartial observer presenting "just the facts," you were an *interested* party interpreting what remains from the past in order to explain that past to other interested parties (viewers) in the present. You were subtly and not so subtly influenced by your own historical, religious, social, political and economic history. How could it be otherwise? To stand outside the human condition (i.e., outside history, religion, society, politics and economics) would mean becoming in-human, ceasing to be human. Now, at last check, only humans were writing and watching the news, and, as it seems that only humans seem interested in doing so, we humans are left with the discomforting knowledge that we have no disinterested news. (But you can keep the Emmy, anyway.)

Now, the temptation remains for people who hold very strong opinions to see only what they want to see, and to hear only what they want to hear. If some of these people happen also to write the news, they could easily misinterpret the evidence. In fact it would be astounding if they didn't. Compare for instance your Emmy-winning story with coverage of the very same event in the *National Enquirer*. Now the writer of this story took the same events, and maybe the same evidence, and came up with a very different and peculiar interpretation. You would immediately notice, however, that the evidence you used so fairly was slightly altered by the *Enquirer*. Parts of quotations were used; some things were ignored completely, while others were blown all out of proportion. Just as people can be careful and scrupulous as you were in your news story, so people can be careless and unscrupulous in their interpretations of the news. Sometimes this is deliberate, and sometimes people are so biased they really believe they are telling the truth.

Now history is very much like the evening news. History is,

oddly enough, not the past, but a particular present understanding
of the past. History even changes. Different historians interpret the
different writings and monuments surviving from the past in very
different ways. British historians of the early nineteenth century
would present a much different account of the colonial rebellion in
the Americas than British historians of the late twentieth century.
Just as there is no disinterested news, so there is no disinterested
history.

This creates all kinds of dangers, the same dangers you ran
into in doing your news report. You had to constantly check your
own biases, and the biases of your witnesses. So must historians.
Because historians are interested parties, the historical profession
has a demanding set of criteria which must be met if a history is to
be accepted as accurate. Historians need these rules because their
own interests can blind them in their interpretation of the past. The
rules cannot make history "objective"; they can keep historians
critically subjective. No histories are perfectly objective; some histories are unacceptably uncritical. No histories are "just the facts";
some histories are not the facts at all. History, alas, has its own
National Enquirers.

Whose History of the Church?

All the problems raised above seem intensified in writing the
history of religion. Historians are not only interested parties, they
are also usually believers. Often church historians seek not only to
explain the past actions of humankind, but also to interpret God's
hand in those actions. The temptation is very strong to see one's
own present beliefs and structures as God's will, and then go on to
understand the past as the more or less obvious revelation that those
beliefs and structures are indeed God's will. The past then becomes
nothing more than a confused or incipient or mistaken present. In
no case, however, is the past simply different from the present, for
the past must always, in this view, be evaluated in its relationship to
God's present will.

Especially when a Christian group understands a particular
tenet of their belief to be central to their own identity, an historian
from within that group will be tempted to understand that tenet as

central to all of Christian history. Historians of Christian groups for whom a hierarchical priesthood is central will expend much time, energy, and even more ingenuity trying to ascertain a clear hierarchical structure in the church from apostolic times on. Christians for whom a hierarchical priesthood is anathema will set their historians the equally difficult task of demonstrating that true Christians never adopted such a structure.

Roman Catholic historians are tempted to rummage through past documents looking for support for the contention that Thomas Aquinas, Trent, and, more recently, Vatican II or the Medellín Conference, fully embody the teachings implicit in earlier centuries. Anglicans are tempted to look for precursors to the Thirty-Nine Articles or the Book of Common Prayer. Lutherans are tempted to search the middle ages for "Lutherans before Luther." Some evangelical historians go so far as to claim that all true Christians went underground at the time of Constantine and did not reappear until the reformation. That little or no historical evidence supports this claim would only prove (for them) the underground nature of the church.

Many, many historians, of course, do not succumb to these temptations. They explain the past in a way that is intelligent and critical, even when their presentations seem to weaken the historical claims of their own group. This takes courage and, even more, great insight into one's own biases. The temptation always remains, for both historians (and Emmy winning news reporters), to see things as they want them to be.

It may seem a bit odd to bring up this subject in a book which is supposed to be dealing with the history of the eucharist, but this problem has so shaped the way each particular Christian understands his or her own history that to present a part of that history as if it were simple and straightforward would be naive, and, in the end, deceptive. Historians of theology, like the evening news staff, must be selective. They often select their materials and form their interpretations in light of their own faith tradition. Especially when one speaks of the eucharist, however, there is more than one tradition of faith, and hence more than one history. In approaching any history of Christianity, the question inevitably arises of whose history is it that is being written.

Ever since the reformation, historians from the different Christian groups have set out to "reclaim" the past in order to show that their own particular stance best embodies the Christian message. These efforts have been so successful that people speak of the history of the Roman Catholic Church, or Anglican Church, or one of the Protestant churches as if somehow that particular group (and only that group) started with the apostles. They forget that none of these groups existed before the reformation. Before the reformation, Christians were simply Christians—eastern and western Christians sometimes, but mostly simply Christians.

The reasons for the creation of these separate histories are understandable enough. Each of the different groups emerging from the reformation felt itself to be under attack by the other groups, and often quite literally was. History became one part of a much larger intellectual defense network which different groups established in order to justify their own claims and strengthen their members. The more fiercely a group felt itself under attack, the more firmly it would hold to its own justifying view of history. Indeed, persecution itself became historical evidence of the correctness of a stance. Assurance was needed that that for which one was suffering was indeed the eternal truth, eternally recognized by Christians, past and present, to be true. Historians addressed themselves to questions with obvious apologetic intent. Was Augustine, for example, really a Catholic or really a Protestant? Which was the more Christian epistle, Romans or Hebrews? Did history show the papacy to be the vicar of Christ or the whore of Babylon? In the midst of intense suffering, and fierce intellectual challenge, the various histories of Christianity emerged. As much defenses of the present as presentations of the past, they helped to comfort, to justify, to offend, and finally to firmly separate the disunited Christian groups.

Whose History of the Lord's Supper?

This tendency was particularly marked in historians treating of the theology of the eucharist. Historians tended to thematize past understandings of the Lord's supper in terms of the reformation debates. The Roman Catholic historian Joseph Geiselmann categorized early eucharistic theologies as either "spiritualist" or "realist" depending on how each author describes the presence of the Lord in the sacrament.[1] Geiselmann could, for example, condemn the "spiritualist" teaching of Ratramnus, a ninth century writer, as heterodox, even though Ratramnus' teachings received no such condemnation in his own time.[2] On the other hand, the Anglican historian A.J. MacDonald maintained that Berengar of Tours, an eleventh century theologian, was a valiant defender of patristic orthodoxy despite Berengar's multiple condemnations.[3] As recently as 1974, the *Oxford Dictionary of the Christian Church* spoke of the Lateran Council of 1215 as affirming that belief in transubstantiation was required by the Christian faith.[4] No contemporary theologian would have so understood the statement of Lateran IV, and it would be many years after the council before such an interpretation of the document would be put forward. What these writers have in common is a tendency to see earlier history in terms of the great reformation debates about the presence of the risen Lord in the sacrament, a debate which still separates many Christians.

To repeat an earlier claim, historians come to their task as interested, not disinterested, parties. Surely this was the case with Geiselmann, MacDonald and the writers of the *Oxford Dictionary*. Without the imposition on the past of present concerns and categories, there would be no history. These authors interpreted the past in order to make the present stances of the various Christian groups intelligible in terms of that past. One need only read the authors themselves to see how admirably they succeeded. Yet one has the feeling more could be said. If Ratramnus' teaching was indeed so different from the present Catholic position, why did the authorities then let it stand? If Berengar was in fact representing the teaching of the fathers, why was he condemned? To answer these questions, what is needed is not more historical documentation, but a different way of looking at those documents.

The different histories of Christianity, and more particularly of the theology of the eucharist, which arose from the reformation disputes were necessary and valuable contributions to the living communities from which they emerged. They gave a sense of purpose and mission to the oppressed. Sadly, they gave an equal sense of purpose and mission to the oppressor. These histories assumed that the present situation of the church was the final product of long development guided by the Spirit. Careful historians could discern a gradual movement toward certain culminating pronouncements of truth (e.g., Trent, the Thirty-Nine Articles, the Augsburg Confession). Whatever did not fit this slow development was to be seen as inexact, tentative, vacillating or simply heretical. What was heretical was to be attacked—whether it existed in the present or in the past.

The social, economic and religious atmosphere out of which these histories arose has gratefully changed. The Christian groups now see themselves more as brothers and sisters than as enemies. With this change, a new understanding of the Christian past is emerging. Christian historians are beginning to see the past as a past common to all Christian groups. More even than this, historians are beginning to see the thought of our Christian sisters and brothers from the past not so much as pale and inadequate reflections of our own thought but as Christian responses more or less adequate to the problems of their own age. In the words of the French historian Yves Congar: "History [is now] understood less as a continual process of 'development,' that is as progress achieved through a gradual unfolding of what was already implicit, and more as a series of formulations of the one content of faith diversifying and finding expression in different cultural contexts."[5]

Just as the ecumenical movement tends to see the many Christian groups as different but complementary expressions of Christian life, so too are historians seeing the Christian past as a series of different but certainly accepted and acceptable modes of Christian living. As the post-reformation understanding of history gave security and mission, for good and evil, to the different Christian groups, so this newer understanding of history challenges us to break out of our old defenses. This new way of reading our history challenges and jars the smugness of our former security. It presents us with forms of Christian living which surprise, delight and sometimes shock us. Jean Leclerq, the great French medieval scholar, has recently pointed out that liturgies exist from the early middle ages that were clearly intended for para-liturgical services held by women.[6] It has long been known that the medieval theologians felt that it was immoral to charge interest simply for the use of another's money. Excessive wealth was not to be used for further gain, but belonged in justice, not charity, to those in need. Here indeed are modes of Christian thought that radically challenge the assumptions of many twentieth century Americans.

These aspects of the past, these "subversive memories" (to use the phrase of the theologian Paul Ricouer) remind us that it was *not* always so. The Christian past is indeed a storehouse, full of treasures, marvels, challenges. The past, seen in this way, keeps us honest. Maybe the way we now understand Christian life is not the best, and certainly not the only, way of living out the Christian message. If Christians in the past have not only lived differently, but lived differently as good Christians, then Christians now may feel freer to change, to grow, to find strength to face diversity in the present and future by accepting the diversity of the Christian past. History becomes a "launching pad" rather than a "fortress," to use the evocative and exciting language of the historian and theologian Walter Principe.[7]

Different ways of understanding Christian history, and the many different Christian histories themselves, offer different insights into that history. All, of course, are subject to the rules of historical research that keep historians from reading their own biases into the past. Indeed, each different perspective can help to offset and reveal the biases of the others. If an historian of either approach allows his or her prejudices to contradict, distort or arbitrarily dismiss the sources left to us from the past, then that interpretation must be judged as a *mis*-interpretation of the past. There may be different ways of understanding Christian history, but there are even more ways of misunderstanding it. To argue for diversity is not to argue for chaos. The temptation unwittingly and unintentionally to distort the past comes as easily to ecumenically minded historians as to those defending their particular tradition. There are risks inherent in any attempt to interpret the Christian past. Yet it seems that a diversity of approaches, a kind of historical pluralism, will not only allow us to uncover more varied aspects of our multifaceted past, but will also serve as a system of checks helping historians uncover the biases with which they approach their task.

The way in which Christians write about their history has changed since the reformation, allowing a plurality of Christian histories. Historians tend now to write books entitled *A History of . . .* rather than *The History of . . .* As the title indicates, this is one of those books, and one of the presuppositions behind the book is that this sort of pluralism is a good thing for the reasons mentioned above.

This introductory chapter has been an attempt to explain in simple, untechnical language some of the questions and presuppositions that led to the writing of this book. It assumes that the different Christian groups have a single, common past that reaches from the time of the apostles to the time of the reformation. Each of the different groups emerging from that past can find its roots there because the past which Christians have inherited is a pluralistic past. What was lost in the reformation was not just Christian unity, but toleration of pluralism. To see our own past as a unity made up of pluralism can give us the confidence to again recover the lost Christian sense of toleration. This book is written with this hope and from this perspective.

A few more words of clarification must be added. This book is primarily about western Christianity. Neither time, nor space, nor competence is sufficient here for me to do justice to the further problems raised by the breach between eastern and western Christianity. Secondly, this book is about the theology of the eucharist, what Christians thought about the celebration of the Lord's supper. Clearly, thinking about the sacrament is a secondary activity, always subordinate to the actual practice. Because this is so, the separation of practice and theory is quite artificial, and, whenever possible, care will be taken to relate the theology to the ceremonial setting upon which it depends. Yet the major disagreements about the eucharist which have arisen between the Christian groups tend to come from thought rather than practice, and one hopes that this very real concern will justify a division between theology and ceremony which would be otherwise unjustifiable.

2

The Origins of Diversity:
The Early Church

The eucharist is first and foremost a ritual meal, a sharing in the life, death and resurrection of Jesus the Christ by the community founded in his name. It is something one does, not something about which one talks. No more important statement can be made about the Lord's supper. It is a celebration, a way of life: a celebration of a way of life. It should not be too surprising, therefore, to learn that the first book written specifically on what the eucharist means for us, and how the eucharist extends God's offer of salvation to us, did not appear on the scene until the ninth century. Indeed, not much more was written on this subject until the eleventh century. For nearly half of Christian history, people lived the eucharist without, frankly, thinking much about it, at least in a formal theological sense. No one needed to. People knew (more or less) what the liturgy meant, and people agreed (more or less) on what role the Lord's supper played in Christian life. There was no need to be more specific, and Christians seemed to be willing to live with the ambiguities which appeared in theory as long as they felt that they were united in practice. Until some serious challenge appeared to both theory and practice, as it would in the eleventh and twelfth centuries, Christians were content to attend to the much more important task of living, worshiping and celebrating the salvation wrought for them.

This is not to say that no one wrote about the eucharist. Christians could hardly explain, defend, and clarify their beliefs without mentioning the central celebration of those beliefs. Bishops gave lessons on the eucharist to the catechumens preparing for their first

15

experience of the Christian rites. The early Christian apologists described the ceremonies and their meaning to a skeptical pagan world. Theologians adverted to the community's understanding of the eucharist in their attempts to meet the challenges of the early christological controversies. From the time of the earliest Christian writers, references to the eucharist were made in order to explain to members and non-members alike what the Christians intended in their worship.

The Scriptural Basis

The ritual meals which the earliest Christians celebrated were simply a continuation of Jesus' custom of sharing the usual Jewish ritual meals with his closest friends. This was a very old and very important Jewish custom. To share food with a person was to share his or her life, and to pledge oneself to the kind of life which that community lived. In the book of Judges, considered by some scholars to contain the oldest stories in Hebrew scripture, Gideon, leader of the Hebrew army, is described as killing those Hebrew people who refused food to his army (Jgs 8:4–21). They had placed themselves outside the Hebrew community by refusing to share its life, and to ritually pledge allegiance to that life in a ritual meal. So when Jesus, on the night before he died, directly associated his own life and imminent death with the great ritual meal of the Jewish community, the passover, the meaning was clear to his friends. He was asking them to share in that life, and, what is more, he was proclaiming that such a life and such a death would bring about a fulfillment of the promises made to Abraham, Isaac, and Jacob. This life and this death would bring about the kingdom of God and the salvation of those who shared that life.

With the resurrection of the Lord, the meaning of such a pledge became even clearer. To share in the life of the Lord would mean sharing in the life of the risen Lord, as well as in the life of sacrifice and obedience which Jesus had lived while on earth. The link was soon made between living a Christian life and celebrating that life in a ritual reenactment of the meals which Jesus shared with his friends. The earliest accounts of these meals simply speak of the "breaking of the bread," referring to the Jewish custom of starting a ritual meal with the blessing and sharing of bread. The author of the Acts of the Apostles described just such a set of circumstances as existing in the early Jerusalem community:

> These remained faithful to the teaching of the apostles, to the brotherhood, to the breaking of bread and to the prayers. The many miracles and signs worked through the apostles made a deep impression on everyone. The faithful lived together and owned everything in common; they sold their goods and possessions and shared out the proceeds among themselves according to what each one needed. They went as a body to the temple every day but met in their houses for the breaking of bread; they shared their food gladly and generously; they praised God and were looked up to by everyone (Acts 2:42–47).

As the good news of the Christian message spread, however, the Jewish background to the community practice of "breaking bread" became less well known and appreciated. The pagan audiences to which the message of Paul and the other missionaries was given had their own ritual meals with which they were familiar. The most common of these was the feast that would follow the sacrifice of an animal or grain or wine to one of the many gods or goddesses of the ancient world. Certain parts of the carcass were burned as an offering to the deity, and the rest was shared in a sort of dinner party or sold to the local meat market. Certain ancient societies, something like the Chamber of Commerce or the Rotary, would occasionally sacrifice an animal in order to hold a kind of picnic or dinner party for community morale. Some of these parties, then as now, could get out of hand, especially if they were dedicated to one of the more enthusiastic of the mystery cults, the popular secret societies of the Roman empire.

The earliest description of the Lord's supper, that given by Paul in his first letter to the Corinthians (1 Cor 11:17–34), was written, it seems, to warn the Corinthians not to celebrate the eucharist as if it were one of these pagan mystery rites. Paul stressed the community nature of the celebration. Christians participate in the body of Christ which is made up of the community itself. To partake in the bread or the cup without living a Christian life would be to invite condemnation. The "bread of life" passage in the gospel of John (Jn 6:26–66) also describes the meaning of the Christian ritual, and, again, may have been written to respond to certain misunderstandings concerning the breaking of the bread. The author stressed the saving union formed between Christ present in the ritual and the worthy participant. Because of our sharing in the life of Christ present through the ritual meal, the author insisted, we will share in immortal life. These two passages, perhaps the most explicit explanations of the eucharist in the New Testament, contain most of the major themes which echo throughout the literature of the early church.

Early Problems

As the Christians moved out into the Roman empire, they encountered many enemies, who were only too glad to spread rumors of the debauchery and immorality of this latest of the many sects of the empire. The ritual meal of the Christians was the cause of some of this scandal. As already expressed in the sixth chapter of John, Christians felt that the risen Lord was truly present for them in the celebration of the ritual meal. Almost certainly, it was the explicit nature of this claim that earned them the accusation of practicing cannibalism. Writing in the early third century, Minucius Felix, a Christian from North Africa, describes the accusations made against the Christians:

> Now the story of how they [the Christians] initiate recruits is as revolting as it is well-known. They coat a baby with batter, to fool the unwary, and they place it before the one to be initiated. The baby is then slaughtered with hidden and secret wounds by the recruit who has been urged on to strike blows which are apparently quite harmless because of the covering of batter. It is unspeakable: they slurp up the baby's blood, and eagerly hand around his limbs. By this victim are they leagued together; by the shared knowledge of this crime they pledge themselves to silence. These rites are more foul than all sacrileges com-

bined. The nature of their "banquet" is well-known. Everyone talks about it, and the speech of our man from Cirta bears witness to it. They meet for the meal on an appointed day, and all their children, sisters, mothers, people of each age and sex. There, after a huge meal, when the party has really got going, and fire of drunkenness and incestuous lust has waxed hot, a dog, which has been tied to the lampstand, is provoked to rush and leap forward by the tossing of a scrap of food beyond the length of the rope by which it is tied. Thus, when the light, a potential witness, has been overturned and extinguished, they throw themselves haphazardly into couplings of unspeakable lust in the wanton darkness, and if they do not all commit it in fact, nonetheless they are all guilty as accessories to incest, since whatever is capable of happening in individual cases is what the entire group really wants (*Octavius*).[1]

A tiny minority in a hostile empire, the Christians needed to defend themselves, to "apologize" for their practices and beliefs. Thus the Christian writers of the second century are often called "apologists." Also writing in North Africa, only somewhat earlier, the Christian lawyer Tertullian sarcastically responded to such critics. After rehearsing the same strange views voiced by Minucius, Tertullian asks his readers:

Even if you believed all this, I say you would not be willing to act in this way, and, even if you were willing, you would be incapable of it. Why, then, are others able, if you are not? Why are you incapable, if others can? I suppose we are of a different species, dog-headed, or like the bigfoot, with a different arrangement of teeth, or a different musculature, one avid for incestuous lust! If you believe these things about a human being, then you too are capable of them. You yourself are a human, just as the Christian is. If you cannot do these things, then you should not believe the reports of them. For you are human, and the Christian is just what you are (*Apologeticum*).[2]

Justin Martyr, one of the most famous of these writers, attempted to explain Christianity to the emperor Antoninus Pius. He
is careful to point out that the table celebration of the Christians
involves the presence of the risen Lord, but that only bread and
wine are eaten:

> At the conclusion of the prayers we greet one another
> with a kiss. Then bread and a cup containing wine and
> water are presented to the one presiding over the brothers.
> He takes them and offers praise and glory to the Father of
> All, through the name of the Son and of the Holy Spirit,
> and he makes a lengthy thanksgiving to God because He
> has counted us worthy of such favors. At the end of these
> prayers and Thanksgiving, all express their assent by say-
> ing Amen. This Hebrew word, Amen, means "So be it".
> And when he who presides has given thanks, and all the
> people have acclaimed their assent, those whom we call
> deacons summon each one present to partake of the bread
> and wine and water over which the thanksgiving was said,
> and they carry it to those who are absent. We call this food
> the "Eucharist" (literally, the thanksgiving). No one is al-
> lowed to partake of it except him who believes that our
> teachings are true and has been cleansed in the bath for
> the forgiveness of his sins and for his regeneration, and
> who lives as Christ commanded. Not as common bread or
> as common drink do we receive these, but just as through
> the word of God, Jesus Christ, our Saviour, became incar-
> nate and took on flesh and blood for our salvation, so, we
> have been taught, the food over which thanks has been
> given by the prayer of His word, and which nourishes our
> flesh and blood by assimilation, is both the flesh and
> blood of that incarnate Jesus (*First Apology*).[3]

A second accusation made against Christians was that they
were atheists. Since they refused to offer sacrifices to the different
gods and goddesses of the empire, and did not even *go* to temples,
people thought that they did not believe in any divinity at all. After
all, the only churches were temples, and from this point of view the

Christians could be said to never attend church. Municius Felix records the accusation:

> They [the Christians] despise the temples as tombs; they spit on the gods, they ridicule our rites; they are pitiful, yet if one dare to say it, they pity our priests; they treat elective office and the purple with disdain, though they themselves are half-naked (*Octavius*).[4]

Writing toward the end of the second century, another of the apologists, Athenagoras of Athens, wrote to the emperor Marcus Aurelius in defense of Christianity. In his work Athenagoras points out the reasonable grounds for this strange custom of the Christians:

> Because the majority of those who accuse us of atheism have no conception at all of divinity, not even in a dream, and they are untrained and unconversant with scientific and theological thought, they measure out piety by the conventional practice of offering sacrifices, and thus they accuse us of not holding to the same gods as the cities. Concerning both charges, O sovereigns, please consider the following. First, as to our not offering sacrifices: The Fashioner and Father of the universe has no need of blood, nor of the savor of fat, nor of the fragrance of flowers and incense. He is Himself the consummate fragrance, in need of nothing and self-sufficient. Instead, the best sacrifice to Him is that we know who it was who stretched out the heavens, gathered them into a sphere, and fixed the earth as a center, who brought together water into the seas, and divided light from darkness, who adorned the sky with stars, and made the earth to cause every seed to spring up, who made animals and fashioned men. But what to me are whole-burnt-offerings of which God has no need? Indeed, to offer sacrifices is necessary, but to offer an unbloody sacrifice, a spiritual worship (*The Plea*).[5]

Because of this concern not to be confused with either the pagan priests or the Jewish priests, Christians did not call their leaders "priests." Priests were technically people whose job it was to offer animal or food sacrifices, and Christians did not do this. For the first two centuries of Christianity, the followers of Jesus used the title "priest" only metaphorically for either Jesus as the risen Lord or for the people as a whole.

Not until the third century did Christians speak readily of the Lord's supper as a "sacrifice" of praise, or of the celebrant as a "priest," or of the ceremony itself as a "representation" or "re-creation" or "participation in" the one sacrifice of the high priest Jesus. At a time when these words referred to a literal animal sacrifice of some kind, Christians had to make it clear that they intended to be understood metaphorically or spiritually. Cyprian, bishop of Carthage in the middle of the third century, more clearly than most early writers identified the sacrifice of Jesus with the Christian celebration:

> For if Jesus Christ, our Lord and God, is Himself the High priest of God the Father, and first offered Himself a sacrifice to the Father, and commanded this to be done in remembrance of Himself, certainly the priest who imitates that which Christ did offers the true and full sacrifice in the Church of God the Father; if he offers according to what he sees Christ Himself to have offered, he truly acts in the place of Christ (*Letter* 63).[6]

Christians for the first few centuries would be cautious in their use of such language, however. A second cause of concern for the earliest Christians came from groups of pseudo-Christians called "gnostics" (literally, "those in the know"). Basing themselves on popular religious and scientific thought, the gnostics held that nothing material could be of any benefit to humans, since it was only the "spirit" that was of lasting value. The gnostic teachers differed among themselves, but basically they agreed that Jesus could not possibly have had a human body, and the "man" people saw on earth was only an illusion. The gnostics had their own gospels and epistles to back them up, and when confronted with orthodox teaching, they would respond that Jesus had passed on a secret knowledge to certain of the apostles, who in turn secretly passed it on to them. Conspiracy theories involving a "secret knowledge" were as popular in the second century as they are in the twentieth.

Of course, the gnostics denied that baptism or the Lord's supper could have any value, since these actions involved mere matter. On the whole, the gnostics attributed little value to any actions, and understood salvation as arbitrary, limited to those to whom the secret knowledge was imparted, provided, of course, that the recipient was capable of understanding the secret knowledge in the first place.

The problem of gnosticism is a constant threat to any understanding of both the incarnation and of the sacraments for Christianity. There always seem to have been a group of Christians who were impatient with the humdrum, messy business of earthly existence and wished to vault over the material directly into a spiritual realm. In the second century, the gnostic groups threatened to turn early Christianity into one more esoteric form of Near Eastern secret religions. In the fourth century the teachings of gnosticism were joined to those of Buddhism and Zoroastrianism (native Persian religion) by a brilliant teacher named Manes. The religion he founded, Manicheeism, was extremely popular in the fourth century, and still manages to find advocates today. Again and again these groups offered Christians an understanding of life that denied value to the mundane, the earthly, the sensual—the whole messy business of being human. And each time that some form of gnosticism took hold, the value of the eucharist was attacked. After all, what possible good would it do to be joined to the body and blood of the Lord, if bodies and blood in themselves were evil, material things? And if even the body and blood of the risen Lord were worthless (and, for most gnostics, non-existent), then surely to attribute spiritual value to mere reception of bread and wine was a joke.

Some scholars feel that the sixth chapter of John, which insists so strongly on the value of receiving the body and blood of the Lord, was a response to an early group of gnostics. At least this passage makes it clear that by the time it was written, participation in the eucharistic meal was understood by the early church to be a sharing in the immortal and divine life which the Lord already enjoys. Irenaeus, the second century bishop of Lyons, was one of the strongest adversaries of the gnostics, and he appealed to Christian thought on the eucharist in his attack on the teaching of the gnostics. Irenaeus claimed that the gnostics could not be correct when they said Jesus had no body since in the Lord's supper Chris-

tians take on the immortality already experienced by the body of
the risen Lord:

> Then, again, how can they say that the flesh which is
> nourished by the Lord's body and blood goes to corrup-
> tion, and does not partake of life? Let them, therefore,
> either change their opinions, or refrain from offering the
> things just mentioned. But our opinion agrees with the
> Eucharist, and the Eucharist, in turn, establishes our opin-
> ion, for we offer to Him what is his own, proclaiming
> fittingly the fellowship and union of the flesh and the
> spirit. For, as the bread which is produced from the earth,
> when it receives the invocation of God, is no longer com-
> mon bread, but the Eucharist consisting of two realities,
> the earthly and the heavenly, so also our bodies, when
> they receive the Eucharist, are no longer corruptible, but
> have the hope of resurrection (*Against the Heretics*).[7]

> So wholly foolish are they who disdain the entire Econ-
> omy of God, and deny the salvation of the flesh, and
> reject its regeneration, saying that it lacks the capacity for
> incorruptibility. Rather, if this flesh is not saved, then the
> Lord has not redeemed us by His blood, and the cup of
> the Eucharist is not a communion in His blood, and the
> bread which we break is not a sharing in His body (1 Cor
> 10:16). For there is no blood except from veins, and from
> flesh, and from the rest of the substance of human nature
> which the Word of God came to be, and redeemed by His
> blood. . . . He declared that the cup, which came from
> His creation, is His own blood, from which he strength-
> ens our blood; and He affirmed that the bread, which is
> from creation, is His very own body, from which He
> strengthens our body (*Against the Heretics*).[8]

This form of very realistic language was used to refute the
claim made by the gnostics that, first of all, Jesus himself had no
real body, and, secondly, Christians were not saved physically, but
only spiritually. The language of Irenaeus and others like him

worked well in opposing the gnostics, but, when read by later authors, the strong realism of their language could be disconcerting or even downright confusing. This, however, was not the concern of the second century. Besides, as will be explained in greater detail in the next chapter, people throughout much of Christian history had a much different concept of "real" than we do in the twentieth century, and this makes their "realistic" language mean something very different than ours.

There were Christian writers, of course, who pointed out that the reception of the Lord's body and blood was a purely spiritual affair. Typical of this sort of writing are passages found in the scriptural commentaries of the third century scholar Origen. Writing in Alexandria and in Caesarea in Palestine, Origen was the greatest Christian scholar of his day, and still ranks as one of the most brilliant Christians of all times. His commentary on the gospel of Matthew demonstrates the philosophical approach of this great writer:

> For God the Word was not saying that the visible bread which He was holding in His hands was His body, but rather the word, in whose mystery the bread was to be broken. He was not saying that the visible drink was His blood, but the word, in whose mystery the drink was to be poured out. For what else could the body and blood of God the Word be except the word which nourishes and the word which "makes glad the heart" (Ps 103:15)? But why did He not say "This is the bread of the new covenant"? Because the bread is the word of righteousness whereby those who eat it are nourished, but the drink is the word of the knowledge of Christ, according to the mystery of His Nativity and Passion. But since the covenant of God with us was placed in the blood of Christ's Passion, that believing that the Son of God was born and suffered in the flesh we should be saved—and not by righteousness, for by that alone, without belief in the Passion of Christ, there could be no salvation—on that account, only of the cup was it said "This is the cup of the covenant."[9]

Teaching in the Community

Origen was speaking to his fellow Christians here, not to the gnostics or pagan opponents of Christianity. He could assume that his hearers understood the basic beliefs of Christianity, including an understanding of the saving and spiritual presence of the Lord in the eucharist. Writers other than Origen also addressed their remarks about the eucharist to fellow Christians. The bishops (*episcopoi*) taught their new converts before they were baptized and addressed their congregations as to how to understand this central ritual in their lives.

Following the teaching of Paul to the Corinthians, Cyprian, the third century bishop of Carthage mentioned above, appealed to the eucharist when he wished to stress the unity of the community. In the first Christian work devoted exclusively to the eucharist, Cyprian wrote to a fellow bishop to explain that water alone could not be used in the Lord's supper, but wine mixed with water. In the letter, he insists that the commingling of the two demonstrates the unity of congregation with each other and with Christ:

> But thus, in consecrating the cup of the Lord, water alone cannot be offered, just as wine alone cannot. For, if anyone offers wine alone, the blood of Christ is without us; but if the water is alone, the people are without Christ. But when both are mixed and are joined to each other in the indiscriminate union, then the spiritual and heavenly sacrament is completed. Thus the cup of the Lord is not water alone, or wine alone, but both are mixed together, just as flour alone or water alone cannot be the body of the Lord, unless both have been united and joined and made solid in the structure of a single bread. By this very sacrament our people is shown to be united. Just as many grains, collected and milled and mixed, make one bread, so let us know that in Christ, who is the heavenly bread, there is one body, to which our number has been joined and united (Letter 63).[10]

In a different letter, Cyrpian would make the same point:

Finally, the very Sacrifices of the Lord demonstrate that Christian unanimity is bound to itself with a firm and inseparable charity. For when the Lord calls Bread made from the union of many grains His Body, he indicates our people whom He bore united; and when He calls Wine pressed from the clusters of grapes and many small berries and gathered in one His Blood, He, likewise, signifies our flock joined by the mixture of a united multitude (Letter 69).[11]

A further theme, present in both Paul and John, was always central to the community's understanding of the supper and rarely absent from any discussion of the eucharist by the early church. Christians are recalled again and again to the commitment to a life of faith and love of which the sacrament is a sign. So close did the association of Christian life with the celebration of Christian life become that Ignatius, the second century bishop of Antioch, movingly spoke of his own martyrdom as a eucharistic celebration:

I am writing to all the Churches to tell them all that I am, with all my heart, to die for God—if only you do not prevent it. I beseech you not to indulge your benevolence at the wrong time. Please let me be thrown to the wild beasts; through them I can reach God. I am God's wheat; I am ground by the teeth of the wild beasts that I may end as the pure bread of Christ. . . . Make petition, then, to the Lord for me, so that by these means I may be made a sacrifice to God (Letter to the Romans).[12]

Ignatius wrote his series of letters to different Christian churches while a prisoner on his way to Rome to be killed in the arena. For the brave Ignatius, such language was not figurative. He truly lived and eventually died what he would have called a "eucharistic" life. In another passage, Ignatius identified the body and blood of the Lord with faith and love, again implying that the Christian life itself was eucharistic:

And so, put on the armor of forbearance and refresh yourselves in faith, that is, in the body of the Lord, and in

love, that is the blood of Jesus Christ. Let no one be down
on his neighbor. Let not the folly of a few give occasion to
the pagans to calumniate your pious community (Letter to
the Tralians).[13]

Ignatius was hardly alone in his admonitions. Justin, the second century writer mentioned earlier, included charitable works as
part of his description of Christian ceremonies:

On the day which is called the day of the Sun we have a
common assembly of all who live in the cities or in the
country, and the memoirs of the apostles or the writings of
the prophets are read, as much as there is time for. Then,
when the reader has finished, the one presiding provides,
in a discourse, admonition and exhortation to imitate
these excellent things. Then we all stand up together and
say prayers, and as we said before, after we finish the
prayer, bread and wine are presented. He who presides
likewise offers up prayers and thanksgiving, to the best of
his ability, and the people express their assent by saying
Amen, and there is the distribution and participation by
each one in those things over which thanksgiving has been
said, and these are sent, through the deacons, to those not
present. The wealthy, if they wish, contribute whatever
they desire, and the collection is placed in the custody of
the president, and he helps the orphans and widows,
those who are needy because of sickness or any other
reason, and the captives and the strangers in our midst; in
short, he takes care of all those in need (*First Apology*).[14]

It is amazing how little the celebration of the Lord's supper has
changed in two thousand years. Justin's description, written probably as a description of the Roman church around 150 A.D., is a
decent general description of most Christian Sunday liturgies today. Justin was kinder to the donors than Luke in his description of
the early Jerusalem community, where Ananias and Sapphira are
struck dead by the Spirit for holding back some of their wealth from
this earliest of Christian communities. Living a truly Christian life,

or, rather, having Christ living in and through individual Christians, was the heart of the eucharistic celebrations. Each celebration was both a celebration of such a life, and a strengthening for such a life in the future. For the early church (as for every period of Christian history) one was called to live the eucharist. In the early centuries, that could often mean facing the kind of death which Ignatius described as the eucharist itself.

A series of themes appear and reappear in the writings of the early church writers, blending and intertwining with no clear distinction. Early Christians called their ritual meal either "the breaking of the bread" or the "giving thanks" (in Greek, *eucharistion*). The term "body of Christ" could refer equally to the bread used in the supper, or to the now present risen Lord, or to the Christian community, or, as in the passage of Ignatius quoted above, to the Christian life itself. The celebration of the eucharist could be described as the celebration of the salvation already won for us by the Lord Jesus, or as the cause of that salvation. The Lord's supper was described as contributing to salvation by forming us into the community of the saved, or by mingling Christ's now risen life with our own; but whatever terms might be used to explain the eucharist, Christians were reminded that only those who lived a truly Christian life could worthily participate in the ritual celebration of that life.

A certain pattern did emerge, however, in the many discussions of the Lord's supper which occurred during those early years. First, the early Christians firmly believed that the risen Lord was present in the celebration of the supper, and, second, they believed that the presence itself was instrumental in bringing about the salvation of both the body and the soul of the believer. More than this, however, the early Christians spoke of the eucharist as forming the community of believers, that the eucharist both celebrated and effected the life of faith and love to which Christians dedicated themselves in the ceremony of sharing the life of the risen Lord. Finally, in the third century, the language originally reserved to discussions of animal sacrifices was applied metaphorically to the supper as a reminder of the saving offering of Jesus' own life and of the similar pledge which each Christian makes in the celebration of the ritual meal.

The Celebration

In order to understand more fully of what the early writers were speaking when they wrote about the Lord's supper, some idea of what the early liturgies were like seems essential. Since these liturgies have been described at length in other books (see the bibliography at the end of the book) just a brief overview will be given here.

The very earliest Christians, like the ones to whom Paul wrote in Corinth, actually had a full-blown meal, as Jesus did at the last supper. The most important part of the meal, however, was the blessing of the bread and wine. Sometime in the first hundred years of Christianity, however, the meal seems to have been separated off from the blessing of the bread and wine. The meal still took place, but as a separate ritual, sometimes called the "agape meal" or meal of Christian love. The practice of having such a meal, especially at the tombs of the martyrs, would continue at least into the fourth or fifth century.

The description of a Sunday liturgy given by Justin and quoted above seems to fit what we know about the liturgies of the first few centuries. There were readings and a sermon, prayers were said, the bread and wine were blessed and distributed. Justin allows for a great deal of freedom in his service. There seem to have been no fixed prayers, and Justin just says that the presider does the best he can. Perhaps in some places the liturgy had become more fixed, but the best evidence we have indicates that there was a great deal of regional variation and freedom in the choice of liturgical prayers throughout this period.

There also seems to have been a good deal of freedom about who presided at the liturgy. There is some evidence that in the very beginning the prophets in the community presided. Justin refers merely to "the presider" or "the president." The earliest celebrations of the liturgy were truly community celebrations, and there seems that there was no clear distinction between those who led the liturgy and those who did not. More accurately, no one led the liturgy; everybody seems to have worshiped together.

Gradually, however, Christians began to model their communities on the secular institutions surrounding them. The freedom and spontaneity of the earliest decades of Christianity succumbed to the human tendency to organize, and people naturally turned to those structures with which they were most familiar. This pattern of organizing Christianity according to whatever structures the surrounding culture employs has been operative throughout Christian history and prevails even today. (Unfortunately, even today some Christian groups have become locked into one particular historical pattern of organization and refuse to change even when the society around them has long abandoned the organizational structures involved.)

As you might imagine, the organizational structures that most attracted the early church were those used by the surrounding Greek and Jewish societies. By the third century at least, two groups had become responsible for the liturgy. The most important was the *episcopos*. Literally, the word in Greek means "overseer" and was a secular term for anyone who had a charge of a group of people (the foreman of a ranch, for instance, might be called an *episcopos*). Particularly in the Greek communities, the overseer became the person who did the teaching and directed the affairs of the community. When the gnostics threatened the authority of the church, it was the overseers who could claim that they had been taught by the apostles, or at least by the students of the apostles. As time went by, the overseers became the most important personages in the church and the ordinary celebrants of the liturgy.

The Jewish communities of the first centuries had a different structure. In these communities a group of elders—in Greek, *presbyteroi*—led the people. The early Jewish-Christian communities followed this custom, and by the second century most Christian communities had a group of elders as well as an overseer. The relationship between the two offices seemed to differ from place to place and time to time, but it seems that the elders played the role of judges, while the overseers were more like the executive branch of the community. By the end of the third century, however, it was clear that the elders were becoming less and less independent of the overseer. Gradually the elders would be seen as the helpers of the overseer, and they would lead the liturgy only when for some reason the overseer could not.

Liturgies were usually held in someone's house at this time. Especially in the very early church, people went to someone's house for a meal, and later for the readings, the prayers, and the sharing of the bread and cup. It seems that some people donated houses to be used as churches, and maybe even had some built as places for Christians to worship. At times, too, the Christians would hold liturgies in secret places, like the catacombs, but this was not the usual practice.

So, if you wanted to attend a Christian liturgy in, say, the third century, you would first find out at whose house the Christians were going to meet. Next, you would have to be a baptized member of their church, or perhaps visiting from another church, but certainly the members would want to know that you were baptized. Once you got to the place, you would find one of the more respected members of the community leading the prayers. He (and by the third century it would unquestionably be *he*) would also be the one whom the deacons (servants) assisted in aiding those in need, and even probably be the teacher for those interested in joining the community. You might find this strange, because in your church the teachers were a quite separate group from the overseer and the deacons, but you would be used to diversity. After all, the Christian churches were very small groups, quite independent of one another. After exchanging the kiss of peace, or some other greeting, you would settle in to listen to the readings. As there was not a fixed body of scripture, you might hear something read, like the book of Revelation, that your own community did really not think of as sacred.

The presider would then do a little teaching by way of a sermon. Surely talents were as diverse then as they are now. Perhaps one of the prophets would speak, moved by the Spirit. The bread and wine would then be blessed and passed out, the deacons taking them to the sick and imprisoned. Finally, the overseer would ask all those who could to help out the community. This was a very serious obligation, and the Christians were renowned for their charity. Aristides, one of the apologists, described actions of the Christians in his defense of his beliefs to the emperor in the middle of the second century:

> Falsehood is not found among them; and they love one another, and from widows they do not turn away their esteem; and they deliver the orphan from him who treats them harshly. And he, who has, gives to him who has not, without boasting. And when they see a stranger, they take

him to their homes and rejoice over him as a very brother; for they do not call them brethren after the flesh, but brethren after the Spirit and in God. And whenever one of their poor passes from the world, each one of them according to his ability gives heed to him and carefully sees to his burial. And if they hear that one of their number is imprisoned or afflicted on account of the name of their Messiah, all of them anxiously minister to his necessity, and if it is possible to redeem him they set him free. And if there is among them any that is poor and needy, and if they have no spare food, they fast two or three days to supply to the needy their lack of food. Every morning and every hour they give thanks (*eucharistion* in Greek) and praise to God for His loving-kindness toward them; and for their food and their drink they offer thanksgiving (*eucharistion*) to Him (*The Apology*).[15]

These acts would be seen as part of the liturgy in a very real sense, as would the supreme sacrifice or martyrdom. The martyrs were very highly regarded in the early church. Prayers were said at their tombs as well as liturgies celebrated. Those who had witnessed to their faith by trial and imprisonment, and had not been killed as martyrs were called "confessors" and had equal or greater standing than the overseers or elders, including the right to lead the liturgy.

In short, it was a very dramatic and lively time for the church—exciting, but dangerous, too. Persecutions were sporadic. In some places and at some times, to be a Christian was to court certain death. Most of the time, Christians were more despised than actually killed, but one never knew when the political winds might change. It was a time of great enthusiasm, of great vitality, of great diversity, and the liturgies, and the understanding of those liturgies, mirrored this great movement of the Spirit.

GLOSSARY OF PERSONS

Athenagoras. Little is known of Athenagoras' life. He was probably born in Athens. Formerly a teacher of platonic philosophy, Athenagoras was converted to Christianity. He kept on teaching, however, and started a school for Christian philosophy in Alexandria. His school had many famous teachers, including St. Clement and Origen. He wrote his apology, called the *Embassy for the Christians* sometime between 176 and 180. In it he tried to convince the emperor Marcus Aurelius of the value of Christianity. He is considered the ablest of the apologists.

Aristides. Like Athenagoras and Justin, Marcus Aristides was a philosopher before his conversion to Christianity. He wrote an apology during the reign of the emperor Hadrian (117–138) or possibly Antoninus Pius (138–161). We know nothing else about his life except that he, like Athenagoras, was probably born in Athens.

Cyprian. Thascius Caecilianus Cyprianus was a pagan rhetor (lawyer and teacher) who had received an excellent education as a youth in Carthage. He was converted to Christianity in 246 and immediately distributed his wealth to the poor and undertook a serious study of scripture. He became *episocopos* (overseer) of Carthage in 249. He wrote a great deal, and was involved in two nasty persecutions, as well as rallying his people during a plague. His ideas on penance, baptism, and the unity of the church had a great deal of influence on later thought. During earlier persecutions, Cyprian directed his flock from hiding, but during the persecution of Valerian he gave himself up to the authorities as an example to his people. He was martyred on September 14, 258.

Gnosticism. Scholars disagree whether gnosticism existed apart from Christianity or was an offshoot of Christianity, but certainly it was an important influence and rival to the church in the early centuries, particularly the second century. Gnosticism is a mixture of Christianity, astrology, myth, and neoplatonic philosophy. Apparently there were many groups which followed different combinations of these ingredients, and which violently disagreed with each other. Gnostic sects did, however, share some common characteristics. They were thoroughly dualistic; that is to say, they held that matter is evil and absolutely separate from spirit, which is good. Since matter is evil and God is good, the world must have come from some cosmic disorder or conflict or fall, and the world must have been built by some lesser spirit (often associated with the God of the Old Testament). According to the gnostics, there is a spiritual element in all or some people which yearns to be released from matter and return to God. This redemption comes through knowledge—in Greek, *gnosis*. Christian gnostics taught and believed that Jesus passed on an esoteric, spiritual knowledge to the disciples who passed it on to them alone. Jesus was a spiritual being having no body (of course) and no birth, His earthly existence was a mere illusion for lesser men, He did not really suffer or die. To many, gnosticism seemed to be a more intelligent and intellectually and scientifically satisfying version of Christianity than that generally taught and contained in the gospels of Matthew, Mark, Luke and John and the epistles of Paul.

Ignatius. Born c. 35, probably in Syria, Ignatius was either the second or third *episcopos* (overseer) in Antioch. Sometime between 106 and 110 he was taken under guard of ten soldiers from Antioch to Rome after being arrested as a Christian. While on the journey, Ignatius wrote seven very moving letters to other churches. When he arrived in Smyrna, the overseer, Polycarp, received Ignatius with great honor. Polycarp, who may have heard John preach as a youth, himself was martyred at the age of 86. When Ignatius arrived in Rome, he was condemned to death.

Irenaeus. Born c. 140 in Asia Minor, Irenaeus heard Polycarp (see Ignatius) preach. He studied in Rome, and eventually became a *presbyteros* (elder) in the city of Lyons in southern France. When the *episcopos* (overseer) was martyred in 177, Irenaeus took over. Irenaeus was a skilled opponent of the gnostics during his lifetime. He died sometime around 200.

Justin Martyr. Justin was born in the city of Flavia Neopolis (now Nablus) in Samaria, of Greek parents. He spent his life in pursuit of wisdom, studying all the different philosophies of his day. He was finally convinced around the year 130 that Christianity was the greatest philosophy. He taught Christianity as a philosophy first in Ephesus, and then in Rome. He wrote two apologies for Christianity as well as a dialogue with the Jew, Trypho. He was martyred in Rome c. 165.

Minucius Felix. Marcus Minucius Felix was probably born in North Africa, but he studied and later practiced law in Rome in the early third century. In his book *Octavius* he refuted the common accusations made against Christians by the pagan Romans. Nothing else is known about his life.

Origen. Unlike most of the other writers mentioned here, Origen was born to Christian parents. The oldest of seven children, Origen received a thoroughly Christian education in his home in Alexandria. His father Leonides may have been taught by St. Clement, who was head of the catechetical school in Alexandria. In 202 Leonides was martyred, and Origen was only prevented from following his father by his mother, who hid his clothes so Origen would stay home. Origen took over the catechetical school from Clement, as well as teaching to support his family. Origen lived a life of strict asceticism and scholarship. He taught both in Alexandria and in Caesaria. He underwent several journeys and was considered the greatest scripture scholar of his time. Unfortunately, not all of his work has survived. In 250 he was imprisoned and tortured in hopes that the great man would retract his religion. Despite prolonged punishment, Origen never denied his faith. When he was finally freed from prison, however, his health was broken and he died a few years later at the age of sixty-nine.

Tertullian. Quintus Septimus Florens Tertullianus was the son of a Roman centurion. Born in North Africa c. 160, Tertullian received an excellent education and became an advocate in the courts of Rome. He was converted to Christianity c. 195, taking over as instructor of catechumens for the church in Carthage. By 212–213, he had joined an heretical Christian group called the Montanists, who were a puritanical and apocalyptic movement which expected a great outpouring of the Spirit followed by the end of the world. Tertullian died c. 220. By his own admission, Tertullian was an impatient and irritable man, and he tended to take extreme stands. Yet Tertullian was also a brilliant writer in his native tongue of Latin and is considered the father of later Latin Christian writers.

3

The Origins of Diversity:
The Patristic Church

The period between the fourth and sixth centuries is sometimes referred to as the "golden age" of Christian writers. Christianity over these centuries came out of the shadows to become first a tolerated, and finally a respected, religion in the Roman empire. Christians appeared on the scene who were well educated writers, trained in the great classical traditions of Greece and Rome. Great causes forced the most brilliant of these writers to produce their best work. Augustine, Ambrose, and Hilary in the west and Athanasius, Cyril of Alexandria, and the Cappadocians in the east all produced brilliant defenses of orthodox Christianity in opposition to the challenges of Arianism, Nestorianism and Monophysitism.

The cause for this momentous change in Christianity came about for reasons that are purely and simply political. Constantine, who laid claim to the empire in 306 A.D., defeated his opponents by calling on the God of the Christians, the God whom his mother worshiped. After becoming sole ruler of the Roman empire in 324 he founded a dynasty which reigned supreme until 363. With the exception of Julian, the last of the Constantinian emperors and a supporter of the old Roman gods, Constantine and his family strongly supported the new religion in return for their continued victories over enemies both internal and external.

The emperor's favor took very tangible forms. Constantine had beautiful basilicas built for the Christians. Basilicas were ordinarily government buildings which housed deliberative or judicial bodies. Since the Christians didn't have temples, the emperor substituted elaborate civil buildings, somewhat the equivalent of our present state capitol buildings. The emperor also gave the Christians money, respect, and, above all, peace.

Slowly but surely during this period, Christians were drawn into the actual administration of the empire. The *episcopoi*, once overseers of small house churches, now became true bishops with increasing power over their dioceses. The bishops eventually were even given juridical power and could (and did) try civil cases. Ecclesiastical disputes now became political disputes as well, and the great Arian and Nestorian controversies of the fourth and fifth centuries were as much disputes over imperial power as they were theological discussions. By the end of the period under discussion, the church and empire (while often not in agreement) were inextricably linked.

The loosely knit structure of the early Christian communities changed as well. Not only were the *episcopoi* now the virtual rulers and leaders of their dioceses, but certain of the bishops gained ascendency in prestige and authority over their fellow bishops. At least by the fifth century, five great centers of orthodoxy were recognized as the leading cities of Christianity. The bishops of all these cities were referred to as "popes" or "fathers" (the word has the same root as the English word "pop" or "papa"). These "patriarches" formed a kind of federation. Agreement among them was usually considered essential for determining the orthodoxy of any question. The leaders of the Christian communities of Rome, Jerusalem, Antioch, Alexandria, and later Constantinople were expected to meet and determine both pressing doctrinal and administrative questions at the great councils of the church. This is not to say that the bishops of other cities were always subservient to the patriarch. A bishop like Ambrose of Milan was quite ready to tell the patriarch of Rome to mind his own business if he felt the situation called for it. In general, this period is marked by governance by consensus. The ideal council was considered to be that of Nicea in 325, where it was believed that the Holy Spirit inspired the many different bishops present to unanimously accept one statement of unity in belief.

Like the earlier Christian writers, the great authors of this era did not write works specifically on the Lord's supper. This does not mean that they did not write about the eucharist. They did, and some of the authors, like Augustine, wrote so much it is difficult to pick out even the major themes in their writings. When they did write, however, they never intended to put forward a well thought out explanation of the purpose of the Lord's supper. Often, on the contrary, they would refer to already accepted belief about the eucharist to support their defense of other Christian claims, as did Irenaeus in the passage quoted in Chapter 2. As in earlier centuries, the understanding of the Lord's supper was fairly well accepted. The great problems of the age were the controversies over the nature of Jesus as both divine and human. What the fathers[1] did write on the eucharist was to have important long-range effects on the understanding of the sacrament, however, and it would be to these authors that later writers would always return for both inspiration and authority.

Platonism

In order to truly understand the teachings of the fathers on almost any subject, however, it is necessary to point out some fundamental differences between these writers and ourselves. The early Christian writers had a much different view of reality than do most people in the late twentieth century. Throughout the period we will be discussing in this book, in fact, people in general would think of the world quite differently than we do, and this difference is crucial in understanding what they have to say about the eucharist. During the period of the late Roman empire, educated people were more and more turning from the classical religions of Greek and Rome, and adopting as their personal beliefs the teaching of the great philosophers of ancient Greece.

Several of the writers mentioned in the last chapter were philosophers who were converted to Christianity as part of their search for truth. Most of them were converted from one particular kind of philosophy, Platonism. Justin Martyr, Athenagoras, and Aristides were Platonists before their conversion, and Origen studied under one of the greatest of the Platonists in Alexandria. There were other philosophies available to the Christian writers. Tertullian, for example, was heavily influenced by Stoicism, and teachers at the Christian school in Antioch would follow the teachings of Aristotle. It was Platonism, however, that most attracted the Christians. There was an excellent reason for this. Platonism offered a sophisticated and respectable way to explain Christian beliefs.

In this, the Christians were following a precedent. Even before the time of Jesus, Jewish scholars had used Platonism as a framework to explain their faith. Writing in Alexandria at the same time that Jesus was teaching in Palestine, the Jewish scholar Philo used Platonism to reconcile the Jewish scripture with contemporary philosophy. Later, Clement of Alexandria and his student Origen would both borrow freely from the work of Philo.

What made Platonism so attractive to Christianity? Even a simple glance at the form of Platonism taught during the first centuries of Christianity makes this clear. The founder of Platonism, Plato, lived in Greece from about 429 to 347 B.C. The essence of Plato's philosophy is his theory of knowledge. According to Plato, knowledge cannot come from sense data because this is too variable and hence untrustworthy. Knowledge comes from the transcendent, non-sensible world of forms which are grasped by the intellect alone. To most modern ears this sounds at worst like nonsense and at best simply wrong. Twentieth century people trust sense data almost implicitly. For us, something is "real" if we can touch, taste, smell, but most of all see it.

What, then, did Plato have in mind when he denied what seems obvious to us? His problem was quite simple. Suppose you look at a field of cows. Some are red, some are black, some are black and white, others are red and white. Clearly color does not define a cow. Some of the cows appear large (those closest); others appear tiny (those way off on the hillside). Clearly, then, size does not determine what a cow is either. (Now you're cheating if you say that you "know" they are all the same size, because you are supposed to be relying on your senses here, and according to them you only know that the things you see are different sizes.) Plato would then ask you how you know all these wildly different things are cows.

Again the answer seems obvious. Cows have four legs, you can milk them, they have hooves, etc. Plato, being a very bright man, would then say, "Aha, then if a cow is missing legs, hooves, or if it's dry, etc., it is no longer a cow." Dead cows, to use an extreme example, aren't cows. Worse yet, you shouldn't even be able to recognize them as cows. Plato wouldn't be finished yet. He would hold up a picture of a green cow and ask, "So, please tell me, modern person, what is this?" You might say, "Why, Plato, that's a picture of a cow, of course." Plato would be stunned. How do you know that? Here we have something that is two dimensional, has no hooves, no legs, no sense data in common with any of the other things we insist on calling cows. Surely, if you recognize a cow in the picture, it cannot be because of sense data. The sense data in all these different things called cows just differs too much to provide any reliability.

Plato would then begin to explain that the reason you know that all things are cows (or pictures of cows) is because your mind has grasped the essence of "cowness" underlying the sense data. Of course, this "essence" is not sensed. That's the whole point. It is intuited by the mind. The mind recognizes the essence of things, just as the eyes (and other senses) recognize the shape, size, color, smell, touch, etc. of things. Now this may seem very odd to you, but, to be honest, Plato has a point. In fact, many modern philosophers would at least agree that things are real for us because we *decide* (a mental process) that they are real. The sense data alone *can* be wrong. There may be times that people *sense* pink elephants, but they decide (for very good reasons), and therefore *know*, there are no pink elephants at this particular party.

Most modern people have a terrible time trying to grasp this concept of what is "real." If you are one of the many, try this little experiment. Turn on a light. Stare at the naked bulb for a second or two. *Not too long—you will hurt your eyes!* Now look at a blank wall, and ask yourself where are the little dots that you see? If you say nowhere, Plato's right about sense data. You see something, but it's not there. Now that could be true for everything you see. All sense data *could* be an illusion. If you say that the dots *do* exist somewhere, and you can figure out where, you may well be on your way to a great philosophical and medical breakthrough.

Nothing is more important in understanding Christian thought on the eucharist than the simple insight that for most of Christian history, people who wrote about the eucharist just assumed Plato was right. The most "real" things were those grasped by the mind; the least "real" things were those things that were sensed. "Essences" (or "substances" or "forms") were *always* more real than sense data. Keep this firmly in mind throughout this book. When the writers talk about what is "real," they mean that which the mind grasps, either through reason or in faith.

Now for Plato, the forms actually existed in their own world, and originally our souls (which are our essences) were part of this world, the world of the forms. In fact, every individual thing only exists because it shares in the world of the forms. Humans beings are individual manifestations of "humanness," the essence of being human. The One or the Good is the one form in which every other form participates, and hence it is the highest form or God. From the first century before Christ to the second century after Christ, a group of philosophers, particularly in Alexandria, revived the teaching of Plato. They are now called the "middle Platonists" because they stand midway between the teaching of Plato and that of "Neoplatonism," the teaching of the third century philosopher Plotinus. The middle Platonists thought of the One and the Good as the source of all movement and order in the universe, and they identified this power as God. For them, the world of the forms existed in the mind of God. Since God, however, must also be unchanging as the One, the middle Platonists talked of different "levels" of divinity. There was one God, but since God was immaterial, it was possible to talk of a hierarchy within God. At the highest level was the One and the Good unchanging and unchanged. Sometimes this aspect of God was called the first mind. At a lower level was the second mind, or that reason which was the "soul" of the universe, the principle by which all things moved and were alive.

Now one of the words which the Greeks used for "reason" was *logos*, sometimes translated as "word." Especially for Philo, the Jewish writer, that aspect of God which interacted with the universe, and which communicated with humans (say, in the burning bush), was called the logos. It became fairly common, then, to speak of the logos as the intermediary between the unchanging, transcendent God and the universe. Christians who were educated in the philosophy of the first few centuries would immediately identify the logos (word) of John's gospel with the intermediary aspect of God spoken of by Philo, by the Stoics, and by some of the middle Platonists.

Plotinus, a Greek-speaking Egyptian who studied in Alexandria and later taught in Rome from 244 to 270, created another very popular version of Platonism called Neoplatonism ("new" Platonism). Plotinus conceived of reality as a vast hierarchical system with grades descending from what is beyond being to what falls below being. The highest principle is God, designated as the One. Beyond being or mind, it is the source from which all comes and to which all strives to return. Below the One stands mind or thought, which includes the world of forms which it contemplates in its effort to return to the One. Below mind is soul, which is divided into the higher soul, which is like mind and transcends the material order, and the lower soul, or nature, which is the soul of sensed things. Matter in this system, unilluminated by form, is darkness or non-being.

Each person in this philosophy is urged to ascend to the One by purifying oneself from the body and sense perception. Rising to the level of the mind through the study of philosophy and science one eventually rises to the level of the One through ecstasy, in which the distinction between the One and the self is lost.

Not only did Plotinus' philosophy offer an ascent to God similar to Christian teaching, it also put forward an understanding of God as a triad. The Trinity, the ascent of the soul to God, the idea of the soul itself, as well as the notion that Jesus was somehow connected to the logos who was part of God from before time; all these concepts took shape in Christianity due to the influence of Platonism. Now there were differences, of course, but by the end of the fifth century most Christians would say their prayers and state their beliefs using language and concepts that were inherently Platonic in nature. Christianity borrowed heavily not only from Plotinus, but from all forms of Platonism. It offered a ready-made and respectable tradition which gave academic justification and impressive clarity to what was really a very recent religious movement. It is in terms of Platonism as well that the theology of the eucharist would develop.

More Problems

Just as in the early period, when scholars did turn their attention to the eucharist, it was sometimes due to misunderstandings of Christianity. Unlike the earlier period, however, the problems during the fourth through sixth centuries did not come from outside the church, but rather from within it. The Manichees did exercise some influence during these centuries (Augustine was a Manichee for nearly fifteen years), but the Manichees never claimed to be Christians, nor did they ever seriously challenge the growing dominance of Christianity in the Roman empire.

The great problems of these centuries came from an ever more sophisticated understanding of Christianity. If, as Platonists held and more and more Christians accepted, God must be unchanging if God is to be perfect, then how could it be possible for God to become incarnate in the person of Jesus of Nazareth? For Platonists, this was an easy question to answer. God couldn't and didn't do this. For Christians, however, the claim that Jesus was the incarnate logos formed the center of their beliefs. The question occupied the greatest minds of the time for several centuries, and even caused, as one contemporary historian tells us, fights in the markets and barber shops. Sadly, people were exiled and sometimes killed over the question.

The first great challenge came from a presbyter from Alexandria, Arius, who, beginning in the early third century, began to teach that the "logos" (the word) who became flesh was not quite fully God, and thus could be subject to change, while the Father, who was fully God, remained unchanged. Arius himself was condemned by his own bishop and several councils, but his teaching found support, sometimes even by the emperor. For more than fifty years the debate continued over the full divinity of the Son. It would not be solved until 380 when a council meeting at Constantinople declared once and for all the full divinity of the Father, Son and Spirit.

One of the most ardent defenders of the full divinity of the Son was yet another convert from Platonism, Hilary, who became bishop of Poitiers in France c. 354. Writing in the middle of the fourth century, Hilary was concerned to demonstrate the full divinity of the Son in opposition to those who claimed that, although one in will, the Son and the Father were different kinds of beings. In the eucharist, Hilary argued, we are joined to the very nature of Christ. There would be no point to this union unless Christ's life was the same as that of the Father, thus forming a saving union of natures between the Father, the Son, and the Christian:

> If the Word has indeed become made flesh, and we indeed receive the Word as flesh in the Lord's food, how are we not to believe that He dwells in us by His nature, He,

who, when He was born as man, has assumed the nature
of our flesh that is bound inseparably with Himself, and
has mingled the nature of His flesh to His eternal nature
in the mystery of the flesh that was to be communicated to
us? All of us are one, because the Father is in Christ and
Christ is in us (*On the Trinity*, book 8, c. 13).[2]

Hilary assumed that his adversaries agreed with him about the
eucharist, and then proceeded to turn that belief into an argument
against them. The general theme underlying Hilary's statement
here is that pointed out a century before by Irenaeus. Sharing in the
life of the risen Lord, already present to us in the eucharist, the
Christian is transformed, allowing him or her to join in immortal
life. For Hilary this process entails a form of deification because of
the union of Father and Son.

Even when the church accepted the full divinity of the Son in
380, problems remained. How was the human being, Jesus of Nazareth, related to the divine Son and word? The theologians in Antioch argued that Jesus remained a fully human being and independent of the word, although always acting in cooperation with the
divine. The theologians of Alexandria, on the other hand, argued
that the human Jesus was divine, completely overshadowed in both
body and soul by the power of the word. Both groups of theologians had recourse to the Lord's supper in making their arguments.
The argument, which began in the early fifth century, continues to
the present day and is usually referred to as the "Nestorian" controversy after Nestorius, the patriarch of Constantinople from 428 to
431. Arguments between Nestorius and Cyril, patriarch of Alexandria from 412 to 444, started the debate.

The Alexandrians were the first to appeal to the sacrament.
Writing in the early fifth century, Cyril, the patriarch of Alexandria
wished to demonstrate the unity of the divine and human natures in
Christ. In his commentary on the gospel of John, Cyril insisted the
body of Christ was so inseparably linked to the second person of the
Trinity that, through contact with the Lord's body in the eucharist,
Christians shared in divine immortality:

For He [Jesus] is Life by Nature, inasmuch as He was
begotten of a Living Father: no less quickening in His

Holy Body also, being in a manner gathered and ineffably united with the all-quickening Word. Wherefore It is accounted His, and is conceived of as One with Him. And since the Flesh of the Saviour hath become life-giving (as being united to That which is by Nature Life, the Word from God), when we taste It, then have we life in ourselves, we too united to It as It to the indwelling Word (*Commentary on the Gospel According to St. John*).[3]

Like Hilary, Cyril assumed his readers thought of the eucharist as imparting immortal life. Cyril goes on to point out that this could only happen if there were an intimate, insoluble union between the human and divine natures in Jesus Christ. So intimate is this union that the reception of the body of Christ in the sacrament necessarily entails a life-giving union with the word, the second person of the Trinity.

Cyril emphasized this point in one of his many letters to Nestorius, the patriarch of Constantinople:

We will necessarily add this also: Proclaiming the death according to the flesh of the Only begotten Son of God, that is, Jesus Christ, confessing His Resurrection from the dead, and His Ascension into heaven, we celebrate the unbloody sacrifice in the churches, and so proceed to the mystical consecrated gifts, and are sanctified, having become partakers of the holy flesh and precious blood of Christ, the Saviour of us all. And not as common flesh do we receive it, not at all, nor as a man sanctified and associated with the Word according to the unity of dignity, or as having had a divine indwelling, but as truly the lifegiving and very flesh of the Word Himself. For He is life according to His nature as God, and when He became united to His flesh, He made it lifegiving. Thus, even if He said to us "Amen, I say to you, unless you eat the flesh of the Son of Man and drink His blood" (John 6:54), we must not think that it is flesh of a man like us—for how can the flesh of man be life-giving by its own nature?—but as having become truly the very own of Him who for us both became and was called the Son of Man (*Third Letter to Nestorius*).[4]

The Antiochene writers would argue that the eucharist also supported their position that Jesus was fully human, and independent of the logos, although working in cooperation with him. Theodoret, the bishop of Cyrrhus in Syria, was one of the most brilliant of Cyril's opponents, and eventually even Cyril accepted a compromise creed written by Theodoret. One of the few works left by the bishop of Cyrrhus is written in the form of a dialogue in which Theodoret's position is taken by the character Orthodoxos. In this passage, Eranistes, a heretic, tries unsuccessfully to convince Orthodoxos of his eucharistic beliefs:

> *Eranistes:* And you believe that you partake of the body and blood of Christ? *Orthodoxos:* That is my belief. *Eranistes:* Therefore, just as the symbols of the Lord's body and His blood are one thing before the priest's invocation, but after the invocation are changed, and become something else, so too was the Lord's body changed, after the Ascension, into the divine essence. *Orthodoxos:* You have been caught in the nets which you have woven, for not even after the consecration do the mystical symbols depart from their own nature! They continue in their former essence, both in shape and appearance, and are visible, and palpable, as they were beforehand. But they are considered to be what they have become, and are believed to be that, and are adored as truly being those things which they are believed to be. Juxtapose, then, the image to the archetype, and you will see the likeness, for the type must bear a likeness to the truth. For too the body possesses, the earlier one, appearance, and shape, and outline, and generally the essence of a body. But after the Resurrection it has become immortal, and stronger than corruption, and was counted worthy of enthronement at the right-hand, and is adored by all creation, in that it is the body of the Lord of nature (*Dialogue 2*).[5]

Despite the fact that Cyril and Theodoret would disagree about the relationship of Jesus to the word, and hence the relationship between Jesus' body and the word, they had one important thing in common. Both understood the risen body of the Lord as a special kind of body. This new kind of body was unlike ours in that it was suffused with divinity and transmitted that divinity to those who received the body in the Lord's supper. Certainly, for both men, what was sensed in the sacrament was the least important aspect of the eucharist. As one might expect, this is how the bishops explained the rite to the catechumens in their care.

The Teaching of the Newly Baptized

During these centuries it was common practice for people to put off baptism until late in life. The emperor Constantine was baptized on his deathbed. The great bishops Augustine and Ambrose were not baptized until they were adults despite the fact that both came from Christian families. One of the duties of the bishops was to instruct these potential Christians (catechumens) on the Christian sacraments. Fortunately for us, some of the lectures which the bishops gave to the newly baptized Christians about both baptism and the Lord's supper have survived intact. These lectures provide an excellent witness to the understanding which Christians had of the central rituals in their lives.

During the fourth century, three great teachers appeared in Cappadocia (now central Turkey). All trained in the great universities of their day, they form a formidable force in Christian history. Two were brothers, Basil, bishop of Caesarea in Cappadocia and Gregory, bishop of Nyssa. The third was Basil's schoolmate and friend, Gregory, bishop of Sasima, who is more commonly known as Gregory of Nazianzus because his father was bishop of that city.

The lectures of Gregory of Nyssa, written c. 385 AD, offer a model presentation of the Christian faith to be used by catechists in their teaching of the newly baptized. In describing the eucharist, Gregory gives a very clear and simple explanation of how the sacrament effects our salvation:

> But since human nature is twofold, a composite of soul and body, those who are being saved must grasp Him who leads the way towards life by means of both. Now the soul, being blended with Him by faith, received from

it the beginnings of its salvation. For the union with Life involves a sharing of life. But the body comes into an association and blending with its Saviour in a different way. Those who have through treachery received poison neutralize its destructive force by means of another drug. But the antidote, like the poison, must enter the vital organs of the person, in order that the effect of the remedy may, by passing through them, be distributed through the entire body. So, when we had tasted of that which brought destruction to our nature, of necessity we needed in turn something to restore what was destroyed, in order that such an antidote passing into us might, by its own counteracting influence, repel the harm already brought into the body by the poison. What was this, then? It is nothing else but that body which was shown to be mightier than death and which inaugurated our life. For just as a little leaven, as the Apostle says (1 Cor 5:6), makes the whole lump like itself, so the body which was made immortal by God, by passing entire into our body, alters and changes it to itself. For just as when a deadly drug is mingled with a healthy body, the whole it is mingled with becomes as worthless as the drug, so also that immortal body, passing into him who receives it, changes the entire body to its own nature (*The Great Catechetical Oration 37*).[6]

According to Gregory, in order for our bodies to be saved as well as our souls, we need to be infused with the body of the risen Lord. Just like Cyril and Theodoret, however, Gregory was thinking here of the special, unique form of spiritualized body that the Lord had taken on after the resurrection. Just as our natures are overshadowed and mingled with the Lord's body through reception, so too the bread and wine are overshadowed by the Lord's body and become the medium through which the Lord contacts and transforms our bodies.

A very similar idea is contained in the set of catechetical lectures given c. 380–390 by Ambrose, the bishop of Milan. Quite possibly one of the newly baptized Christians to hear his sermons was Augustine, who was baptized by Ambrose in 387. In a famous passage, Ambrose describes the change that takes place in the bread and wine, as well as in the believer, during the ritual:

> The Lord commanded, the heaven was made. The Lord commanded, the earth was made. The Lord commanded, the seas were made. The Lord commanded, every creature came to be. You see then how effective is the word of Christ. If, then, there is so great a power in the word of the Lord Jesus that things which were not began to exist, then how much more effective, that those things which were exist, and are changed into something else! The heaven was not, the sea was not, the earth was not, but hear David as he says "He spoke and they were made, He commanded and they were created" (Psalm 148:5). Therefore, to answer you, there was not the body of Christ before the consecration; but after the consecration, I tell you, it is then the body of Christ. He spoke and it was made, He commanded and it was created. You existed, but you were an old creation. After you were consecrated, you began to be a new creation. Each, he says "is a new creation in Christ" (2 Cor 5:17) (*On the Sacraments*, book 4).[7]

For Ambrose, all things have been given a new identity in Christ. As the catechumens became new people through baptism, so in the celebration of the eucharist, the bread becomes the body of Christ. Now both Gregory and Ambrose were Platonists, and the change that they refer to here is not a "physical" change in *our* sense of the word. For us, physical means sensed, and clearly nothing sensed here has changed. What has changed is the essence, the true reality of the bread and wine, just as our true reality has been changed through baptism and through the reception of the Lord's body and blood. Of course, for Gregory and for Ambrose, this *would* be both "physical" (in terms of Platonic physics) and real. What really counts has changed, and what is sensed certainly counts very little.

This becomes even clearer in the catechetical lectures of Cyril, bishop of Jerusalem. Writing c. 348–349, Cyril has left a remarkable record of the kind of sermons a bishop would give to recent converts, including a description of the eucharist used in Jerusalem in the fourth century. Describing the bread and wine, Cyril tells his audience:

> Do not think of the elements as mere bread and wine. They are, according to the Lord's declaration, body and blood. Though the perception suggests the contrary, let faith be your stay. Instead of judging the matter by taste, let faith give you an unwavering confidence that you have been privileged to receive the body and blood of Christ (*Mystagogical Catechesis* 5).[8]

And Cyril adds later on:

> You have learned and become quite convinced that the perceptible bread is not bread, though it is bread to the taste, but the body of Christ, and that the perceptible wine is not wine, though taste will have it so, but the blood of Christ; and that it was of this that David sang of old: "Bread strengthens the heart of man, to make his face shine with oil" (Psalm 103:15). Strengthen your heart, partaking of this bread as spiritual, and make cheerful the face of your soul (*Mystagogical Catechesis* 5).[9]

Augustine, bishop of Hippo in North Africa at the close of the fourth and beginning of the fifth centuries, often mentioned the eucharist in his many works. A series of Augustine's lectures on the eucharist to the catechumens of Hippo have survived, dating from the early fifth century. Not surprisingly, many of the same themes found in Cyril and Ambrose also appear in Augustine's sermons. Like his contemporaries, Augustine also points out the importance of distinguishing what is seen from what is believed:

> These things, my brothers, are called sacraments (in Latin, the word *sacramentum* means "sign") for the reason that in them one thing is seen, but another is understood. That which is seen has physical appearance, that which is understood has spiritual fruit. If, then, you wish to understand the body of Christ, listen to the Apostle as he says to

the faithful "You are the body of Christ, and His members" (1 Cor 12:27). If, therefore, you are the body of Christ and His members, your mystery has been placed on the Lord's table, you receive your mystery. You reply "Amen" to that which you are, and by replying you consent. For you hear "The Body of Christ," and you reply "Amen." Be a member of the body of Christ that your "Amen" may be true (Sermon 272).[10]

In a second sermon, Augustine is even more explicit about the relationship between what is sensed and what is real in the eucharist:

Great mysteries are these, very great indeed! Would you like to know what importance is assigned to them? The Apostle says: "Whosoever eats the body of Christ or drinks of the cup of the Lord unworthily shall be guilty of the body and blood of the Lord" (1 Cor 11:27). What is it to receive unworthily? To receive in contempt, to receive in mockery. Let it not seem common to you because you can see it. What you see is transitory, but the invisible reality signified does not pass away, but abides. Behold, it is received, eaten, and consumed. Is the body of Christ consumed? Is the church of Christ consumed? Are the members of Christ consumed? Not at all! Here, on earth, His members are purified, there they are crowned. Thus what is signified will endure eternally, even though what signifies it seems to pass away (Sermon 227).[11]

At the risk of redundancy, listen again as the great bishop of Hippo explains to the recent converts the importance of inward efficacy of the sacrament which seems on the outside to be no more than common bread and wine. Remember that at this time ordinary bread and wine, brought from people's homes, were used in the ceremonies:

What you see on the Lord's table you are accustomed to see on your own tables, as far as outward appearances go. It has the same appearance, but not the same efficacy. You too are the same people you were before, for you do not present new faces to us. Nevertheless, you are new, your old selves in physical appearance, but new by the grace of holiness. So also is this something new. Until now, as you see, it is bread and wine. But once the consecration is added, this bread will be the body of Christ and this wine will be the blood of Christ. The name of Christ, the grace of Christ brings it about that even though it looks as it looked before, yet its efficacy is not what it was before. Had you eaten thereof before the consecration, it would have filled your stomach; but now, when it is eaten, it builds up the soul (Sermon Wolfenbüttel 7).[12]

The fathers quoted above all shared a common overview of the presence of the Lord. The spiritual reality, perceived through faith, of the eucharist was the risen, transformed body and blood of the Lord. This presence transformed our own bodies, giving them the immortality which the Lord's body and blood had already attained. Notice, however, the comparison made by the authors. The change taking place on the altar is the same sort of change which takes place in the "essence," the soul of the believer in baptism. The true reality of the new Christian makes him or her a truly new form of being, because his or her "essence," his or her soul, has changed. Imagine, then, that the "essences" or, if you like, the "souls" of the bread and wine have changed here, so that the risen body of the Lord can come into contact with each believer, and grant him or her immortality.

Living the Eucharist

As Augustine points out, however, the presence of the risen Lord exists not only in the bread and wine, but in the community itself. The eucharist *is*, for the fathers, the community acting in faith and charity. The body of Christ exists just as really and "physically" in the community of faith and love as it does in heaven and as it does in the eucharist. Why? Because the spirit, the essence, the soul, of the risen Lord animates the community as surely, as "really," as it animates the risen body and as surely as this spirit is mediated by the bread and wine. Just as for the earliest writers of the church, the fathers assumed and demanded that the life of faith and love which is Christianity was central to worthy participation in the eucharist. In fact, in a real sense, such a life was the eucharist. Many of the writers of this period write about this subject and all assume it, but for the sake of brevity only two will be discussed here.

Later writers, both in the middle ages and reformation periods, would remark on the close identity which Augustine saw to exist between a true Christian life and participation in the sacrament. This was a theme so central to Augustine that in a passage from Augustine's commentary on John's gospel, he comes close to identifying the two completely:

> Wherefore, the Lord, about to give the Holy Spirit, said that Himself was the bread that came down from heaven, exhorting us to believe on Him. For to believe on Him is to eat the living bread. He that believes eats; he is sated invisibly, because invisibly he is born again (*Tract.* 26, c. 1).[13]

Further on in the same commentary, Augustine remarks:

> For we have said, brethren, that this is what the Lord had taught us by the eating of His flesh and drinking of His blood, that we should abide in Him and He in us. But we abide in Him when we are His members, and He abides when we are His temple. But that we may be His members, unity joins us together. And what but love can effect that unity should join us together? (*Tract.* 27, c. 6).[14]

And finally, in a passage from the same commentary, Augustine tells his congregation what it means to truly eat and drink the body and blood of the Lord:

> Finally, He [Jesus] explains how what He is speaking of is to come about, and what it is to eat His body and drink His blood. He who eats my flesh and drinks my blood abides in me and I in him. Therefore, to eat that flesh and to drink that drink is to abide in Christ and to have Him

abiding in oneself. And so he who does not abide in Christ and in whom Christ does not abide is, beyond doubt, one who neither eats his flesh nor drinks His blood, but instead eats and drinks the sacrament of so great a reality unto condemnation for himself (1 Cor. 11:29), because, though unclean, he has presumed to approach the sacraments of Christ which no one receives worthily except him who is clean, concerning whom is said: "Blessed are the clean of heart, for they shall see God (Matt 5:8)" (*Tract.* 26).[15]

Although only one strand in Augustine's thought, these passages demonstrate how closely the early Christians tied a true Christian life to a worthy celebration of the eucharist. Of all the brilliant writers and speakers of this period, none was more eloquent than John, the patriarch of Constantinople from 398 to 403. John is usually known by the phrase that best describes him, John of the Golden Tongue, or, in Greek, John Chrysostom. Fifteen hundred years and an English translation have done nothing to tarnish the gold. To read St. John is to be thrilled and challenged by the Christian call. Like Augustine, John insists that to receive the eucharist demands a Christian life, and he is unrelenting in his challenge to his flock:

Let there be no Judas present, no one avaricious. If anyone is not a disciple, let him go away. The table does not receive such ones, for "I keep the passover," He says, "with my disciples" (Matt 26:18). This table is the same as that, it has nothing less. It is not the case that Christ created that one, and man this one. He Himself creates this one also. This is the upper room where they were then, whence they went out to the Mount of Olives. Let us also go out to the hands of the poor, for that is the Mount of Olives. The multitude of the poor are olive-trees planted in the house of God, dripping the oil which is needful for us there. The five virgins (Matt 25:1–13) had it, and the rest, who did not, perished for that reason. With it, let us go in, that with bright lamps we may meet the Bridegroom. With it, let us go forth from here. Let no

inhuman person be present, no one who is cruel and merci-
less, no one at all who is unclean.

Chrysostom continues on to admonish the celebrant to take care
that only those actually dedicated to a Christian life be allowed to
receive the life-giving body and blood of the Lord:

> I say these things to you who receive, and also to you who
> minister. For I must address myself to you also, so that
> you may distribute the gifts with great care. There is no
> small punishment for you if, conscious of any wickedness
> in any man, you allow him to partake of this table. "His
> blood shall be required at your hands" (Ez 33:8). Even
> though someone may be a general, or a prefect, or even
> the one who is invested with the diadem [*sc.* the emperor],
> if he approaches unworthily, forbid him. Your authority is
> greater than his. If you were entrusted with the task of
> keeping a spring of water clean for a flock, and you saw a
> sheep with much mire on its mouth, you would not allow
> it to stoop down into the stream and foul it. But now,
> entrusted with a spring, not of water, but of blood and
> Spirit, if you see any who have sin on them, something
> more grievous than mire, approaching it, and you are not
> indignant, and do not drive them off, what pardon can
> you have? (*Homily on Matthew*).[16]

One can imagine that John's congregation, which commonly
interrupted his sermons with applause and shouts, was very quiet
that day. Yet John was only articulating the same theme as Paul, as
the Acts of the Apostles, as Cyprian of Carthage and as Ignatius of
Antioch. Many things would change in the liturgy and in the understanding of the eucharist throughout history, but the connection
between living a Christian life and worthy reception of the sacrament has remained a constant refrain and challenge.

Other themes also appeared in the teaching of the bishops
during these years, of course. Continuing the custom of the late
third century, Christians would describe the action of the eucharist
as a form of spiritual reenactment of the crucifixion. Borrowing
from Hebrew scripture, they would describe the actions of the

liturgy as a form of spiritual sacrifice which gave the faithful access to the salvation effected on Calvary. Gregory I, pope in the late sixth century, merged two themes in describing the effects of the celebration of the liturgy. In a passage in his *Dialogues*, he not only stressed that the body and blood of the Lord were present in a saving way by participation in the sacrament, but also included a striking description of the Lord's supper as mediating for us the sacrifice of Calvary:

> The Sacrifice alone has the power of saving the soul from eternal death, for it presents to us mystically the death of the only-begotten Son. Though He is now risen from the dead and dies no more, and "death has no more power over him" (Rom 6:9), yet, living in Himself immortal and incorruptible, He is again immolated for us in the mystery of the holy Sacrifice. Where His Body is eaten, there His flesh is distributed among the people for their salvation. His Blood no longer stains the hands of the godless, but flows into the hearts of His faithful followers. See, then, how august the Sacrifice that is offered for us, ever reproducing in itself the passion of the only-begotten Son for the remission of our sins. For, who of the faithful can have doubt that at the moment of the immolation, at the sound of the priest's voice, the heavens stand open and choirs of angels are present at the mystery of Jesus Christ (Book 4, c. 60).[17]

Just as in the passages quoted above Augustine and John Chrysostom identified the eucharist with authentic Christian living, here Gregory identified the Lord's supper with the redemptive action of the crucifixion. It is this unique saving action of Christ that touches us and saves us in the eucharist. Again, Gregory would not have meant this as a magical act. One would have to incorporate the crucifixion into one's own life in order for the grace of redemption to be truly present. As in the writings of Hilary and Cyril of Alexandria, however, Gregory understood contact with the risen Lord in the Lord's supper as linking us with the salvation he has won for us.

If the above passages seem a rather scattered collection of various, and even irreconcilable, thoughts about the eucharist, it is because they are meant to be. Discussions of the eucharist sprang up in the fathers' works in the midst of other topics. They did not sit down and carefully work out a consistent understanding, nor did they compare notes with their fellow theologians and bishops to see if everyone was teaching the same thing. The result is, of course, that when one places these random thoughts side by side, one is faced with a number of common themes, but no common theology. What the fathers of the early church bequeathed to their followers was not a theology of the eucharist, but a pluralism of themes out of which any number of theologies could develop. By the early ninth century this process had begun.

The Celebration

Once again, traveling back in time to witness a liturgy of the patristic period can help us understand why the writers just discussed saw the eucharist in the way that they did. If we entered the great basilica of Constantinople or Milan at the time of John Chrysostom or Ambrose, we would be amazed at the difference between this grand and noble ceremony and the simple and sometimes furtive meetings of the first few centuries. The first difference would be the buildings themselves. Immense, dark, and cavernous, the basilicas were meant to impress the visitor. We would be faced with a huge mosaic of, perhaps, Christ in glory, looking like the emperor in his majesty. In the apse (the rounded back of the building) a throne would be placed. Here only the bishop could sit, just as judges and rulers did in the secular basilicas of the time. Paintings and tiles would tell us that we were in imperial surroundings.

This impression would not be lessened upon the arrival of the bishop as celebrant. Privileges associated only with the highest ranking officials of the empire would be accorded to the leader of the church. The bishop would be met at the church by a chorus, a rite reserved only for the emperor. He was waited on by deacons with covered hands, again a mark of imperial dignity. People would genuflect in front of the bishop and kiss his feet. By the seventh century, a procession would precede the patriarch, at least in Rome, and the clergy would sit around the bishop's throne just as the emperor's advisors sat at his side. The bishop would be dressed as an imperial dignitary with not only special clothes but also special shoes and head gear. All of these clothes were marks of imperial dignity, and clearly secular and political in origin. As fifth century Christians, we would probably be delighted to see our leaders treated like emperors out of respect for God. Of course, such dignity could, and sometime did, go to the head of the person who was bishop. A few important bishops, like Hilary of Poitiers and Augustine of Hippo, thought that such honors were not appropriate to men of God. On the whole, however, people probably would have expected to see God honored in the way that they best knew, that is, by imitating the honor due to the secular ruler.

The liturgy itself would be longer than in earlier centuries, with an entrance song and a song of praise (*Sanctus*) among the additions. Ambrose loved to teach his people new songs, and one can imagine that there were enthusiastic, but dignified, liturgies in Milan. The central part of the liturgy changed little: readings, followed by the offering of bread and wine, the blessings of these gifts and their distribution. Everything, however, became more stylized and formal, as one can imagine in such a setting.

To give one example of how reception became stylized, listen to the description of a proper reception given by Cyril of Jerusalem:

> Coming up to receive, then, do not have your wrists extended or your fingers spread, but making your left hand a throne for the right, for it is about to receive a King, and cupping your palm, receive the body of Christ, and answer "Amen." Carefully hallow your eyes by the touch of the sacred body, and then partake, taking care to lose no part of it. Tell me, if someone gave you gold-dust, would you not take the greatest care to hold it fast, so as not to lose any of it and endure its loss? How much more carefully, then, will you guard against losing so much as a crumb of that which is more precious than gold or precious stones? After partaking of the body of Christ, approach also the cup of His blood. Do not stretch out your hands, but, bowing low in a posture of worship and reverence as you say "Amen," sanctify yourself by partaking of the blood of Christ. While it is still moist upon your lips,

touch it with your fingers, and so sanctify your eyes, your forehead, and other senses. Then wait for the prayer, and give thanks to God who has counted you worthy of such high mysteries (*Mystagogical Catechesis*, 5).[18]

Of course, not all liturgies would be so elaborate as those described above. In the countryside, one imagines, small groups would gather much as in earlier centuries. They would still use small buildings; and perhaps even houses as churches. Yet the ideal was the formal liturgy with the bishop presiding. More and more court ceremony would be added to the liturgy until even the responses to the liturgical prayers were made by a trained choir rather than by the people. Christianity would have been closely integrated into imperial society by the end of the fifth century. Christian liturgies would have used imperial civic buildings; bishops, priests and deacons would have had special standing in imperial law, and they would have worn court dress in performing the liturgy. All of these things would survive into the following centuries. Only one thing would have disappeared, at least in the west. That, unfortunately, would be the empire itself. Slowly, but inexorably, tribes from Asia and eastern Europe pushed their way into the Roman empire, cutting off the west from the emperor and his armies centered in Constantinople.

One imperial institution held firm, however, and that was the church. Augustine died at the venerable age of seventy-six while his community was being besieged by the Vandals. Leo, the patriarch of Rome from 440 to 461, convinced Attila the Hun not to sack Rome in one of the greatest feats of diplomacy in history. Gregory, his successor in Rome at the end of the sixth century, used his family fortune to set up refugee camps and to pay the police and soldiers. More and more people looked to the church as the last bastion of stability, justice and learning in a world torn apart by the barbarian invasions. It was into such a world that the very first books written exclusively on the eucharist appeared.

GLOSSARY OF PERSONS

Ambrose, bishop of Milan. Ambrose was the son of the Roman prefect of Gaul (France). He was trained in law and was eventually appointed governor of the region of Italy centered in Milan about 370. When the bishop of Milan died in 374, Ambrose was proclaimed bishop by popular acclaim, despite the fact that he was not yet baptized. After some hesitation, he submitted to baptism and ordination. Bishop until 397, Ambrose was one of the leading figures of his day. Known as one of the four great doctors of the western church, he fought to keep the church free of government control, wrote beautiful sermons and hymns, and helped to make the Greek theologians available to the Latin-speaking west.

Arius and Arianism. Arius was a presbyter and teacher in Alexandria who, early in the fourth century, began teaching that the logos (the Son of God incarnate in Jesus) was not fully divine. His teachings were condemned at several councils, as well as by his own bishop. Arius died c. 336. The questions he raised, however, continued to be discussed for another fifty years after his death. "Arianism," the heresy named after him, teaches that because God is perfect and unchanging, it is impossible for God in God's perfection to interact with nature or humanity, and so the incarnation of God in the human Jesus must be of some lesser form of divinity. Arianism was finally condemned at the Council of Constantinople in 380.

Athanasius, patriarch of Alexandria. Athanasius, patriarch from 328 until 373, was the leader of the opposition to Arianism, insisting throughout his long life that the Son of God incarnate in Jesus was fully divine. Athanasius suffered much for his beliefs, spending over fifteen years of his episcopate in either exile or hiding. (He was one bishop who kept his bags packed!) Beloved by his community, he was never handed over to the authorities while in hiding, and often he found his way out into the desert, where the famous monk, Antony, supported his cause. Along with his numerous writings against Arianism, Athanasius wrote a famous life of Antony which did much to popularize monasticism.

Augustine, bishop of Hippo.   One of the greatest of the Latin Christian writers, Augustine was born in North Africa in 354. His mother was a fervent Christian and his father was a pagan. Both agreed that Augustine should become a successful rhetor (lawyer). By the age of thirty Augustine had succeeded beyond his parents' dreams in becoming rhetor of the city of Milan. Disillusioned with the Manicheeism he had picked up in his youth, Augustine was converted by reading Neoplatonism and listening to the sermons of Ambrose. He retired as a rhetor and eventually became bishop of the North African city of Hippo (modern Annabis). He spent the rest of his life writing on almost every important topic of the time and influencing not only the North African church, but the entire western church. He died at the age of seventy-six while the city of Hippo was under siege by the Vandals.

Basil, bishop of Caesarea.   Born c. 330 in Cappadocia (now central Turkey), Basil was educated in Caesarea, Constantinople, and Athens. He gave up his career, however, to lead the life of a hermit. Only when his bishop asked him to debate the Arian emperor Valens did he come out of his retirement. He was elected bishop of Caesarea in 370 and spent the rest of his life defending orthodoxy against the claims of the Arians. Basil was also an excellent administrator and organized the monastic communities in Turkey. He convinced both his brother (Gregory of Nyssa) and his good friend (Gregory of Nazianzus) to aid him in his efforts. He died in 379 shortly before the Arian controversy was settled at the Council of Constantinople.

Constantine.   The son of the emperor Constantius Chlorus and St. Helena, Constantine was proclaimed emperor in 306. He defeated his chief rival for the throne at the battle of Milvian bridge where Constantine adopted the Christian cross as his battle standard. Constantine, although not baptized until his death in 337, supported Christianity as his favored religion. He worked to integrate the Christian faith into Roman law and society and gave generously to constructing basilicas for Christian worship. He moved the capital of the empire from Rome to the city of Constantinople (modestly named after himself) in 324.

Cyril, patriarch of Alexandria. Chosen as patriarch of Alexandria in 412, Cyril fervently, if somewhat unscrupulously, defended orthodoxy against all forms of heresy and paganism. He is perhaps best known for his attack on Nestorius, the patriarch of Constantinople, whom he accused of heresy because of Nestorius' teaching concerning the relationship between the logos and the man Jesus. A brilliant theologian, Cyril finally reached a compromise position with the supporters of Nestorius. Cyril enforced the compromise until his death in 444, at which time the whole issue was raised once more.

Cyril, patriarch of Jerusalem. Cyril was patriarch of Jerusalem from c. 349 until his death in 386. Twice banished during the Arian controversy because of his faith, Cyril seems to have been instrumental in forming the creed written at the Council of Constantinople in 381. He is best known for the catechetical lectures given during Lent and Easter c. 350 which describe the rites used in Jerusalem during the fourth century.

Gregory I, patriarch of Rome. Known as Gregory the Great, Gregory was the son of a Roman senator and became prefect of the city of Rome in 573. He gave up his position, however, and distributed his wealth to the poor, entering a monastery c. 574. Elected pope in 590, Gregory immediately moved to negotiate a settlement with the Lombard tribes who were harassing Rome and used the church's wealth to aid the poor refugees streaming into Rome due to the barbarian invasions. Gregory was also a gifted writer and an avid supporter of monasticism. He died in 604.

Gregory, bishop of Nyssa. The younger brother of Basil of Caesarea, Gregory originally practiced law as a Roman rhetor. He soon left his profession, however, to join his brother's monastery. In 371 he was consecrated bishop of Nyssa and worked closely with his brother to defend the orthodox faith against the Arians. Much in demand as a preacher, he traveled a great deal in his later years. He died c. 395.

Gregory of Nazianzus. Born in 329, Gregory was the son of the bishop of Nazianzus in Cappadocia. He was a fellow student of

Basil of Caesarea at the university in Athens. Like Gregory of Nyssa, Gregory of Nazianzus followed Basil of Caesarea into the monastery. Truly of a monastic spirit, Gregory was ordained and became bishop of the small village of Sasima in 372 only under duress. He never even visited Sasima, but helped his father in Nazianzus until his father died in 374. In 379 Gregory attended the Council of Constantinople, where he was elected patriarch, but resigned after the council, returning to the monastic life until his death in 389.

Hilary, bishop of Poitiers. A convert from Neoplatonism, Hilary was elected bishop of Poitiers in southern France c. 353. He was exiled by the emperor for four years (356–360) for his defense of orthodoxy against the Arians. While in exile in Asia, he was in contact with the other leaders in the struggle against Arianism. He was the most respected of the Latin Christian writers of his day. He died in 367.

John Chrysostom. Originally trained as a rhetor (lawyer), John gave up his profession to become a hermit. He retired first to his home, and later to the desert. Ordained by the bishop of Antioch, he was assigned as a preacher, a task at which he was so successful that he gained the nickname "Golden Tongue" (in Greek, *Chrysostom*). Against his wishes John was made patriarch of Constantinople in 398, where he made powerful enemies by his preaching against the corruption of the imperial court. His enemies first framed him on heresy charges and when this strategy failed, they had him banished. He finally died in 407 when, despite poor health, he was forced to travel during inclement weather.

Julian (the Apostate). The nephew of Constantine, Julian suffered the murder of all but one of his male relatives under the brutal policy of the emperor. Julian turned violently against Christianity. A fellow student of Gregory of Nazianzus, he eventually became emperor in 361. During his brief reign Julian attempted to restore the ancient Roman religion to the empire. He died fighting the Persians in 363. His reign was the last attempt to remove Christianity from its favored position in the Roman empire.

Manes and Manicheeism. Manes was born c. 216 in Persia. Raised in a Christian community which still practiced Jewish customs, Manes founded his own religion based on his studies of Persian religion, Buddhism and Christianity. Manes was put to death by the Persian emperor in 276, but by the time of his death Manicheeism was already spreading rapidly throughout the Roman empire. Manichees teach that there is a radical dualism in the world. All matter is evil, and all spirit is good. The purpose of life is to remove the spiritual part of ourselves (the soul) from the matter (the body) in which it is trapped. Buddha, Jesus and Manes had all been sent from God to aid this process. Eventually the effects of creation (a great cosmic mistake) would be reversed, and all spirit would be finally separated from matter. Severe asceticism, celibacy, and vegetarianism were practiced by the truly dedicated (the elect).

Monophysitism. The teaching that Jesus had no human nature of his own, but only the divine nature of the logos. In Greek, "monophysite" means "one nature." The Monophysites refused to accept the Council of Chalcedon in 451 which reaffirmed the compromise position reached by Cyril of Alexandria and Theodoret of Cyrrhus in 433. The Monophysite communities were an important part of the African and Asian church until the advent of Islam. The Copts in Egypt, the Armenian Christians, and the Syrian Jacobites are important monophysite groups in the present day.

Nestorius. Patriarch of Constantinople from 428 to 431, Nestorius was a monk from Antioch famous for his preaching. A student of the biblical school at Antioch, he was accused by Cyril of Alexandria of teaching that there were two separate persons in Christ, a human person and a divine person. Although it seems that he never really taught this heresy of "Nestorianism," it has become associated with his name. Nestorius was deposed and died in exile sometime after 436.

Philo. Born into a prominent Jewish family in Alexandria c. 20 B.C., Philo was the leading Jewish intellectual of his time. He developed a form of biblical interpretation which used contemporary philosophical sources to interpret the hidden (spiritual) meaning of scripture.

Philo's influence continued in Alexandria long after his death c. 50. The early Christian writers in Alexandria, like Clement and Origen, borrowed freely from Philo.

Plato. A native of Athens, Plato gave up a political career to become a student of the philosopher Socrates and eventually a philosopher in his own right. Except for one unsuccessful venture in politics, Plato spent his life teaching in his school outside Athens. One of the greatest of western thinkers, Plato's thought has influenced philosophy down to the present day. His students include the equally great Greek philosopher Aristotle.

Plotinus. Plotinus studied under the many different philosophers teaching in Alexandria in the early third century, where he may have studied under the same teacher as Origen. At the age of forty, c. 244, he established his own school in Rome. He died in 270. Usually considered the greatest of Neoplatonic philosophers, his teaching influenced such important Christian writers as Ambrose and Augustine.

Theodoret, bishop of Cyrrhus. Born in Antioch c. 393, Theodoret distributed his wealth to the poor and entered the monastery at about the age of twenty. Some five years later, he was consecrated bishop of Cyrrhus in Syria. A friend and defender of Nestorius, the patriarch of Constantinople, he eventually reached a compromise with Cyril of Alexandria, who had accused Nestorius of heresy. After Cyril's death, Theodoret was accused of heresy and exiled from 449 to 451. After his return to his see, Theodoret ruled his diocese in peace until his death c. 466.

4

Diversity in Practice: The Early Middle Ages

In the seventh and eighth centuries, one of the greatest spiritual movements in history swept through the regions which first produced Christianity. Islam, the doctrine of submission to the one God, sister religion to Judaism and Christianity, swept through the Middle East, threatening to engulf western Europe and the Roman empire based in Constantinople. The effect on Christianity was devastating. Three of the five great centers of Christianity, the patriarchates of Jerusalem, Antioch and Alexandria, were now dominated by Islam.

Only the two most distant of the patriarchates remained to lead the church, Rome and Constantinople. These two centers were separated by a great distance, filled with dangers from the Islamic armies. Constantinople continued the refined, elaborate learning and ritual inherited from Greek thought. Rome, always a center of Latin rather than Greek thought, more and more adopted the ways of the barbarian tribes who dominated the west. The two leaders of Christianity slowly drifted apart, politically, intellectually and ritually.

This book will follow developments in the west, since this is the history that affects most directly most Christians in the United States and western Europe. It is well to remember, however, that all during the period of which we are speaking, great theologians will be writing in Greek, in Byzantium, as the Roman empire in this period will be known. Sometimes scholarly exchange will be both possible and welcome between the sister churches; sometimes excommunications will be hurled back and forth. But the theology of the eucharist from this point on takes a different form in the west and in the east, and so we reluctantly turn from the beauty of Greek thought to the more rough and ready Latin west.

The First Treatises on the Eucharist

Very little was written on the eucharist between the death of Gregory in 604 and the appearance of the first treatises on the eucharist in the ninth century. In fact, very little theology was written at all. The Roman empire was torn asunder by wave after wave of invasions from the Germanic tribes to the east. Augustine died in 430 while the Vandals besieged the city of Hippo. Gregory spent the wealth of the church to pay the imperial soldiers and provide care for the refugees flooding into Rome. Except for a brief respite under the emperor Justinian, the western half of the Roman empire was pretty much left to its own devices, while the emperors in Constantinople were hard pressed to defend themselves in the east. As imperial officials themselves, the bishops and especially the patriarch of Rome took upon themselves the task of first placating and then Christianizing the Germanic tribes.

The year 800 marks a turning point in the history of western Europe. First of all, for the first time since the Roman empire had come under attack in the fifth century, a kind of unity and peace had been enforced on central Europe by the powerful warlord and leader of the Franks, Charles the Great (or in French, Charlemagne). Secondly, in a dramatic move, the west officially and formally broke diplomatic ties with the east when Pope Gregory III crowned a reluctant and astounded Charlemagne emperor on Christmas Day, 800. Charlemagne was not just crowned emperor in the west, but the true Roman emperor, successor to Julius Caesar and Caesar Augustus. Needless to say, this did not go down well in Constantinople, but by this time, there was little the empress Irene could do. The west turned traitor to the old empire and began to chart an independent course.

Charlemagne was chosen by the papacy to restore order and Christianity to western Europe. Even before his coronation, Charles had set about the reformation of his empire with the same vigor and resourcefulness that he once used to smash his enemies. One of

Charlemagne's first orders of business was the preaching and teaching of Christianity to his people. For this purpose, he imported to his court the best scholars to be had and even borrowed the pope's own mass book so that copies could be made and sent out to all the bishops. To an illiterate people the liturgy was extremely important, as here the common folk could see the central mysteries of Christianity acted out in a kind of pantomime.

Rosamund McKitterick, in her excellent book on the reforms of Charlemagne and his successors, describes the importance of the liturgy to this effort:

> The motives for the remarkable liturgical activity in the ninth century are quite clear, and they are those of the Carolingian reform programme generally; the extirpation of paganism, promotion of unity, the proclamation of Christianity, and above all, the instruction of the people. The liturgy was one of the most crucial elements in the shaping of the Frankish society.[1]

One of the scholars instrumental in the attempt to reform the liturgy was Amalarius of Metz. A highly original and exuberant scholar, Amalarius not only set out to reform the liturgy of Laon while acting bishop there, but also wrote an elaborate commentary on the liturgy, describing the mass as a tableau of the life of Christ. The deacon of Lyons, Florus, objected to the innovations of the chancellor, and, partly from personal spite and partly from true concern for orthodoxy, had some of the teachings of Amalarius condemned for heresy at the Council of Quierzy in 838.

One of the teachings condemned centered around the explanation of Amalarius for the breaking of the bread into three parts during the canon of the mass. Amalarius asserted that the three parts of the host stood for three bodies of Christ: the first, the presence on the altar, the second, the church itself, and the third, the risen body of Christ now in heaven. Florus accused Amalarius of dividing the one body of the Lord. The problem is, of course, not irreconcilable. Earlier writers had spoken of all three presences as yet being one. The charge of Florus may not have stemmed only from spite, however. More literal minds were now approaching the mysteries, and Florus would certainly not be the last person to wonder which of the "bodies" spoken of by the fathers was really present to the faithful.

It is against such a background that the first theological work written specifically on the eucharist appeared. Writing c. 831–833, Paschasius Radbertus, a monk at the monastery of Corbie, composed a book entitled *On the Body and Blood of the Lord* for the education of the Saxon monks. It seems that the barbarian monks were having trouble understanding exactly what use the Lord's supper might have. Although relying heavily on the theology of Hilary and Ambrose, Paschasius would be the first writer to attempt a consistent theology of the eucharist, and it would be here that his major contribution to the theology of the eucharist would lie.

Like Irenaeus, Hilary and Cyril, Paschasius asserted that Christians are saved by a kind of natural union formed between the recipients of the supper and the body of the risen Lord. For this reason, Paschasius also insisted that the body of Christ present in the eucharist was the same body as that born of Mary. Paschasius' reasoning was simple and straightforward. God took on human nature, thus transforming human nature itself in the person of Jesus. It is this transformed human nature, the same human nature born of Mary, which is present, and which Christians receive, in the eucharist. By this reception, our human nature, body and soul, is taken up and joined with Christ's nature, thus sharing in its transformation. Paschasius paraphrased Hilary when he asserted:

> If the Word had become flesh, and we truly consume the Word as flesh in the Lord's food, how can it not be justly judged that He dwells in us by His nature, who being God born as a human, has assumed the inseparable nature of our flesh, and has mingled the nature of His flesh to His eternal nature in the sign of the flesh that was to be communicated to us? And therefore in this way, we all are one in God the Father and the Son and Holy Spirit, because it has been shown that the Father is in Christ and Christ is in us. On this account it is that we are made one body naturally with Christ.[2]

Paschasius would repeat this claim several times but perhaps he was clearest in a letter explaining his thought to a young monk:

"[Christ] however lives on account of the Father, because he was born the only-begotten one of the Father, and we live on account of Him, because we eat Him."[3]

At first glance, this seems a crude way of describing the reception of the Lord's body, and at least one of Paschasius' contemporaries accused him of a realism bordering on cannibalism. But this is to misunderstand Paschasius. He went out of his way to insist that the reception of the Lord's body is always to be understood in a spiritual sense. The body of the Lord to which Paschasius referred was the spiritual body of the risen Lord—still the body born of Mary—but now transformed by the resurrection.

When faced with difficulties in understanding how bread and wine could be the body and blood of the Lord or how the Lord's body could be present in many places simultaneously, Paschasius referred to divine omnipotence. God was the author of the laws of nature, and could, and in this case does, break them to ensure our salvation. Nor was salvation for Paschasius a simple matter of some sort of magical contact with the risen Lord. Only those already united to Christ by living a life of faith and love would be naturally joined to the risen Lord through reception of his body and blood.

Paschasius united an understanding of the incarnation, an understanding of salvation, and an understanding of the Lord's supper into a unique and consistent, if somewhat simplistic, whole. In a sense, Paschasius reversed the arguments of Irenaeus, Hilary and Cyril. They used a particular understanding of the eucharist to demonstrate their teaching concerning the nature of Jesus the Lord and Christ. Paschasius took the now accepted understanding of the Lord and used it to demonstrate what role the Lord's presence in the sacrament must play in Christian salvation. Paschasius' clear, consistent and simple little book for Saxon monks, for better or worse, would long influence the theological interpretation of the Lord's supper.

Yet if Paschasius in some sense preserved the themes highlighted by Irenaeus, Hilary and Cyril, his fellow monk and theologian Ratramnus based his understanding of the sacrament on the thoughts of Cyprian, Ignatius and Augustine. Ratramnus was a well-known theologian who was also a monk at the abbey of Corbie. He wrote a short treatise on the eucharist in answer to a letter written by the newly crowned emperor Charles the Bald, grandson of Charle-

magne. Charles wrote Ratramnus asking him to answer two questions concerning the eucharist. First, did the faithful receive the
body and blood of Christ in truth or in mystery? Second, was this the
same body and blood as that born of Mary? That the emperor should
write to Ratramnus of Corbie on just these two questions is interesting, since Paschasius, now abbot of Corbie, had sent a special copy of
his own work on the eucharist to the emperor for his coronation.
Historians for centuries have assumed that Charles read Paschasius'
work and then wrote to Ratramnus for clarification. The situation
certainly would have been an awkward one. The monk and theologian Ratramnus would have to respond to the emperor concerning
the theology of his own abbot.

Ratramnus' response, if it is intended as response to the theology of Paschasius, showed little tact. Ratramnus' approach to the
sacrament proved to be very different from that of his abbot. Because of this, and also because of the role these works would play in
later controversies, scholars in the eleventh century, the sixteenth
century, and on into the twentieth century would speak of the
"controversy" over the eucharist between Paschasius and Ratramnus. Heriger, abbot of Lobbes from 990 to 1007, would be the first
to point out that two such different theologies must have been
written in contention.

Certainly, Ratramnus' theology was different from that of his
abbot Paschasius. Ratramnus answered the emperor by stating,
first, that we do indeed receive the body and blood of the Lord in a
real manner in the eucharist, but that this reality is a reality "in
sign" or "in figure." This figure points to the interior reality of the
spiritual presence of the risen Lord. It is this spiritual reality, not
the signs that we receive, that saves us. These signs could even be
changed, as when God used the manna in the desert to symbolize
his saving presence for the ancient Hebrews. Ratramnus would
explain his thought in this way:

> This is confessed most plainly by saying that in the sacra-
> ment of the body and blood of the Lord, whatever exterior
> thing is consumed is adapted to refection by the body.
> The mind, however, invisibly feeds on the Word of God,
> Who is the invisible bread invisibly existing in that sacra-
> ment, by the vivifying participation of faith.[4]

So, too, Ratramnus answered the emperor's second question by asserting that the physical body born of Mary could not be present in the eucharist. How could there be bones, nerves and flesh present on the altar? No, it is the spiritual body and blood that are present under the signs of bread and wine. This second, spiritual presence of Christ is present to us in faith, sensed by our minds, and it is this presence that saves us.

The differences between the theology of Paschasius and Ratramnus are obvious. For Paschasius, the actual contact between the risen body of the Lord and our bodies is a necessary part of the process of salvation. We actually need this contact to be saved. For Ratramnus, whatever might be present to our senses in the Lord's supper is only a sign of the presence of the Lord known in faith, and it is this presence known in faith that saves us. The positions are not mutually exclusive; after all Paschasius insisted that he was speaking only of the *spiritual* body and blood of the risen Lord in his explanation. Most people who have read the two works down through the centuries have noticed (and emphasized) the differences, however, and not the similarities of the two theologies.

Yet, if there was a controversy at Corbie in the mid-ninth century, it was a very quiet one. A few mumblings by other theologians, which may or may not have been directed at the two Cluniacs, are the only witnesses to the struggle. No council was held; Paschasius remained as abbot; Ratramnus remained a well-respected theologian. As far as can be determined, the two men went on living together in peace, attending the same liturgy, but obviously thinking about it in quite different ways. A letter from Paschasius to a young monk who read both works and was understandably confused demonstrates that Paschasius was aware of Ratramnus' work, and did in fact disagree with it. It is hard to interpret motives on such scant evidence, and yet it seems quite likely that two different theologies of the eucharist were simply able to exist side by side in the same monastery without the charges of heresy being hurled. Florus did not hesitate to drag Amalarius up to the judges for condemnation. Paschasius and Ratramnus seemed to have accepted their differences with rare equanimity.

For the next two hundred years, Europe found itself once again fighting for its very existence against the chaos caused by the collapse of Charlemagne's empire and the invasions of the Vikings and

Moslems. Theologians had little time to think or write about the Lord's supper (or anything else, for that matter). When they did, however, they tended to read Paschasius, and slowly the theology of the abbot of Corbie became the standard way of thinking about the eucharist, when anyone had time to think about it. When a teacher named Berengar, in the eleventh century, revived the teaching of Ratramnus, theologians were surprised and, at first, appalled. The eucharist became one of the hottest topics of the age, and literally dozens of books appeared which addressed this issue. A prolonged and serious discussion of the meaning of the Lord's supper began in earnest for the first time.

Cultural Background

The eleventh through thirteenth centuries saw one of the most creative and formative eras in the history of Christian theology. As Europe recovered from the onslaughts of the Vikings and the Moslems, western Christians turned from the more narrow and defensive outlook of the ninth and tenth centuries. In art, music, literature, and especially law, philosophy and theology, a great awakening shook the west and changed its history and culture profoundly. Perhaps few epochs have so definitely shaped the western character as have these three centuries.

In literature, the first stirrings of vernacular literature appeared, introducing the great legends of King Arthur and the Round Table, the Cid, Robin Hood, and Charlemagne. Even more radically, these authors introduced the notion of "courtly" love, even going so far as suggesting the novel idea that one might marry for love! The first true autobiographies were written in the twelfth century, including the bittersweet tale of Abelard and Heloise, and the western peoples slowly began their strange fascination with the individual that would become almost an obsession in our own era.

Devotional life, too, changed. The saints, and especially Mary and Jesus, were seen as more and more human. The awesome earlier crucifixes, the risen Lord glaring in majesty against the background of the cross, gave way to sensual portrayals of the suffering man Jesus slumped in death. Mary, too, was metamorphasized from the reigning "mother of God" into a truly human mother. Mary appears in the art from this era both as a graceful young woman and as an earthly queen. This personal form of devotion would have a dramatic effect on the understanding of the eucharist.

Even more important for the theology of the Lord's supper would be the fascination with learning and law which, beginning in the eleventh century, swept like a wildfire throughout Europe. Scholars were convinced, with what now appears as incredible naiveté, that all learning could be reconciled with Christian belief. What is more, they believed that all church law, starting with the law of the gospel, could be formed into a workable system of justice which would produce, if not a perfect society, at least some remedy against the terrible effects of sin.

To some extent, these extravagant ventures succeeded. In learning, brilliant syntheses of the thought of the early church with Greek philosophy appeared in the works of such men as Hugh of St. Victor, Thomas Aquinas, and Bonaventure. In law, an ever more elaborate church structure provided protection against the whims of the local lords and offered the poor of Europe a form of relief unparalleled until the present time.

By the fourteenth century, it would become clear to the people of Europe that the naive hopes of earlier centuries could not be met, and the scholars and lawyers forged new directions—directions which would eventually lead to the modern world. In the eleventh, twelfth and thirteenth centuries however, the enthusiasm was infectious, and for good or evil (or more accurately, for good *and* evil), this youthful, exuberant, sometimes puritanical, and wryly earthly period shaped the problems of both the reformation and of the present.

The Berengarian Controversy

One of the many scholars to be stung by the desire for new forms of learning was the eleventh century teacher of the choir school of St. Martin in Tours, named Berengar. Berengar was renowned for his knowledge of the arts of grammar and of dialectic, skills which were being slowly recovered from the newly found texts of Aristotle, the great Greek thinker of the fourth century B.C. Berengar was, alas, also an irascible character, who formed as many enemies among his fellow scholars as he had followers among the students. When Berengar turned his hand to theology, he took up the question of the eucharist, basing his thought on that of Ratramnus.

Berengar proposed that the Lord was present in the sacrament only in a spiritual sense, and that the body of the risen Lord, that born of Mary, could not be present, for obvious physical reasons. His theology is similar to that of Ratramnus, but with several important differences. Ratramnus believed that spiritual realities were more real than physical realities, and like the Neoplatonists before him he held that all physical realities participated in and pointed beyond themselves to another more important spiritual reality.

For Berengar, the matter seems to have been much simpler. Physical realities were sensible, things you could touch and see and smell and taste, things that had bulk and took up space. Spiritual things were quite different. They were real and certainly existed, but they were not sensible, and the two realms remained distinct, and unconfused. To say that the physical body and blood of Jesus were present in the eucharist was absurd. In the one complete work we have from Berengar, he ridiculed his opponents mercilessly on just this question.

To believe that the Lord was physically present in the eucharist would mean that "little bits" of Christ's flesh would daily be subject to the indignity of eating and digestion. It would mean that the body of Jesus would be subject to cannibalism, to digestion, to desecration by rot, fire and animals. If the body of the Lord appeared every day in every liturgy all over the world, then surely every day the body of the Lord would grow bigger and bigger, and finally there would be a mountain of Jesus' body.

For Berengar, this was foolishness. Clearly, the bread and wine used in the liturgy remained simple bread and wine, and became signs of the reality of Jesus' spiritual presence, perceived in faith:

> External salvation is produced in us if we accept with a pure
> heart the body of Christ, that is, the reality of the sign while
> we accept the body of Christ in sign, that is, in the holy
> bread of the altar, which has a temporal function.[5]

The controversy lasted some thirty years, and involved not only theological but also political intrigue. Several councils were held to dispute the issue, and Berengar would sign statements of faith, only to return home and continue his earlier teaching, railing against his enemies. Two of these statements became important for later discussions of the eucharist because they were included in most collections of church law, and so were seen as official statements of the church.

The first of these, the oath Berengar was forced to take at the Synod of Rome in 1059, is perhaps one of the most unfortunate and theologically inept statements ever put forward by the church on the subject of the eucharist. Written by Cardinal Humbert of Silva-Candida, the oath was intended not only to put Berengar in his place, but also to insult the Greek Christians, whom Humbert had some five years earlier excommunicated in a bitter quarrel. The central section of the oath reads:

> . . . the bread and wine which are laid on the altar are after consecration not only a sacrament but also the true body and blood of our Lord Jesus Christ, and they are physically taken up and broken in the hands of the priest and crushed by the teeth of the faithful, not only sacramentally but in truth.[6]

Never would the presence of the Lord in the eucharist receive such a crudely physical interpretation. For hundreds of years theologians would do their best to interpret this blunder in a manner consistent with Christian tradition and common sense. The second oath taken by Berengar, also recorded in canon law, was the oath taken at the Synod of Rome in 1079:

> . . . the bread and wine which are placed on the altar . . . are changed substantially into the true and proper vivifying body and blood of Jesus Christ our Lord and after the consecration there are the true body of Christ which was born of the virgin . . . and the true blood of Christ which flowed from his side, not however through sign and in the power of the sacrament, but in their real nature and true substance.[7]

At first reading there may appear to be little difference between these two statements. Both clearly condemn the teaching of

Berengar, and both insist on the real presence of the body and blood of the risen Lord. The discussions of the previous twenty years had introduced an important difference, however. The second oath, that of 1079, described the Lord as "substantially" or "naturally" present. This was a reference to the philosophy of Aristotle, which was slowly being recovered, and discussed in the medieval schools. "Substance," for Aristotle, was the "essence," or "soul," of a thing or person, distinct from its "accidents" or sensible qualities. A "substance" was nothing you could touch or feel or taste or smell but it gave form and individuality and life to that which was touched or tasted or felt. In 1079 the understanding of this concept was vague, and often not well understood, but it did provide a technical language which was capable of asserting a real presence of the Lord without insisting on a sensible presence.

To most modern readers it must seem that it would have been simpler just to say, as Berengar had, that the Lord was *spiritually* present in the Lord's supper. After all, that would have been a perfectly traditional way of speaking of the Lord's presence, and would have avoided the embarrassing and even sacrilegious implications of asserting the kind of physical presence declared in the oath of 1059. However, the matter was not so simple in the eleventh century and would become even more difficult in the twelfth and thirteen centuries. To understand, one must turn to the writings of Berengar's opponents.

Berengar followed at least what he thought was the teaching of Ratramnus on the eucharist; his opponents followed quite explicitly the teaching of Paschasius. They quoted extensively from Paschasius, and considered Berengar's reinterpretation of Ratramnus not only a threat to the theology of Paschasius, but also a threat to salvation itself. The opposition to Berengar was centered in the monastery of Bec in Normandy. Several of the monks there wrote tracts against Berengar, the most famous of these being the abbot of Bec, Lanfranc, who later became archbishop of Canterbury.

The monks based their opposition to Berengar on the very simple thesis that the physical (or, as they preferred to put it, the "natural") body of the risen Lord must be present in the sacrament, for it is the natural contact with this glorified body which saves us. In other words, our bodies would be transformed into glorified bodies by sharing in the glorified body of the risen Lord, and this necessitated actual physical contact. Rupert, a theologian writing some fifty years later, would even insist that the souls of the just who had died before the time of Jesus would all have to receive the eucharist before they could be saved. In order to enter heaven, Rupert suggested, all the just would have to line up for communion so that their bodies could be prepared for heavenly bliss.

This is, of course, precisely the teaching of Paschasius (and not unlike that of Cyril and Hilary). Just, however, as Berengar had misunderstood the intricate relationship between the spiritual and the physical in the writings of Ratramnus, so too his opponents (with the possible exception of the brilliant and subtle Lanfranc) saw an unbridgeable divide between the material and the spiritual. If Berengar was correct, then our bodies could not be saved, for we would lack the necessary contact with Jesus' risen body. Hugh of Langres, one of Berengar's opponents, described the problem:

> Nevertheless, then, if from their essences and natures, they [the bread and wine] do not have the power of salvation, they have the contrary of it, and thus, as long as they remain in their nature, it [the eucharist] will be an impotent sign (*sacramentum*).[8]

Both Berengar and his opponents shared a similar problem. How could one affirm that the presence of the Lord in the eucharist was a saving presence (i.e., *real*) and yet also admit the obvious fact that the Lord was not present to the senses? For the writers of the early church, for Ratramnus, and, to a great extent, for Paschasius, this was not a problem, for there was a continuity between the spiritual and the material, and in fact spiritual things were the more "real" part of which the sensed reality was a mere shadow. The eleventh century writers saw the problem more as we might. If something is "real," it must be sensed; if it is "merely" spiritual, it is not real. From the eleventh century until the present day, the problem of the "real presence" in the eucharist has been more accurately a question of what is "really real," and in many ways the rest of this book will be a discussion of the different answers Christians have given to this question.

Berengar raised several important questions in attacking the position of Paschasius, and his opponents were sometimes hard pressed to find answers to his often satirical rejoinders. First, there was the problem of sacrilege. If the body of Jesus was really present in the sacrament, how did one explain the digestion of the bread and wine, or, even worse, what would happen if an animal ate the consecrated elements? Some theologians merely responded that no harm could come to a glorified body. Others, especially the monk Guitmund from the monastery of Bec, took the problem quite literally. Guitmund understood the consecrated bread and wine to be merely appearances, a sort of covering which the risen Lord took on so that we could consume his body without repulsion. If a mouse broke into the sacristy and ate the bread, well, Guitmund suggested, Jesus had been in the tomb, which was just as bad. Few theologians would be as materialistic in their understanding as Guitmund, but such literal understanding of the presence of the risen Lord persisted.

A more sophisticated understanding of the problem suggested that the sensed reality of the bread and wine could undergo any sort of abuse or change without affecting the "substance" or "essence" of the risen Lord signified by the sensed reality. This sort of distinction led theologians to differentiate between the "sign" (*sacramentum*) of bread and wine which a person sensed in the eucharist, and the "reality" (in Latin, *res*) of the presence of the risen Lord. Again, the Aristotelian distinction between "accidents" (sensed perceptions) and "substance" (essence of a thing) would become very handy as a way to explain how the saving presence of the Lord could be affirmed without resorting to the crass materialism of the kind Guitmund suggested.

A second problem suggested by Berengar's challenge, although not specifically raised by him, involved the way in which the presence of the Lord in the eucharist could be salvific. It would appear at first glance that according to the teaching of Paschasius all that was necessary for salvation was that one received the consecrated bread and wine, which would automatically transform one into a glorified body. This contradicted the insistence of the church that the true purpose of the sacrament was to be a sign of the life of faith, hope and charity which was made possible by sharing in the life of the risen Lord. In short, why bother to be good if you could get salvation automatically through the sacraments?

No theologians suggested that such automatic salvation was

possible, although in the later middle ages, as we shall see, a similar belief would become popular. The opponents of Berengar did, however, find it difficult to respond to this dilemma. The best they could suggest was that a life of faith and love was absolutely essential for salvation, and that without this kind of a life, the transformation of our bodies into glorified bodies could not take place. Even literalists like Guitmund never wavered in asserting the importance of a good Christian life as the real purpose of the presence of the Lord in our lives and in the eucharist. Later theologians would abandon Paschasius' theology entirely and explain the intricate link between a good Christian life and participation in the Lord's supper as the real key to understanding the liturgy.

The Cathars and the Real Presence

The controversy surrounding the teaching of Berengar was the first major discussion concerning the eucharist in the history of Christianity. In many ways, it set the pattern for discussion of the Lord's supper for centuries to come. Particularly important was the introduction of the philosophy of Aristotle to explain the real, but not sensed, presence of the risen Lord in the sacrament. The term "change in substance" or in Latin *transsubstantiatio* would become a common way of referring to the way in which the risen Lord became present during the liturgy. Now, at first, this term "transubstantiation" was very vague and referred to no more than the teaching that the "essence" of the sacrament was the saving presence of the living Lord in the devout participation in the liturgy. For writers of the thirteenth and fourteenth centuries, this term could take on a very precise meaning, but the theologians of the twelfth and early thirteenth centuries were not yet concerned with such precision.

The theologians who lived immediately after the time of Berengar had a much more important problem with which to deal. Beginning in the late eleventh century, bands of wandering teachers appeared who taught different forms of dualism, the belief that all reality is divided into two powerful forces, one good and one evil. One name by which these medieval teachers were called was "Cathars," "the perfect ones," and consisted of several different groups, some directly descended from the followers of a dualist sect in eastern Europe called "Bogomils" who sent missionaries to western Europe in the early twelfth century. The teachings of the groups were very similar to those of the fourth century Manichees, and were thought to actually be Manichees by many medieval writers.

Although the Cathars differed among themselves, basically they agreed in teaching that all material things were evil, and that salvation consisted in freeing the spiritual reality of each person (the soul) from the material and evil reality of the body. All of life was a struggle between the evil realm of matter and the good realm of the spirit. The "Cathars" were the ones who had freed themselves as far as possible from all forms of materialism. They ate no meat, or any dairy products or eggs, and underwent special rituals even for the eating of vegetables. They, of course, were celibate; sex was the greatest evil for the Cathars, as this act might result in the entrapment of spiritual reality (a soul) in the realm of matter (a body). Not all followers of this teaching were "perfect," however. The less than perfect ones, the "Hearers," were still allowed to marry and live a normal life. The ideal, however, was to live the perfect life, and generally people hoped to be saved by adopting the more rigorous life of a "perfect one" sometime before their death.

This teaching was very attractive for the same reasons that a life of severe dedication has attracted people for centuries. Here was a clear and straightforward way to heaven, unclouded by the gray areas of right and wrong. Nothing could be simpler: matter was evil and spirit was good. The legacy of the dualists has persisted throughout Christian history, and there are still many Christians who think of their religion in ways that are really more dualist than Christian. One has only to think of the fixation with sexuality as evil in several Christian groups to realize that this legacy is still very much with us.

The eleventh and early twelfth centuries were times of great change and spiritual revival in the church, and this aided the Cathars in their missionary efforts. A movement to reform the clergy, enforced by the papacy, had been joined to the enthusiasm for a personal devotion mentioned in the beginning of this chapter. The result was an explosion in interest in the "apostolic life." Bands of wandering ascetics could be found all over Europe. Up until this time, the monastic life, basically that regulated by the Benedictine order, was the only alternative to the life of a lay Christian. Now there were dozens of new experiments in Christian living going on. Groups of men and women formed together to attempt to live more closely the life described in the gospel.

Some of these groups lived together in the middle of towns, like the Augustinian canons and the holy women known as Beguines. Others took to the highways, preaching the word of God and living as beggars. The most famous of these groups were those founded by Francis of Assisi (the Franciscans), and Dominic Guzman (the Dominicans). Oftentimes church officials, especially those with limited imaginations, did not know what to do with these groups. Their teaching on poverty and a simple lifestyle made the wealthy clergy very uncomfortable.

Furthermore, it wasn't always easy to tell which of these groups were truly holy men and women, and which were heretical, or even just crazy. Eudes of Brittany, for instance, claimed that he shared dominion over the universe with God, and he spent his time robbing people who came too close to his hideout in the woods of Brittany. The transcripts of his trial demonstrate that Eudes and his "merry men" were probably ignorant and disturbed people who nevertheless believed themselves to be leading a religious revival.

The Cathars unquestionably fit into this milieu. The "perfect ones" were often admirable and humble people who contrasted sharply with the many worldly clerics of medieval Christianity. The Cathars gained many followers, especially in southern France and northern Italy. By the beginning of the thirteenth century, the different groups of Cathars controlled both of these two regions, and orthodox Christianity felt itself severely threatened.

The Cathars, of course, rejected all the sacraments. The very idea that any material things could be of spiritual value was completely alien to their teaching. The eucharist came in for special attack, for not only was this the most common of Christian sacramental practices, but the very idea that the risen Lord had a body and that this body could be involved in salvation was the greatest heresy for the Cathars. Many of the Cathars, in fact, denied that Jesus was ever really human. They taught that the body which people saw in Palestine in the first century was sheer illusion for the benefit of the ignorant. Certainly, Jesus never suffered or underwent death. Records which survive of the Cathars' teachings come mostly from their enemies and therefore are suspect. It does seem, though, that the Cathars used the old arguments of Berengar to convince the common folk that to believe in the presence of the risen Lord in the eucharist was utter nonsense.

Orthodox theologians, in response, felt themselves called upon again and again to answer these objections, and especially to insist that the body of the risen Lord was present in the sacrament, and that this body could be a saving presence. Theologians took as an article of faith that the body of the risen Lord was present in the eucharist, and in fact this belief, and the insistence on this belief, is a hallmark of the medieval theology of the Lord's supper. This insistence, however, should be understood against the background of the Cathar challenge.

Many of the strongholds of the Cathars were destroyed in the early thirteenth century by a cruel "crusade" led by the French leader Simon de Montfort, but for over a century they were a force to be reckoned with in Christian Europe. In fact, the first official use of the term "transubstantiation" appeared in a creed directed against the Cathars at the Lateran Council of 1215. Some later theologians (and historians) would read this document as an official endorsement (a "definition") of the term, but to the theologians of the time it was seen only as a strong assertion of the saving presence of the Lord in the eucharist in opposition to the anti-materialistic claims of the Cathars.

The Teaching of the Schools

During the late eleventh and early twelfth centuries a new institution appeared in western Europe. Associations of scholars and students banned together to regulate the certification of teachers and the payment of fees. They called themselves *universitates*, the Latin word for a community. They were the forerunners of all modern universities. Medical students flocked to Salerno, law students headed for Bologna, but theologians and philosophers went to Paris. At first the cathedral schools in cities like Laon, Liège, and Chartres attracted good students in competition with the larger university towns. By the middle of the thirteenth century, however, Paris, Bologna, Salerno, Oxford, and the other university centers dominated the intellectual scene.

Most of the eleventh and twelfth century theologians teaching in either a cathedral school or a university had something to say on the eucharist. In one recent study of this period, over one hundred and fifty different works treating the eucharist were identified.[9] Clearly not all these works can be discussed here. Two examples will have to suffice, but these two men would be perhaps the most frequently read and quoted of the many twelfth century theologians who wrote on the eucharist.

The Augustinian canon Hugh taught in one of several smaller schools, that of St. Victor, which would eventually make up the University of Paris. From 1127 to his death in 1142, he lived and worked at this famous school, known for its theology and biblical scholarship. Hugh of St. Victor was the most influential of the several scholars of this period who labored to recover the teaching of earlier centuries on the eucharist. Hugh was particularly influenced by the writings of St. Augustine.

According to Hugh, salvation consists of a growing union with God in faith and love. The possibility of this union was restored by Jesus through his incarnation, crucifixion and resurrection. Humans participate in the graces won by Christ through a whole series of outward signs that mediate this salvation by signifying and effecting a union with God. Presumed in this theology, of course, was a life which exemplified such a union through acts of devotion and charity.

The Latin word *sacramentum* was used by Hugh to refer to any act which mediated the union between God and humans. In the opening of Hugh's major work, *On the Signs [Sacramenta] of the Christian Faith*, he explains that there are two great signs of salvation: the creation and redemption of humankind. Hugh then goes on to describe the process and history of salvation. In one section of his book, he treats of the ceremonies which mediate salvation. These too he calls *sacramentum*. Clearly the word *sacramentum* did not yet mean the same as the English word "sacrament" in the sense of a particular rite. Nor did Hugh and his colleagues agree about what might be called a "sacrament." Some, for instance, included the anointing of kings and the rituals of knighthood among the *sacramenta* of the church.

For Hugh, all these outward signs were used by God to lead us to him. Each outward sign appealed to our senses, drawing us toward the inner reality to which the outward sign pointed. It was the inner reality which saved us, however, not the outward sign. In this understanding, Hugh was very close to the Neoplatonists and was in fact influenced greatly by the "Pseudo-Dionysius," a Christian Neoplatonist writer of the early sixth century. Hugh went so far as to say that even Jesus' human life was an outward sign meant to lead us to an inner union with God. Hugh was very concerned that his students understand this relationship between outer sign and inner reality. With gentle persuasion, Hugh responded to his students' questions about the physical presence of Christ in the Lord's supper by using this distinction:

> Your heart says to you: What becomes of the body of Christ after it has been taken and eaten? I hear you. Do you seek the bodily presence of Christ? Seek it in heaven. Here Christ is sitting at the right hand of the Father. He wishes to be with you at those times when and where it is necessary. He showed Himself to you at the time of His bodily presence in order that He might draw you to His spiritual presence. This is why He came to you in bodily form and showed Himself to you during the time of His bodily presence in order that through this presence you might find His spiritual presence which is not taken away. Thus He came into the world at a certain time by assuming flesh, and by means of this bodily presence lived with humans, in order to rouse them to seek after and then discover His spiritual presence. After having completed this mission, He left in His bodily presence, but remained in His spiritual presence. . . . So too, in His sign [*sacramentum*] He comes to you in a temporal way, and in it is with you in a bodily way, in order that through this bodily presence, He might urge you on to seek His spiritual presence, and aid you in finding it.[10]

The most important thing in the eucharist was the spiritual union with God that this ritual signified. So important was this for Hugh (and several like-minded theologians of the twelfth century) that he distinguished between the sign alone of the eucharist (in Latin, *sacramentum tantum*), the thing signified in the sacrament (in

Latin *res tantum*) and that which both signifies and *is* signified (in Latin *sacramentum et res*). The signs alone were the bread and wine. The thing signified was, of course, the union of God and the believer in faith and love. That which was both signified (by the bread and wine) and which signified (the union in faith and love) was the presence of the Lord in the eucharist. This format:

bread and wine→	real presence→	union with God
(*sacramentum*)	(*res et sacramentum*)	(*res*)

would remain the standard way to describe the different realities present in the Lord's supper right up to (and, in some traditions, far beyond) the reformation.

Using this schema, Hugh, and many other theologians in the middle ages, argued that since the really important thing in the eucharist was the union with God in faith and love, it was not absolutely necessary for one to receive the sign of that faith and love. If a person, out of devotion or reverence or hardship, could not or did not wish to participate in the Lord's supper through reception, then she or he would be saved by means of the union which already existed between her or him and God.

Taking this thought one step further, these theologians argued that some other act of devotion during the liturgy could take the place of reception, and a popular custom grew up during the twelfth century of "spiritual reception." Certain ritual actions or prayers which took the place of the eating of the bread and wine were understood as being just as effective for the believer's salvation as long as the person performing the action was leading a life of faith and charity.

This devotional practice, which continued into the twentieth century among some Christian groups, would seem odd both to the early church and to most modern Christians. To the medieval mind, however, the practice was considered both devout and, most importantly, safe. The insistence on the real presence of the risen Lord in the eucharist, directed against the Cathars, had the effect in popular understanding of terrifying the congregation. They understood that the Lord of heaven and earth, the judge of all, stood before them in majesty during the Lord's supper. To recklessly receive this, the Lord of lords, would bring about certain damnation. Commentaries on the mass from the middle ages stress again and again that one should only approach the Lord's table after purifying one's life. The custom grew up (and was made law in 1215) that Christians needed to receive the body and blood of the Lord only once, at Easter, after the proper preparation of the Lenten season. Of course, some people continued to receive more frequently, but most spiritual advisors urged their flocks to receive infrequently, only after having attempted to purify their lives through acts of faith and charity.

In order, then, to still feel part of the action of the liturgy and to join oneself to God in prayer, the devout medieval person would rather receive "spiritually" than risk approaching the sacrament while still living a less than perfect life. Most, but not all, modern Christian groups encourage frequent reception at least partly because the medieval practice of infrequent reception was one cause for the separation of laypeople from the ceremony of the liturgy. As we will discuss below, the medieval lay person was really more of a spectator than a real participant in the liturgy.

On the other hand, the medieval writers had a point. Most modern people trot off to the Lord's supper without much thought about whether their own life or that of their community or nation is really a loving and charitable one. The medieval authors were quite right in their insistence (like that of the Christian writers before them) that it was courting damnation to receive the sign of a Christian life while not seriously attempting to live such a life. Acts of charity were closely joined to the liturgy for the medieval mind, just as they had been for the early church. In the words of Baldwin, the archbishop of Canterbury from 1184 to 1190:

> We many are one body through the love of our neighbors; one body through the love of God. The one bread of God (who delights in the fraternal love by which we love one another) is in some sense restored through us. . . . Our mutual love is mutual consolation to us, and is our mutual reception. Therefore we are individually members one of another (Romans 12:5), because we console one another and rejoice with one another. Our misfortune and our good fortune, which seem the individual's own, through the feelings of fraternal charity are considered to be com-

munal. We are one body through charity, by which Christ
is loved as a bridegroom, and who loves the Church as his
own body (*Tract on the Sacrament of the Altar*).[11]

By far the most influential of the many theologians who taught
and wrote during this period was Peter the Lombard. Peter, who
was named for his birthplace in northern Italy, taught in the cathedral school in Paris from before 1144 until his election as bishop of
Paris in 1159, and is best known for his book of *sententia* or sayings.
Organized into four books, Peter gathered quotations from both
past and present theologians on almost every imaginable theological
question and then arranged them by topic. Books of *sententia* were
very popular in the twelfth century, for they offered the reader a
collection of all the best material in one handy book. Good libraries
were hard to come by, and books were very expensive, so the more
material contained in one book, the better.

The Lombard's book was so popular that, by the early thirteenth century a custom had grown up of using his book as the first
text in theology. Those who taught such courses became known as
"masters of the *sententia*," the first step to becoming a "doctor"
(literally in Latin, "one who teaches"). Doctors in theology taught
the greatest of books, the Bible, but masters taught Peter the Lombard, and since one became a master first, everyone eventually
learned from the *sententia* of Peter. For some three hundred years,
the first task of a budding theologian would be to lecture on the
sententia of Peter the Lombard.

(By the way, yes, this is where we eventually got the "master's"
and "doctoral" degrees. Physicians, who of course are not teachers,
were not called "doctors," unless they taught medicine, until fairly
recently. Law teachers in Bologna were the first to use the term, but
for most of history "doctors" were understood to be those who
taught, especially university professors.)

Peter's theology was in many respects similar to that of Hugh.
Like Hugh, he insisted that the bread and wine were transformed
into the body and blood of the Lord. In the same way as Hugh, he
emphasized the intellectual and invisible nature of the eucharistic
presence. A good summary of Peter's position is contained in his
explanation of how this presence signifies the body and blood of the
Lord that is visible and palpable in heaven:

This visible outward appearance of bread is called by the name of flesh, and the visible outward appearance of wine is called blood. Invisibly and intellectually this is said to be the flesh of Christ, because according to its outward appearance, it does not seem to be flesh, but is intellectually understood to be, and the same for the wine. The invisible flesh is said to be a sign (*sacramentum*) of the visible flesh, because the appearances of bread, according to which that flesh is not seen, is a sign of the visible flesh; because by the invisible flesh, that is the appearances, according to which the flesh of Christ is not seen as a body, signifies the body of Christ, which is visible and palpable where it appears in its proper form. The same can be said for the wine (*The Sentences*, book 4, dist. 10, c. 1).[12]

Like Hugh, Peter also used the schema *sacramentum, res et sacramentum*, and *res* to describe the different elements present in the eucharist. Unlike Hugh, however, Peter understood the term *sacramentum* in a somewhat narrow sense. Peter used the term to refer in particular to seven of the church's ritual actions. When Peter's book became the standard text in theology, it also became common to speak of the church having seven (and *only* seven) "sacraments." Peter also understood that the *res*, the reality signified by the eucharist, somewhat differently than Hugh. For Peter the *res* was the church itself, the congregation of all the just. In his commentary on the first letter to the Corinthians, Peter explains:

Through this we are one with Christ, for we all participate spiritually and worthily of the one bread, of course, the body of Christ, and of the one chalice, of course, the blood of Christ; even though we are many, we are one bread, in a union of faith, and hope and charity. And we are one body of that head who is Christ, by providing works of charity; that is to say we are one, one Church, united by bonds of faith, hope, charity and mutual support in the work of God. By the unity of the bread, and the unity of the body, faith and charity ought to be understood; for if these are absent, a person receives unto judgement (*Commentary on I Corinthians*).[13]

Like Hugh and Baldwin, Peter emphasizes the necessity of living a life of active faith and charity in order to truly be united to God in the liturgy. Like them, he too will insist that one not necessarily receive the bread and wine in order to form such a union with God. Peter does differ from them, however, in his understanding of how the saving union with God takes place.

For Hugh, Baldwin and other like-minded theologians salvation is individual. Each person is saved by a personal union between himself or herself and God. For Peter, and most other theologians of the late twelfth and early thirteen centuries, it is not the individual but the church that is saved. Each individual is saved because he or she is a member of the church. Now, of course, for Peter, the church is made up of individuals united by faith, hope, and charity, so there is a great deal of similarity between Hugh and Peter. Yet the different understandings of salvation which they represent have fairly practical consequences.

Hugh's approach to the sacrament can lead to practices like spiritual communion which, taken to extremes, can isolate the individual from the community. Each person sits in his or her own little place in the pew, wrapped up in a personal contemplation of God. Peter's approach, again taken to extremes, can lead to a fascination with the absolutely minimal requirements for membership in the church. What can I get away with and still be saved (or participate in the Lord's supper)?

There were, then as now, people who were quite ready to take things to extremes. As more and more study was done in the area of church law, and as church law became more widely enforced, theologians came to see worthy reception in terms of what sins might keep a person from receiving. Even more importantly, participation in the eucharist on feast days became seen as a test of membership in the church. If someone in the parish didn't come forward to receive, he or she might be in big trouble, for it would be clear to everyone in town that that person had committed a serious sin.

If the parish was in the territory of the Cathars, the people who didn't receive might be suspected of heresy. If it was an ordinary parish, and some poor farmer's cow was missing, the one person who didn't come forward at communion time could be suspected as the thief. Stephen Langton, who taught at Paris before he became the archbishop of Canterbury from 1207 to 1228, advised priests not to deny the sacrament to anyone, even if the priest knew that the person was a sinner privately, "not only because of scandal, but especially that his crime not be made public."[14]

Just as the fascination with the presence of the risen Lord in the eucharist caused people to stay away from the sacrament out of reverence, social pressure made sure that at least at Easter they came forward to proclaim their membership in the church. These two forces created some interesting new ways of participating in the liturgy. Some of the customs developed during this period would have a tremendous impact, for good and evil, on the rest of the history of Christianity. It is to these practices that we now turn.

The Celebration

Since there are really two different periods in church history discussed in this chapter, you will need to imagine yourself attending two liturgies in this section. In the ninth century, the time of Paschasius and Ratramnus, there would have been great diversity in the liturgy. Roman liturgy would still have retained the elaborate rites of the fourth century. French liturgies would have included long penitential prayers preceding the main part of the ceremony. Celtic liturgies would have been different again, perhaps including the strange custom of private confession of sins, a practice which the Celtic missionaries would introduce all over Europe.

The liturgy we will attend, however, will be in a small church in the countryside of Saxony (northwestern Germany). The church building itself is heavy and dark with thick walls. Burn marks on the outside show where the Vikings had attacked the week before when everyone crammed into the only stone building in town for protection. People slowly assemble, bringing fruit, vegetables and cattle with them into church. These will be the offertory gifts, the means by which the priest makes a living. The prayers begin, but attention is scattered, for the Latin of the liturgy is foreign to almost everyone but the priest. The actual prayers come from the Roman prayer book and include references to Roman saints who mean little to this congregation. When the priest mentions St. Grizzled, however, a cheer goes up. St. Grizzled was a somewhat strange but holy man who lived and died in a cave near town. Many miracles had been ascribed to the venerable old man, although a few had to do with love potions.

The people understood little of what is going on, really, and when the priest blesses all the wheat, turnips, cows and beets assembled around the altar, as well as the bread and wine, it might not even be clear to him whether some or all this now contains the presence of the risen Lord. Some of the people still think the Lord about whom the priest is speaking is Woden, the chief Saxon god. This is particularly confusing since the priest used to offer the town's sacrifices to Woden.

This is not to say that the people are inactive or uninvolved. Since we happen to arrive on Good Friday, we are in for a little show. People from the congregation come up after the consecration and take the consecrated bread, wrapping it in a cloth. A short pantomime is played out where the bread is buried, as was the body of Christ after the crucifixion. On Easter the bread will be "resurrected" with townsfolk taking the parts of the angels, the women at the tomb, and the apostles. For illiterate people, this would be a dramatic way of teaching them the basics of their new religion. It would also be the very beginnings of modern theater in the west.

In the ninth century, especially on the outskirts of Christianity, things could be pretty crude, and one stressed only the basics. A few hundred years later a much different picture emerges. It is now the early thirteenth century and our first impressions upon entering a church in a town in northern France are of beautiful colored light and mass confusion. Instead of the dark thick walls of the ninth century, the tall brilliant stained glass windows of the earliest Gothic cathedrals meet our eyes. Still illiterate, we can at least make out the stories of the Bible in the windows, which are called, appropriately enough, the bibles of the poor. We stop for a minute under the window where our Lady is depicted in a beautiful blue dress. A peasant mother herself, we feel much more comfortable praying to her than to the overpowering Son of God who will soon be present before us.

All around there is activity. Small altars are set up around the walls, and priests are busy saying masses with no one present but a server. In the back of the church, two merchants are haggling over a couple of goats. It's a rainy day this Easter, and since the church is the largest building in town, it's a dry place to strike a bargain. A few dirty looks and nasty comments don't seem to stop the discussion until the priest enters to start the liturgy at the high altar.

The liturgy now is pretty much the same all over France, and even in England, Germany, Spain and Italy. A few wealthy people have prayer books in Latin or French, but most people don't understand the Latin prayers of the priest. We all know, though, that the liturgy is a pantomime of the life of Christ, a life we should all imitate. We also know that the moment that the priest pronounces the words of consecration, the bread and wine will somehow be the body and blood of the Lord. Recently the church has installed candles near the metal box where the consecrated bread for the sick is kept. This is to let people know that the Lord is there. Immediately after the words of blessing, two new actions occur. The priest raises up the bread so we can all see the Lord, and the server rings a bell to call everyone's attention to it.

Abashed to be in the presence of the Lord himself, we fall to our knees and hope that our Lenten penances have made us worthy to receive him. We vow to add an extra barrel of beer for the poor when the Easter banquet is held for them and to make sure that a few cheeses each week go to the orphans living next door. Now comes the moment of truth. Despite the fear in their hearts, people mob the altar to receive the body and blood of the Lord. Several years ago, in the mad rush, it was common to knock the chalice out of the priest's hand. Now we receive only the bread, which the priest tells us is just as good; this avoids the horrible sacrilege of the wine spilling.

A quick look around shows us that the baker is hanging back. "I always knew he was a crook," a voice nearby whispers. But then the baker proceeds to the altar and takes the eucharist without being struck dead, and our noisy neighbor blushes. As soon as, or almost as soon as, the liturgy ends, the celebration erupts, right in church. A procession begins with music and pantomime and even pig bladders inflated like balloons. It's been a long and pious Lent and it's time to rejoice that the Lord is risen. The priest objects to all this uproar and has twice threatened to throw the whole carnival out of church. He is a learned man from Paris and is constantly reminding us that this is the Lord's house and deserves our respect. Today, however, is a feast day. His warnings are forgotten, and the procession moves into the street and toward the feast prepared the day before.

Both the ninth century and the early thirteenth century liturgies were very different from those of the early church in tone and in the understanding of the congregation, yet the central prayers and action of the Lord's supper remained relatively unchanged. Exuberant, lively, and intensely devout, the liturgies of the middle ages could get out of hand, and by the end of the middle ages they sometimes did. Along with the devotions and extravagances, however, came a new and exacting professional theology of the eucharist, and it is to this theology that we now turn.

GLOSSARY OF PERSONS

Amalarius of Metz. Amalarius was a liturgical scholar during the renaissance of learning fostered by Charlemagne and his successors. A student of Charlemagne's foremost scholar, Alcuin of York, Amalarius is most famous for his allegorical interpretation of the liturgy. According to this interpretation, the Lord's supper is actually a reenactment of the life of Jesus. This novel understanding of the mass was very popular during the middle ages, although some of Amalarius' ideas were condemned by the Council of Quiercy in 838. Amalarius lived from approximately 780 to 850.

Aristotle. The most famous student of Plato, Aristotle lived from 384 to 322 B.C. He studied under Plato in Athens from 367 until Plato's death in 347. After spending some years first with the ruler Hermeias in Asia Minor, and then with the court in Macedonia (where he taught the young Alexander the Great), he returned to Athens and established his own school. Aristotle, unlike his teacher Plato, stressed scientific investigation and invented the science of logic. Many of Aristotle's texts were lost in the west, and only slowly recovered during the eleventh through thirteenth centuries when they then provided an important tool for medieval theology.

Baldwin of Canterbury. A very devout and austere man, Baldwin was elected abbot of the Cistercian monastery of Ford in England in 1175, only a year after he joined the monastery. He was later appointed bishop of Worcester in 1180 and archbishop of Canterbury in 1184. He was not particularly popular with the clergy because of his ascetic ways. In 1190 he died while on one of the crusades.

Berengar of Tours. Berengar was born of an influential family from Tours in France c. 1010, and by the age of twenty he already held a post in the church there. A very popular and successful teacher of grammar and rhetoric, he turned to the teaching of theology in his later years. His teaching on the eucharist aroused a great deal of opposition and was condemned in several councils, the most important being those held in Rome in 1059 and 1079. Berengar continued to teach, however, until near the end of his long life. He died in retirement in 1088.

Bonaventure. See entry in the glossary at the end of Chapter 5.

Charlemagne. A huge man with a talent for both warfare and organization, Charles "the Great" was the son of Pippin, the king of the Franks. Inheriting his father's kingdom in 771, Charles went on to conquer the Lombards, the Saxons, and some of the Moslem kingdoms in Spain. In the areas he conquered, Charles spread order, law, learning and Christianity, though not always by gentle persuasion. On Christmas day in the year 800, Charles was crowned Roman emperor by Pope Leo III. This was the beginning of the "Holy Roman Empire" which would last in one form or another until the end of the First World War.

Charles the Bald. The grandson of Charlemagne, Charles the Bald was crowned Holy Roman Emperor only for the last two years of his life, from 875 to 877. Charles spent most of his life fighting with his three brothers for control of the empire which his grandfather had established. Although he (and his brothers) to some extent tried to enact and extend the reforms initiated by Charlemagne, the empire which existed under Charlemagne and his son, Louis the Pious, remained hopelessly divided.

Dominic Guzman. Born in 1170 in Castile, Spain, Dominic at the age of twenty-one sold all his possessions to help the poor. He soon became a priest of the diocese of Osma in Spain, and in 1203 went on a preaching crusade against the Cathars in France. For the next eleven years, Dominic worked ceaselessly and often in danger of his life to convert the Cathars. In 1214 he started the Order of Preachers, a religious group whose mission was to preach against heresy. This order received official approval in 1215 and quickly attracted a large following. The order, dedicated to learning, is now known more popularly as the Dominicans. Dominic died in 1221, spending his last years journeying through Europe, organizing the Preachers.

Florus of Lyons. Florus lived in Lyons in France from c. 790 to 860. A learned scholar, he wrote works on church law, scripture and liturgy. Florus was involved in a number of theological controversies, most particularly with Amalarius of Metz, who served as archbishop of Lyons for a short time.

Francis of Assisi. Surely one of the most charismatic and beloved of medieval saints, Francis dedicated himself at a young age to serving the poor. He gradually formed a group of followers around him, all dedicated to living in poverty and preaching to the poor. This group was eventually organized as the Order of Friars Minor (Little Brothers), more popularly known as Franciscans. Francis was renowned for his love of poverty, his humility and his deep regard for nature. He died in 1226 and was canonized less than two years later.

Guitmund of Aversa. Guitmund was a student of the abbot Lanfranc while a monk at the abbey of Corbie in Normandy. While still a monk (c. 1073–1075) Guitmund wrote a book, *On the Truth of the Body and Blood of Christ in the Eucharist,* in which he attacked the teachings of Berengar of Tours. Guitmund later became bishop of Aversa in Italy from 1088 until his death c. 1090–1095.

Heriger of Lobbes. After a long teaching career at Liège, Heriger became abbot of the monastery of Lobbes from 990 until his death in 1007. One of the greatest scholars of his age, contemporaries referred to his school in Liège as the "Athens of the North." He wrote, among other things, a treatise on the eucharist in which he tried to reconcile the theologies of Paschasius and Ratramnus.

Hugh of Langres. Scholars know that someone named Hugh of Langres wrote a treatise about the eucharist directed against Berengar of Tours during the eleventh century. Unfortunately, there are two people with that name who could have written this work. One is Hugh, the bishop of Langres, who was deposed as bishop in 1049 and died in 1050. The second is Hugh-Renard, bishop of Langres from 1065 to 1085. I think it was probably the second man (the timing seems better), but feel free to do a little detective work yourself if you like.

Hugh of St. Victor. Very little is known about Hugh. He was already a canon at the school of St. Victor in Paris by 1127. He taught there until his death in 1142. Hugh was a great and gentle teacher who influenced the theologians well into the fifteenth and even sixteenth century through his writings on theology, spirituality and scripture.

Humbert of Silva-Candida. Humbert was a scholar and monk at the monastery of Moyenmoutier when he was created cardinal-bishop of Silva-Candida in 1050. An enthusiastic reformer, he was also something of a one-man disaster. He headed the embassy to Constantinople in 1054 which led to the formal and official break between eastern and western Christianity; he also wrote the oath which Berengar of Tours was forced to sign in 1059. This oath has been an embarrassment to most theologians since its writings because of its extremely physical language. Humbert died in 1061.

Lanfranc. One of the greatest scholars of the eleventh century, Lanfranc taught at the monastery of Bec in Normandy until he became abbot of St. Stephens in Caen in 1063. In 1070 he was made archbishop of Canterbury under the auspices of William (the Conqueror) of Normandy. Lanfranc was not only a brilliant teacher and writer but also an excellent organizer, and he did much to improve not only Bec and Caen but the church in England as well. Lanfranc died in 1089.

Paschasius Radbertus. As a monk at the monastery of Corbie in 831, Paschasius wrote the first treatise directed entirely to the eucharist. He wrote it in order to instruct the Saxon monks who were entering the monastery without, it seems, a proper understanding of the sacrament. Paschasius became abbot of Corbie in 843/844. Ratramnus, who also wrote on the eucharist, was the leading scholar at Corbie while Paschasius was abbot. Paschasius died in 865.

Peter the Lombard. A native of Lombardy in northern Italy, Peter studied theology in Italy and in France before settling in Paris. He taught there from at least 1144 until he was chosen bishop of Paris in 1159. Peter is most famous as the author of the *Sentences*, a book of short theological discussions divided by topic. Introduced as the standard textbook of theology by Alexander of Hales (see Chapter 5) in the early thirteenth century, Peter's book was the required introductory book in theology in most universities up until the sixteenth century. Peter was perhaps better known in his own time as a scripture scholar. Particularly important were his lectures on the epistles of Paul. Peter died in 1160 after only one year in office as bishop.

Pseudo-Dionysius. A Christian Neoplatonist whose works influenced many later writers. A tradition identifies this writer with Dionysius the Aeropagite who was converted by Paul the apostle. Since the writings of Pseudo-Dionysius can be dated as coming from the early sixth century, Dionysius the Aeropagite could not have written them. We have no other name for this author, so most scholars simply call the author the "pseudo" or fake Dionysius.

Ratramnus of Corbie. A scholarly monk from the monastery of Corbie who died in 868. Ratramnus' learning was highly respected and his opinion was sought on most of the controversial issues of his day. He is best known for his short work on the eucharist, written c. 844, the theology of which differs sharply from that of his abbot Paschasius.

Rupert of Deutz. From an early age Rupert was a monk of the abbey of St. Laurent in Liège. He taught there on and off until 1120 when he was elected abbot of the monastery at Deutz near Cologne. Rupert's many writings involved him in one controversy after another. On the whole he tended to take a conservative stance in opposition to the teachers who represented the newly emerging universities. Rupert died in 1129/1130.

Simon de Montfort. The leader of the "Albigensian" crusade, so called because of the concentration of Cathars in the city of Albi in southern France. Called by Innocent III in 1208 after the assassination of the papal delegate to southern France, the crusade lasted until the death of Simon in 1218. The crusade was carried out with great cruelty, most notably the massacre of the city of Bèzier in 1209. Simon and his supporters used the crusade as an excuse to subdue the south of France for the north. Simon decisively defeated the leader of the Cathars, Peter of Aragon, at the battle of Muret in 1213.

Stephen Langton. Langton was a theologian at the University of Paris until his nomination and consecration as archbishop of Canterbury by Pope Innocent III. King John of England opposed the selection of Stephen as archbishop and refused to allow him to land in England until 1213. Langton was responsible for organizing the barons of England in their attempt to secure basic rights from the king, and it was probably Langton who suggested that the barons force John to sign the Magna Carta. In any case, his name heads the list of signers. Stephen Langton was one of the leading statesmen in England until his death in 1228 and perhaps the greatest of the medieval bishops in England.

Thomas Aquinas. See entry in the glossary at the end of Chapter 5.

5

Diversity in Decline:
The Later Middle Ages

The later middle ages hold a central position in the history of the eucharist because it was during these centuries that the theology and the practices which later divided Christendom came to their fullest development. It is important to point out that this development took place within a larger set of changes both in theology and in devotional practices. One sometimes gets the impression from reading church histories that theology and doctrine smoothly evolved in some sort of cocoon immune to the larger social and institutional picture. This would of course be impossible, and so thinking about the eucharist changed as times changed.

First of all, theology in the thirteenth and fourteenth centuries became a much more professional discipline. The cathedral schools of the eleventh and twelfth centuries became "universities," associations of students and teachers more or less independent of church and state. The requirements for teaching became formalized, and so did the prerequisites for "degrees." University training would become expected of anyone working in the chancellory of a lord or bishop, and so the universities were filled with students looking for career opportunities. Law, medicine, philosophy and theology all became more and more specialized fields with their own language and traditions. The new Dominican order insisted that its brightest recruits be trained in the universities, and the Franciscans, and then the other religious orders, somewhat reluctantly followed suit.

By the thirteenth century, the universities were professional and very well respected institutions, but also hotbeds for new, and sometimes dangerous, ideas. The newest and most suspicious ideas were those introduced by the discovery of texts of Aristotle, lost in western Europe, but slowly recovered by intrepid scholars who journeyed to the east or to Moslem Spain in search of lost learning. The first works of Aristotle to be recovered were those treating of logic and dialectic, and these influenced the work of the eleventh and twelfth century theologians like Berengar of Tours. The metaphysical and scientific works appeared later, often accompanied by Moslem commentaries. These stunned the west. Here was a perfectly rational and coherent picture of the world which disagreed in several fundamental ways with that inherited mostly from scripture. Aristotle, for instance, suggested that the world was eternal, not created. He disagreed with his teacher Plato that the soul and body were separable, and he argued that the soul and body both perished in death. Then as now, anything exciting soon became all the rage in the universities, especially at the center of theological learning, the University of Paris.

Despite formal opposition, and even condemnation, scholars like Albert the Great and Thomas Aquinas worked hard to show that the insights of Aristotle could be compatible with Christian revelation. From this confrontation of Aristotle and Christianity, a new and very technical and professional form of theology emerged. Although not completely out of touch with popular beliefs and devotions, it became more and more a technical field far out of the reach of the ordinary illiterate peasant, or even a fairly literate lord or merchant. Most people, for instance, certainly believed that the risen Lord was present in the eucharist, but, despite the theologians' best effort, that presence was usually understood in a very literal way. At best the eucharist was a relic, making Jesus present on the altar in the same way that St. Andrew the apostle was present in Rome where his head had been taken after the crusaders stole it from Constantinople in the early thirteenth century. This split between theology and popular understanding and devotion could easily lead to abuses, and, like most human beings offered a temptation, many medieval Christians couldn't and didn't resist. Before turning to the exuberant and even exotic devotions of the period, however, a look at what the professionals were up to seems in order.

Thomas Aquinas and Transubstantiation

Perhaps the most widely known (and least well understood) of the theological positions which developed during this period is the teaching known as "transubstantiation." Theologians used the word to refer to several different ways of explaining how the risen Lord could be present, or even as a general term to refer to the real presence. The most famous use of transubstantiation in the latter sense occurred at the Fourth Lateran Council in 1215. In the creed written at the council, the following explanation of the eucharist was included in opposition to the Cathars:

> One, truly, is the faith of the universal Church, outside of which no one is able to be saved, in which the same priest, Jesus Christ, is the sacrifice whose body and blood in the sacrament of the altar under the outward form of bread and wine is truly contained, the bread having been transubstantiated into the body and the wine into the blood by divine power. . . .[1]

Theologians of the time did not read this creed as demanding any particular explanation of the real presence. As late as 1240, William of Auvergne, the Parisian master, could discuss transubstantiation at length and still conclude:

> It suffices for the piety of faith, which we intend to establish here, to believe and hold that after the priestly blessing has been correctly performed, the bread of life is placed on the altar before us under the form of material and visible bread, and the drink of life is placed before us under the form of visible wine.[2]

Not until the mid-thirteenth century would theologians begin to suggest that transubstantiation was the *only* way in which the real presence could be explained. Unfortunately, the creed of the Fourth Lateran Council would be understood during the reformation (and this misunderstanding continues to the present day) to *define* transubstantiation as a doctrine of the church. In fact, it doesn't define anything. It was merely intended to insist on the real presence in opposition to the Cathars.

All of this, of course, tells us little about what this tongue-twister was supposed to mean. Well, in the late twelfth and early thirteenth century the word was only vaguely used to describe the way in which the bread and wine could become the body and blood of the Lord. As theologians became more proficient in the use of Aristotelian philosophy, however, the word took on a very exact meaning. In the hands of Thomas Aquinas, the thirteenth century Dominican, transubstantiation was not only an excellent way to describe the change that took place on the altar, it was the only way that could possibly make sense of this change. In order to understand what Thomas meant by transubstantiation, alas, some understanding of the philosophy of Aristotle is necessary.

Aristotle was a pupil of Plato, and, like Plato, spoke a great deal about the "essence" of things. He disagreed with his teacher, however, about how this "essence" was related to actual individual things. Plato had argued (as you remember from Chapter 3) that the essence of things or their "form" existed independently of individual things and, in fact, gave individual things their reality. Aristotle rejected the idea that form had any existence apart from the individual. For Aristotle, as for Plato, the form or essence of a thing was still the most important part of anything. Form, in fact, is what made matter into a recognizable something. Without form we could never even know anything material. Aristotle insisted, however, that form never exists without matter, and matter never exists without form. Together these two make up individuals.

The issue is somewhat more complex than that, however. Matter and form make up individual things, but together really produce a sort of "generic thing," or, technically, they make up the "substance" of a thing. What makes each individual thing recognizably different is what one senses about that thing: its color, weight, scent, etc. (I am bald and overweight, and you are not, but we both have the substance of a human being.) This sense data is called by Aristotle the "accidents" of things. They are "accidental" to its existence in two ways. First of all, a thing can change color or weight and still be the same thing. A white fat cow is as much a cow as a red thin cow. Secondly, sense data is "accidental" to knowledge.

We know the form and matter of the cow not through sense data, but through the mind. Just as for Plato, the mind grasps the essence behind the sense data, and this essence is the true reality of a thing, or rather it is this essence which we recognize as the "reality" behind the accidents (sense data).

All things then are made up of form, matter and accidents. The form and matter together make up the substance of a thing. Substance played much the same role as form alone did for Plato. It was the true reality which the mind alone grasped. The sense data, which was necessary for the mind to use to reach the substance, was still very much a secondary reality. Sense data grasped by the senses was still not as "real" as the substance grasped by the mind. (If you need a refresher on this particular way of understanding what is real, turn back to Chapter 3 and try the experiment suggested there.)

If all of that seems a bit difficult to follow, then just keep this distinction firmly in mind. *Substance* is the essence of any particular thing, grasped by the mind alone. *Accidents* are sense data which change from individual to individual without changing the substance. For Aristotle, substance and accidents always exist together; you do not find accidents alone, nor substance alone.

Now, if that is clear, we are ready to understand what the theologians of the thirteenth and fourteenth centuries had in mind when they discussed transubstantiation. We will take as an example the Dominican theologian Thomas Aquinas. Thomas is important, first, because he was the most brilliant exponent of this theory, and, second, because it is his understanding that the Council of Trent and most Roman Catholic theologians have adopted as the standard teaching of their church.

Thomas argued that transubstantiation ought to be understood quite literally as a change in substance. More precisely, the substance of the bread and wine are changed by the blessing of the priest into the substance of the body and blood of the risen Lord. The accidents (sense data) of the bread and wine, however, remain exactly as they were before. At first this seems the obvious explanation for this term, but the idea is subtler than it first appears. This means, first of all, that the change Thomas is talking about is *not anything that can be sensed in any way*. For us, it means that it is not a "physical" change, since for us physics has to do with what can be sensed (or at least somehow observed). It is an intellectual change; that is, it has to do with what we grasp with our minds. In his most famous work, the *Summa theologiae*, Thomas responded to the question of whether anyone can see Christ as he is present in the eucharist by answering that this presence is only grasped intellectually, or spiritually:

> . . . the body of Christ is in this sacrament as if it were just substance. But substance as such cannot be seen by the bodily eye, nor is it the object of any sense, nor can it be imagined; it is only open to the intellect, the object of which is the essence of things, as Aristotle says. Hence, properly speaking, the body of Christ, according to the mode of existence which it has in this sacrament, can be reached neither by sense nor by imagination; it is open only to the intellect which may be called a spiritual eye.[3]

One must keep firmly in mind here that for Thomas (and Plato and Aristotle) what the mind grasps *is* what is most real. So, the most real part of the bread and wine (the substance) becomes the most real part of the risen body and blood of the Lord. This particular use of Aristotelian metaphysics solved many problems associated with the medieval teaching that the same body of Christ that lived on earth, died and ascended into heaven was present on each altar during every mass. Since the substance has no quantity (quantity is an accident which underlies all the other accidents) it can be anywhere (or everywhere) at once. Christ can be present in heaven and many places on earth at the same time. Further, anything that might befall the consecrated bread and wine, such as reception by an unworthy person, or fire, or rot, or desecration by an animal, happens only to the accidents of bread and wine, not to the substance of the body and blood.

Thomas felt very strongly that such an understanding of how the risen Lord was present in the eucharist was the best possible protection against both a too physical understanding of that presence (after all, substance was an entity grasped by the mind), and a purely symbolic understanding of that presence (since nothing was more real than substance). Thomas opposed strongly any other understandings on the grounds that they would fall into one or the other of these errors. Further, it was scientific, according to the best standards of his day.

Or rather, it was *sort of* scientific. If you have been following closely, you may have noticed a few problems with Thomas' explanation, nifty as it is. According to Aristotle, you can never have accidents alone, nor substances alone. You have to have a white *something*, not just whiteness, and you won't know that anything is there if you can't sense it somehow. Thomas is saying that in the eucharist you have the accidents of the bread and wine without their substance, and the substance of the body and blood alone without their accidents! How can this be? Well, Thomas argued, it's a miracle.

If that seems like a cop-out to you, Thomas would (and did) reply that Christians have always described the presence as a miracle, and that at least this explanation keeps the number of miracles down to one. Other explanations posited up to twelve separate miracles necessary for the risen Lord to be present. For Thomas, the single act of sustaining the quantity of the bread and wine in which the other accidents adhered was all that was necessary for the substance of the risen Lord to be present under the accidents of bread and wine. If this contradicted the laws of nature and Aristotle's philosophy, so be it.

Actually, transubstantiation, as understood by Thomas Aquinas, is about as neat and clean a way of understanding how the risen Lord can be present in the eucharist as is possible using Aristotelian categories. It also goes a long way to preserve the Platonic understanding of the earlier church writers of that presence. It is worth noting, however, that it does make a further claim that those writers would not have made. Transubstantiation, in this formulation, claims not only that the risen Lord *is* present, but attempts to explain *how* the risen Lord is present in the eucharist. Part of the medieval and reformation debate about the eucharist would be the very touchy question of whether Christians needed to merely assert a belief in the real presence, or whether they needed to believe as well in this particular way of describing that presence.

Thomas' discussion of the eucharist included much more than just an explanation of transubstantiation. He discussed, in fact, almost every imaginable question involved in the theology of the sacrament, and composed beautiful eucharistic hymns and even a liturgy for the feast of Corpus Christi which honored the sacrament. Time and space do not permit a full presentation of all of Thomas' contributions. Thomas' theology, not just on the eucharist but in many areas, was so extensive and so influential that it has often been seen as overshadowing the other great theologians of the middle ages. This is really unfair, as it was a period of great theologians. One of the greatest was Thomas' contemporary and friend, the Franciscan master Bonaventure.

Alexander of Hales, Bonaventure and the Franciscan School

Writing some fifty years ago, the young Jesuit scholar Yves de Montcheuil pointed out that St. Thomas, the great Dominican scholar, and St. Bonaventure, the great Franciscan scholar, disagreed about the eucharist. More precisely, they disagreed about what might happen if the local church mouse broke into the tabernacle and ate a consecrated host. Now, this probably sounds like a pretty silly thing for two great Christian scholars and saints to even think about, much less write about, and then get into a tiff. It would certainly be a strange thing for scholars to spend much time on in the twentieth century, but the thirteenth century had some particular problems.

First of all, it seems that scrupulous pastors really had problems with mice and that they were very concerned for both Jesus and their own souls. Secondly, and far more importantly, it seems that the Cathars used to argue against the presence of the risen Lord in the sacrament by pointing out (or possibly even demonstrating), first, that animals could devour that species, and, second, that this puts Jesus in a pretty nasty fix if orthodox teaching is right. As one early thirteenth century theologian complained,. "We would consider it pointless and excessive to discuss such things if it were not necessary to respond to the relentlessness of the heretics."[4]

Now, both Thomas and Bonaventure agreed that Jesus was in no danger from being gnawed by a mouse, and they agreed that the whole idea was pretty repulsive. They disagreed as to what actually happened to the substance of the risen Lord now under the accidents of the bread and the wine. Thomas, following the teaching of his master Albert the Great, insisted that the substance remained under the accidents, even if the accidents were in the stomach of a mouse. Jesus would be unaffected, of course, and the mouse would get no particular benefit from this divine visit, but still the substance would have to stick with the accidents. This is a fairly radical position, and Albert and Thomas seemed to have been the first to insist that once transubstantiation had taken place, it couldn't be reversed. The presence of the risen Lord remained, no matter what, until the accidents were no longer recognizable as bread and wine.

Albert, and Thomas following him, based his opinion on sound metaphysical principles. One could not just arbitrarily connect and disconnect substance and accidents. One miracle was enough to explain the eucharist, and the simplicity and neatness of transubstantiation would be destroyed if all sorts of modifications, especially involving further miraculous intervention, were introduced.

This was good metaphysics. But was it good theology? Bonaventure, and the majority of teachers at the time, didn't think so. Bonaventure followed his teacher, Alexander of Hales, in holding to the theological principle that the eucharist was fundamentally a sacrament, a sign. Therefore, only those capable of understanding and using signs, that is, human beings, could receive the eucharist. Alexander explained the situation in the following way:

> I would answer that to eat sacramentally, properly speaking, is to be in contact with that which the sacrament symbolizes [the *res* described earlier; see Chapter 4]. Therefore where no form of contact had taken place, neither through faith nor through knowledge, there is no form of sacramental eating, although there may be some form of carnal eating.[5]

Based on this principle, Alexander went on to maintain that neither Jews nor pagans could receive sacramentally either, since they neither believed nor understood what the symbols here meant. What Alexander would insist upon was the excellent theological principle that the eucharist was most fundamentally a sign. Therefore only those creatures capable of understanding signs, that is, human beings, could have anything to do with the presence of the risen Lord in the Lord's supper. Furthermore, the human beings who received had to know what this symbol of bread and wine meant. If they didn't, then they, too, were incapable of receiving the body and blood of the Lord.

Now, Alexander was teaching and writing in Paris some twenty years before Albert the Great at a time when Thomas Aquinas wasn't even born. As a young teacher, Albert seems to have agreed with Alexander, but in Albert's later years he had a problem with Alexander's teaching. The problem is one already mentioned. Once the substances of the bread and wine were changed into the body and blood of the Lord, how could they change back without some miracle? By the time Albert wrote his objections to Alexander's theology, Alexander had died. His students, however, continued his teachings, and when St. Bonaventure, his greatest student, read St. Albert and St. Thomas, he upheld his teacher's position. One argument advanced against Albert and Thomas recalls the comparison between baptism and the Lord's Supper made by St. Ambrose:

Again, if a mouse is baptized in the name of the Trinity, it receives no more than if it were washed in simple water, because it is not capable of performing . . . a sacrament. Therefore it is equally reasonable to hold that a mouse consumes no more than if it had eaten plain bread (*Commentary on the Sentences*, L. 4, dist. 13).[6]

In the last resort, however, Bonaventure accepted Alexander's approach because it was simply better theology:

According to the other opinion, the body of Christ in no way descends into the stomach of a mouse because Christ is only under this sign (*sacramentum*) in so far as it is destined for human use, of course for eating. But when a mouse gnaws it, it becomes unusable (for this purpose) and the sign (*sacramentum*) ceases to exist, and the Body of Christ also ceases to exist here, and the substance of the bread returns. And this opinion is the more usual, and certainly the more respectful and the more reasonable (*Commentary on the Sentences*, L. 4, dist. 13).[7]

Bonaventure was at least right in saying that Alexander's theology was the usual one. Most theologians at the time accepted his theology rather than that of Albert and Thomas. Over the centuries, however, both theologies would continue to be taught.

Challenges and Disputes

Transubstantiation became the accepted term used to describe the way in which the body and blood of the risen Lord became present in the eucharist. By the end of the middle ages, the majority of theologians had no trouble accepting that this was indeed the term which the church definitively used to describe how the change took place. That does not mean, however, that all theologians understood transubstantiation in the same way.

The Franciscan theologians, in particular, continued to take issue with the way in which Albert and Thomas understood that term. John Peter Olivi, writing in the 1280s, found his work censored at least in part because of his attack on Thomas' theology. He argued that Thomas had completely misunderstood what Aristotle had meant by quantity, and that if the body of the risen Lord is present in the eucharist, then this body must have its own quantity. To say anything else would be tantamount to arguing that the body of the risen Lord was really that of a spirit, the ancient teaching of the gnostics and clearly heretical.

A much subtler attack was undertaken by the brilliant Franciscan philosopher and theologian, John Duns Scotus, who taught both in Paris and in Oxford in the very beginning of the fourteenth century. The arguments of Scotus depend on one very important assumption about God. God is omnipotent, and thus free from any constraints of human reason or will. Given this premise, Scotus pointed out that there are several ways in which the body and blood of the risen Lord might become present in the sacrament. Some of these ways are even more reasonable than transubstantiation, and, further, transubstantiation entails several difficult philosophical problems including the problem of quantity mentioned by Olivi. However, since the common teaching of the church makes clear that transubstantiation is the mode that God chose to make the body and blood present, this must be the way God wants to do it.

God doesn't have to be reasonable or efficient in our terms, and, according to Scotus, in this case God chooses not to do things in the most reasonable and efficient way. In short, transubstantiation is not necessary to explain the presence, nor is it even the best way of explaining how the presence comes to be; it is, however, what God chooses to do.

What a strange reversal of Thomas' theology! Thomas defended transubstantiation as the only reasonable explanation of how the body and blood of the Lord could be present. Scotus, some fifty years later, argued that transubstantiation could not be a necessary explanation since that would impair God's free will and, in any case, created more philosophical problems than it solved in explaining the presence.[8]

Perhaps Scotus' approach to the eucharist was taken furthest by Robert Holcot, a student of Scotus, who taught at the University of Oxford from 1330 to 1343. Robert first pointed out that God, in the eucharist, causes one thing to exist (the substance of the body and blood of the risen Lord) under the appearance of another thing (bread and wine). Robert then raised the objection that if this were so, and if all things were possible to God, then God could make any changes God wanted. God could make the entire world fit into one mouse! We could never trust our sense data because we could never be sure if God hadn't made some change. Robert answered this objection in a way that anticipates some modern philosophers:

> It must be said that God is able to do more than the intellect can understand and therefore it is not inappropriate to agree that God could change the entire world and to make it exist under the species of a single mouse. . . . Concerning the certitude of experience, I believe that there is no certitude about an individual created thing as it presently exists, since it is able to become false through [this sort of] change, and it would be hidden from me whether it were true or false (*Questions on the Four Books of the Sentences*).[9]

In conclusion, then, although by the end of the middle ages transubstantiation was certainly the most common theological explanation of how the body and blood of the risen Lord become present in the Lord's supper, it was an explanation which was always seen as problematic. It did a pretty good job of offering a reasonable explanation of how the risen Lord came to be present on the altar, but really wasn't very good Aristotelian philosophy. The first opponents of transubstantiation, like Olivi, pointed out this weakness as its major shortcoming, but later critics like Scotus saw this very flaw as proof of the omnipotence of God. God didn't have to be reasonable. By so arguing, however, Scotus undermined the very purpose for which transubstantiation was put forward in the first place. The criticisms of Olivi, Scotus and others continued to be taught, especially among the Franciscan masters of theology right up until the time of the reformation. Transubstantiation was a very important theological position, which would be both roundly attacked by the reformers and stoutly supported by Roman opponents of the reformers at the Council of Trent. This ambivalence to the idea was not new in the sixteenth century, however. Transubstantiation always had problems, and especially in our own age, which no longer adheres to the philosophy of Aristotle, it still does.

The Sacrifice of the Mass, Purgatory, and Indulgences

During the thirteenth and fourteenth centuries, three somewhat different theological ideas merged in a way that would cause havoc in the sixteenth century. The ideas were not new, but, like the concept of transubstantiation, they attained a precision and acceptance which they lacked in earlier centuries.

As we saw in Chapters 2 and 3, the early Christian writers understood that the eucharist shared in some way in the mystery of Christ's sacrifice on the cross. The particular way in which the once and for all sacrifice of Jesus was connected with the liturgy was not specified, and these writers never intended that the mass should be seen as involving the real death of Jesus or anyone or anything else. The medieval theologians kept this tradition alive. As you probably remember from Chapter 4, starting in the earlier thirteenth century, every new professor of theology had to teach Peter the Lombard's *Sententia* as the standard textbook in theology. The text then that all theologians had to read on the sacrifice on the mass came from Peter. What he had to say is simple and to the point:

After this it is asked if what the priest performs can be properly called a sacrifice or immolation, and if Christ is daily immolated or if He was immolated once only. To this briefly it is able to be said that what is offered and consecrated by the priest is called a sacrifice and oblation because is is a memorial and representation of the true sacrifice and immolation which took place on the altar of the cross. Christ has died one time, on the cross of course, and here He was immolated in His own person; daily, however, He is immolated in sign (*in sacramento*) because in sign recollection is made of that which was done once only (*The Sentences*, l.4, dist. 12, c. 5).[10]

Later theologians followed suit in insisting that the mass was not another sacrifice, but rather a sign of the once and for all sacrifice of Calvary. Amazingly little change took place in this teaching in the centuries before the reformation. Theologians, however, began to add an interesting twist to this teaching. Christ's death once and for all may have freed us from sin, but the application of those benefits to particular people took place through the commemorative sacrifice of the mass. Further, the minister could specify to whom the benefits of a particular mass could be applied. While the commemoration of the living and dead, and even particular living or dead people, was an ancient tradition in the church, the late middle ages saw a proliferation of masses said for particular people.

One of the major reasons was purely financial. People would pay a lot of money to make sure that they had the best possible chance to get into heaven and particularly to get out of purgatory (of which we will speak later). Huge sums were left in wills for masses to be set in "magical" sequences of three, nine, or even up to forty-five masses. Eventually, saying masses for special intentions, and especially for the dead, became a full-time job. By 1521, Strassburg had 120 "chantries" (foundations set up just for the saying of masses), and Henry VIII suppressed 2,374 chantries shortly before his death in 1547. The theology of the period gave partial support to this practice, although there were always theologians and bishops who deplored the abuses to which such a teaching could lead. Gabriel Biel, a theologian at the newly founded University of Tübingen, wrote a very popular commentary on the mass in the late fifteenth century. Going through seven editions between 1488 and 1547, it greatly influenced the young priest Martin Luther. Biel described the theology behind the practice in the following way:

> The priest has the function of offering sacrifice, but in addition he has the office of specifying the application of the sacrifice and oblation, so that the benefit to be given through this sacrifice of the Church may be bestowed on these particular persons in need, or on others (*Exposition of the Canon of the Mass*, Lectio 26, lit. B).[11]

In short, although all theologians agreed that Jesus died once and for all to free all people from sin, the actual application of that salvation took place in the commemoration of Calvary during the liturgy. Further, masses could be offered for specific people, either to help them in some earthly difficulty or to help better their chances in the afterlife. Although the Fourth Lateran Council sternly forbade charging for such services, people were encouraged to make donations to the church and assured that the church would remember such patrons in its prayers. In the final stages of this process, enough money was accumulated for the saying of such masses that priests could be hired full-time to do nothing else but to say masses in the memory of generous donors.

A further complication to the problem of people "buying" masses was the full development of the idea of purgatory. Although the early Christian writers had speculated on the possibility of other places in the afterlife apart from heaven or hell, the actual word *purgatorium*, or, in English, purgatory, did not appear until the end of the twelfth century. The basic idea, even for the earlier writers, was to come up with some scheme in the afterlife that paralleled this life. In the court system of medieval Europe (and even in modern Europe for that matter) forgiveness and restitution were two different things. If you were found guilty of stealing someone's cow, you had to give it back, even if the original owner out of generosity forgave your act. If the original goods could not be restored, say if you killed the cow, you still had to make some restitution. The balance in the community had to be set right, so later thieves wouldn't think that they could get away with theft. More importantly, such an act of restitution demonstrated to the community that the criminal was fit again to live in society. Just as in today's society, punishments were a combination of rehabilitation and retribution.

Well, if this were true for people, why not for God? Sure, God forgave our sins as soon as we were sorry for them, but what about restitution for the evil we committed? Penances of different sorts were imposed on the sinner to prove his forgiveness and to restore the well-being of the community. Since the penances especially in the early middle ages could be very severe, the practice grew up of offering charitable donations to monks to do penance for you if you were too busy to, say, fast on bread and water for three years. As time went on, penances became less severe, but that didn't make matters less difficult. Suppose you died and the books weren't even. You hadn't fully made restitution for your sins. It didn't seem fair to let you go right to heaven, so Christian writers speculated that there was a middle ground, a place where one was purged of the evil left in them, a place to work off the restitution still due to sin. Technically the punishment still due for sins after they were forgiven was called "temporal punishment."

But, said the theologians, there were also people who died with a whole bunch of penance done over and above what was required—the saints, Mary, and especially Jesus. Where did this "treasure" go? The church decided that it reverted to the church, and, even better, the church could dish it out to people for special reasons. The church could be indulgent, and it could give "indulgences." Just like the monks, Mary, Jesus and the saints could do penance for someone else or, rather, had already done penance for everyone. The church could apply this penance to particular people, just as the church could apply the benefits of Jesus' death to particular people in the mass.

The first time the popes made widespread use of indulgences was during the crusades. Any crusader was automatically free from all his "temporal punishment." This very generous form of indulgence was called a "plenary indulgence." Not all indulgences were that inclusive. If you said the Lord's Prayer, for instance, during the elevation of the host during mass, you might receive one hundred days off your allotted time in purgatory. Now, with even a little thought, you can see that you can really rack up days off by whipping off as many Lord's Prayers as you can while the host is up there, or, even better, racing from church to church to get your

Paters in at each of the elevations. People soon figured this out, and Christianity could be reduced on the popular level to something like the collection of "coupons" which you redeemed at the end of your life (or people earned for you after your death) in order to buy off time in purgatory.

The papacy discovered that it could define almsgiving as a penance and then it could barter indulgences for cold cash. As a result, people thought of masses and indulgences in somewhat the same category. Both were necessary purchases to make the afterlife easier for oneself and one's relatives. Just as yuppies now see car phones, Rolex watches, and BMW's as essential to the good life, "yuppies" of the late middle ages collected indulgences, masses and relics to ensure a comfortable next life. Not just the wealthy purchased these things, however. If you loved your family, no sacrifice was too great to ensure their release from the punishments of purgatory. The papacy quickly saw that it had great power in the ability to grant indulgences. Nor should it be thought that the popes always saw indulgences in financial terms. Far from it. This was a way that the pope could alleviate the suffering of his flock even after death. Sir Richard Southern describes better than anyone the late medieval fascination with indulgences:

> A small incident in the year 1476 may serve to illustrate the emotional background to the developments we are discussing. In this year, Sixtus IV, with some cardinals, was paying a visit to the Franciscan nuns at Foligno. The nun's confessor asked him for an indulgence, and he gave then a plenary indulgence for the approaching Feast of the Virgin Mary. Then, feeling moved to give something more, he added, "Besides this, you may have a full immunity from *poena et culpa* every time you confess your sins." "What?" shouted the cardinals. "Every time?" "Yes," said the pope laying his hand on his heart, "I give you everything I have." Then the cardinals went down on their knees crying, "Us, too!" and the pope said, "All right; you too." If this scene had not been recorded by a bystander we should never have known that behind the extraordinary papal privilege for the sister of Foligno, which was finally drawn up in 1482, there lay no searching for prece-

dents and no subtleties of calculation, but just an old man putting his hand on his heart and giving what he could.[12]

All of this could easily become very confused on the popular level. The liturgy not only became a time for celebrating the covenant between the risen Lord and his people, but it was also a time of marvels and great gifts from God. You could get masses said after death to free your soul from purgatory. While alive, you could get indulgences to cut your time short in purgatory by saying certain prayers as the body of the Lord was raised on high at the elevation. And, people reasoned, if spiritual benefits abounded during this great miracle, why not temporal succor as well? The benefits popularly attached to the mass grew and grew. Thomas Brinton, bishop of Rochester until his death in 1389, gave an exuberant and probably very well-received sermon describing the advantages associated with hearing mass:

> If a man serves the Lord daily in honest watchings, in prayers, and especially in hearing Masses, so will the Lord have care of him, that nothing will be lacking to him for his livelihood. It is no wonder, then, that the doctors say that to those who hear Mass devoutly the following privileges are conceded: first, that they have all that is necessary to support life that day; secondly, that they are spared idle gossip and oaths; thirdly, that they do not lose the sight of their eyes; fourthly, sudden death does not befall them; fifthly, that while they are hearing Mass they do not grow older; sixthly, that all the steps they take going and coming to Mass are counted by the angels.[13]

Not surprisingly, people saw mass as a very good deal. They spent a little time and a little cash, and they could be virtually certain of going directly to heaven, without passing purgatory or collecting temporal punishment. This perversion of the eucharist (and of course that's what it was and is) also had terrible consequences. Suppose you were really poor, and couldn't afford to get your parents out of purgatory? Even when you were rich, how many masses and indulgences were enough? No one knew for sure. People in the later middle ages were worried sick about this problem. God became a medieval judge, and salvation an echo of medieval law.

All during this period there were people who knew this was all wrong, and said so. Not everyone bought into the system. The temptation to do so was very strong, though, and the financial benefits to the clergy great. Eventually the vested interests of almost everyone—priest, peasant and pope—made it more and more unlikely that the reform needed could come without a great upheaval. People certainly did try, however, and it is instructive to investigate the movements which to one degree or another anticipated the reformation, especially in regard to the eucharist.

John Wyclif and the Lollards; John Hus and the Utraquists

John Wyclif was a philosopher and theologian who taught at the University of Oxford until his work was condemned by the university in 1381. In many ways he anticipated the later views of the sixteenth century reformers. He argued that the Bible should be the sole source of authority in Christianity and that common people should read it in their own language. He held that the position of the pope had little support in scripture and, in fact, that religious orders had no such foundation. He excoriated the ecclesiastical abuses of his time and was particularly hard on the friars. Most importantly for this study, however, he rejected transubstantiation outright. Wyclif denied that transubstantiation had any philosophical support, using language reminiscent of Robert Holcot some fifty years earlier:

> On this theory [transubstantiation] no intellect or sense proves the existence of any material substance; because no matter what sense-experience or cognition is present, it is possible and consistent that the whole created universe is just a ball of accidents; so someone who wishes to posit material objects must rely on the faith of scripture (*On the Eucharist*).[14]

Holcot, of course, wanted to demonstrate that God could do anything including deceiving our senses, thus proving that revelation alone was reliable. This conclusion infuriated Wyclif, who felt that this made God a liar. Things had to be what they appeared to be, and Wyclif insisted that the bread and wine remained just that at the same time that they were images of the real body and blood of Jesus in heaven.

Wyclif was not just upset by the philosophical absurdity of transubstantiation, however. He also felt that this teaching led to gross impieties. First, it left people worshiping mere accidents hanging in the air, and not God. Second, even stupid and immoral priests were given the power to make God present daily on the altar. Holiness, not ordination, should be required for the presence of the Lord, and Wyclif suggested that worthy laity could also confect the eucharist. Wyclif's attacks on transubstantiation, then, were not just philosophical. He felt that this teaching was an example of a church which used its teaching to deceive and fleece the people of God. Wyclif wanted a purer and more honest church.

The teaching of Wyclif is important for several reasons. First, he felt, unlike previous authors who had attacked transubstantiation, that the arguments against this theory were decisive. The teaching was not just philosophically inconvenient; it was impossible, even for God. Second, his attacks should be understood in the larger context of his disgust with the worldliness and power of the clergy he saw around him. If the clergy kept control by their ability to make the risen Lord present to the people of God, and, worse, they became rich off this power, then there was all the more reason to deny that priests had any such control. Finally, Wyclif's teaching endured long after his death, continuing down to the time of the reformation.

Wyclif's influence started during his lifetime as students of his spread out into the English countryside. Pockets of "Lollards" (as the followers of Wyclif were known) existed, despite their persecution, right up until the time of the reformation. The books used by the Lollards demonstrate their loyalty to Wyclif's ideas of reform. First of all, Lollards used their own English bible. Under Wyclif's patronage, his secretary, John Purvey, translated the Bible into English and some two hundred manuscripts of this Lollard bible survive even today. A Wyclifite book, *How the Office of Curates Is Ordained of God*, illustrates the continued concern of the Lollards with a worldly clergy:

The seventh error [of the clergy] is, that they teach sinful men to buy hell full dear, and not to come to heaven which is proffered them for little cost. For they teach Christian men to suffer much cold, hunger, and thirst, and much waking and despising, to get worldly honor; and a little dirt by false warring, out of charity; if they bring them much gold they absolve them lightly and to think themselves secure by their prayers, and grant them a blessing. But they teach not how their parishioners should dispose themselves to receive gifts of the Holy Ghost, and keep conditions of charity, doing truth and good conscience to each man, both poor and rich. And if they are poor by the chances of the world, or willingly, by dread of sin, they set them at nought, and say they are cursed, because they have not much muck; and if they have much worldly goods, got with false oaths, false weights, and other deceits, they praise them, and bless them, and say God is with them and blesseth them.[15]

When Martin Luther's ideas began to spread in England, the Lollard underground was already in place to help with their dissemination. Perhaps more important than the small groups of Lollards which preserved Wyclif's ideals in England was the influence his teaching had at the University in Prague. How, you might ask, did the teaching of an Oxford professor come to influence distant Bohemia? Czech students had been traveling to Paris and Oxford, and then returning to their native University of Prague for some time, and they brought with them the latest theological and philosophical thought. Contacts became more frequent, both politically and academically, however, when Anne, the sister of the king of Bohemia, married Richard II of England in 1382. Special scholarships for Czech students were set up at Oxford, and Wyclif's works were carried back to Prague and enthusiastically discussed.

(A word of explanation is probably in order here, since the geography of the middle ages is very different from that of today. The modern country of Czechoslovakia is really an artificial union of two different countries and peoples created by the Allies after World War I. The two countries are Bohemia and Slovakia. The people have different histories, languages and traditions. The capital of the ancient kingdom of Bohemia is Prague, and the language of Bohemia is Czech. Bohemia is the western and northern part of modern Czechoslovakia.)

Bohemia already had a growing group of reform-minded clergy when Wyclif's writing arrived to fan the flames. A fiery preacher and reformer, John Hus, became dean of the philosophical faculty at Prague. From his pulpit at the Bethlehem chapel, he addressed his congregation in their native language, ripping into the clergy for their worldliness and greed. He was popular with the students but not with all the clergy, as you might imagine.

In 1407, Hus was forbidden by the pope to preach and was excommunicated in 1411. Meanwhile, the troublesome teachings of Wyclif were also under fire. In 1403 the University of Prague condemned forty-five propositions taken from Wyclif's works. Pope Gregory XII followed suit by prohibiting Wyclif's doctrines in 1408 and again in 1412. This did not stop Hus from writing a scathing condemnation of worldly clerics, including the curia itself:

> Hence the cardinals heap up to themselves ecclesiastical livings and barter with them and take money for their sale either themselves or through others, and so devour and consume in luxurious living the goods of the poor, and if they do not do miracles or preach the Word of God to the people or pray sincerely or fill the place of deacons, whom the apostles appointed, (Acts 6)—by not performing their duties or living their lives—in how far, I ask, are they the vicars of the apostles? (*The Treatise on the Church*).[16]

In 1414, having been granted safe conduct by the emperor, John Hus set out for the Council of Constance, where he hoped to appeal from the curia to the greater authority of the council. The trip was a disaster. On July 6, 1415 he was burned at the stake. Wyclif's doctrines were condemned as well, and as a tragic finale to the whole affair the body of John Wyclif was disinterred in 1428 and then burned, the remaining ashes being cast into the river.

Ideas, however, do not die so easily. Hus immediately became a national hero, and reformers in the Bohemian church continued their fight. Hus' own views on the eucharist were much more moderate than those of Wyclif, but central to the Bohemian reform movement were two important eucharistic practices, frequent communion and reception of both the bread and the wine by the laity. As you may remember from the last chapter, the practice of distributing the cup had pretty much disappeared in western Europe during the thirteenth century. The primary reason seems to have been the prevention of sacrilege, but there soon grew up a theology which supported the practice. Theologians reasoned that since the risen Lord was present in each and every part of the consecrated bread and wine, then receiving any part of the bread and wine constituted full reception of the Lord. The Bohemian reformers insisted that, even if this were so, the people had a right to participation in both signs used in the liturgy. The more moderate of the reformers were named "Utraquists" ("Both-ers" in Latin) because of their insistence on receiving both species.

A league of five hundred nobles rose up against the church under the banner of the martyred Hus and a reformed church. A long period of warfare followed in which the emperor led "crusades" against the Czech lords and people to force their submission to Rome. The Bohemians held out and retained their independence. Despite several attempts to reach some agreement between Rome and the Hussites, Bohemia was to a large extent already practicing a reformed expression of Christianity by the middle of the fifteenth century. Not that all the Bohemians themselves agreed. They were split between more moderate groups like the Utraquists and the revolutionary and violent Taborites, dedicated to bringing in the kingdom of God by force of arms. Despite these differences, just as in England, Luther, Zwingli and others found in Bohemia a country already open to their ideas. In fact, the "Moravian Brethren" (Moravia is a region in Bohemia), who are direct descendents of the Hussites, exist to the present day as a separate church, living a simple and unworldly form of Christianity in rural Europe and North America.

The Lollards were a minority in England, and the Hussites were really quite a small group in comparison with the large number of faithful in Europe. It might seem odd, then, to spend so much time discussing these small groups. After all, Europe had seen larger and more heretical movements, such as the Cathars, come and go without much disturbing the rest of European Christianity. Wyclif and Hus, however, touched on an important theme, one which would become central for understanding why the reformation was so popular so quickly. What Wyclif and Hus both objected to was a selfish and grasping clergy who used the power of the liturgy to oppress, rather than help, their fellow Christians. When Wyclif attacked transubstantiation, he did so because he thought it was wrong, but also because he thought it was part of a larger evil which led the common people to worship the bread and the wine, the indulgences and processions, the pomp and not the substance of Christianity. The technicalities of the theology itself were probably never important to more than a few theologians. As Wyclif pointed out, "The people and a thousand bishops understand neither accident nor subject."[17]

When Martin Luther, Huldrich Zwingli and John Calvin preached, they found willing audiences for the same reasons that Wyclif and Hus had. People felt that they were being taken. They felt that something was wrong with a system which seemed to tell them that heaven could be bought and sold and that one of the things for sale was the mass itself. Not all priests were corrupt, of course. Studies suggest that there was probably no more corruption during the fifteenth century than at other times in the history of Christianity. Nor were Wyclif and Hus always correct in their assessment of popular devotions. Many people built lives of deep faith, hope and charity around the very practices of indulgences, pilgrimages and eucharistic devotion which Wyclif especially despised. It does not take many examples of abuse, however, before people call for reform of the entire system. Wyclif and Hus called out loudly and clearly. The voices would become more insistent as time passed.

The Celebration

But before discussing the split to which the call to reform would inexorably lead, let us look at the last unified liturgy of western Christianity, the lush and lusty liturgy of the late middle ages.

We have arrived in York on an auspicious day in 1472. On a beautiful spring morning the flowers are in full bloom, and today is the feast of Corpus Christi. Walking south from Scarborough on pilgrimage, our little group is tired from the long walk, most a little hung-over from the riotous night in the tavern the night before, and filled with the joyful knowledge that they have all earned a rich indulgence for undertaking the pilgrimage. What a diverse group, too! John, the shepherd, rushes off to the great cathedral, just completed this year, to terminate the pilgrimage by entering the church door. Inconsolable after the loss of his wife, he is too poor to afford the masses necessary to free her soul from purgatory. He is the only traveler to avoid the tavern. He spent his pilgrimage in prayer, hoping God will accept this sacrifice in lieu of the missing masses; the rumor is that he also has no money for food. Brother Cedric, the pardoner, sets up shop close to the cathedral. The entire city will participate in the Corpus Christi celebrations, and he has indulgences to sell at all prices. George Hawker, a wool-dyer, can barely contain his pride and excitement. This year, the wool-dyers' guild of York will lead the procession on Corpus Christi, thus proving both the devotion and social standing of the wool trade. He has been asked to join them as a special favor to fellow dyers in Scarborough.

The feast of Corpus Christi is not an ancient one, as Reginald, the young clerk from Oxford, well knows. Established in 1264 by Pope Urban IV under the inspiration of Blessed Juliana of Liège, the feast became universal in Europe only in the last century. Reginald also knows that the feast is very popular, and of this he disapproves. Rather than calling Christians to worship and imitate the life of Christ (*vita Christi*) it encourages people to worship the body of Christ (*corpus Christi*). The festival itself is raucous and makes for unseemly competition for places of honor in the procession that winds around the town with the bishop holding aloft the host enshrined in a gold reliquary called a monstrance.

Mass is about to begin, and all the pilgrims rush to the Great Minster, as the cathedral is called. After a rather lackluster sermon, with which Reginald is thoroughly disgusted, people become restive for the high point of the liturgy. God's own body and blood are recreated on the altar and raised on high for all to see. A black velvet cloth is draped behind the altar to show up more clearly the small white host. At the moment of elevation, the crowd milling around the outside of the great doors rush forward to see, jostling and crowding, while they pray for the special benefits they know will come from seeing the Lord of lords that day.

At the communion, only a few devout layfolk come forward to receive, along with the cloistered religious. It is dangerous to receive frequently unless one has carefully prepared, as in Lent or Advent. Only the holiest people dare to take the Lord into their bodies and souls except on the high feast of Easter, or maybe Christmas. At the end of the liturgy, however, bread which has been blessed, but not consecrated, is distributed. To receive it is a great act of devotion, and does not require the purity of actual communion. The bishop stands up to begin the procession of this solemn feast. He announces a special privilege for all pilgrims. A plenary indulgence will be granted! John, poor man, is completely overcome and weeps in the corner of the church. He can almost see the now purified soul of his dear wife rise to heaven with the smoke of the incense.

Meanwhile, George pushes his way forward. Proud as a peacock, he stands with the wool-dyers at the head of the procession, behind the clerics who hold God himself aloft. Despite the solemnity of the procession, he cannot help giving a small wave to his family as he passes. After the procession carries the Lord Jesus back into the Minster, all attempts at gravity collapse and pure carnival breaks out.

Here Cedric is in his element. "Have you no mercy, you revelers? How can you so enjoy yourselves when your relatives burn in the fires of purgatory! Save your father; save your mother! They gave you life; now save their souls." His chant continues and the people flock shamefaced to purchase the pieces of parchment that they hope will ease the pain of dear ones now dead. Reginald saunters over to the pardoner's booth. "How did a poor friar with a vow of poverty get so fat?" he shouts to the friar. Earning a dirty scowl, he laughs, and joins his friends outside the church. They exchange secretive glances and proceed down a narrow alley. In a house well back from the street, they meet to discuss the scriptures. The only literate member of this little band, Reginald reads the lesson of the day out of the forbidden English bible. The prayer meeting closes as the festival outside continues on into the night. The final prayer is for a purified church, freed from the corruption of greed and gluttony. Young Reginald alone of the day's pilgrims will live to see this prayer answered, albeit in ways he could never have anticipated.

Conclusion

The thirteenth century started out full of enthusiasm and opti-
mism. Even the seeming threat of Aristotle's philosophy could be
met with the patience and genius of Albert and Aquinas. Theologians thought that God could be shown to be reasonable and consistent with human understanding. Politicians felt that the introduction of law would bring about a new society, the best possible in a
sinful world. The new orders of Franciscans, Dominicans and Car-
melites offered even lay people a chance to share in a great religious
revival. By the end of the fourteenth century, however, most people
had a sense that something had gone wrong. Theologians found
that reason didn't work quite so well as they thought; there were
areas where God didn't seem so reasonable. Politicians found that
laws could be manipulated and bent by wealth. The Franciscans
and Dominicans found more and more of their time taken up with
fund-raising and defense of the status quo, while fewer and fewer of
their order even wanted to "go naked following a naked Christ" as
Francis had.

And then there was the plague. Betwen 1350 and 1400, probably half the population of Europe died. Entire villages disappeared.
Rich and poor, high and low, people died and no one knew why.
Everyone asked what went wrong. Did God hate us? If so, how can
he be appeased? People became fearful or cynical or frantic. The
plague passed, of course, but with it went much of the confidence
of earlier centuries. People looked around and asked: How did we
get here? This is not good. This is not what we intended. This is
not what God intended. People looked for a recovery of old values,
a rebirth of hope. The renaissance and the reformation provided
both.

Theology of the eucharist, not surprisingly, followed this same
pattern. Transubstantiation developed as a refined philosophical
explanation that gave reason and order to the great miracle of the
Lord's presence. By the end of the fourteenth century, severe
doubts had been cast on both the reasonableness and the appropri-
ateness of this explanation. To actually deny transubstantiation, as
Wyclif did, would call down severe ecclesiastical censure; yet one
could accept transubstantiation and still feel it to be unreasonable,
as did Scotus.

Common people cared little for theological niceties. They too often saw the eucharist as a miracle to be manipulated. This was the greatest of the relics, the place on earth where one could meet God face to face, and, as with all great lords, perhaps one could gain a little influence. To say this is not to say that there were not many people who understood and lived the eucharist in a true Christian spirit. The connection between living a life like that of Christ and the reception of communion was never lost. As the author of the popular late medieval work, *The Imitation of Christ*, urged in the voice of the Lord:

> Willingly, with arms outstretched upon the cross where I hung naked, I offered myself to God and Father for your sins, in total surrender, my whole being turned to a sacrifice pleasing to God. So you in your turn should offer yourself to me daily at Mass, with all your powers and affections. A willing offering it ought to be, an offering pure and holy, made with all the power of your inmost heart. There is nothing I ask of you more than this, to strive to surrender yourself entirely to me. I care for nothing that you offer me besides yourself; it is not your gift that I want, it is you. If you had everything else, and not me, you would be unsatisfied; so it is with me; nothing you give can please me if you fail to offer yourself (Book 4, Chapter 8).[18]

Just as there were many good priests and bishops just before the reformation, so too there were many devout Christian lay men and women who had never forgotten that the eucharist was the great sign of union with the risen Lord and with the Christian community. Perhaps the best evidence of that is the reformation itself, which, to a large extent, resulted from the aspirations of devout men and women repulsed by abuses which ill-matched the convictions of their own faith and devotions. It is to the results of this impulse for purification that we now turn.

GLOSSARY OF PERSONS

Albert the Great. A theologian, philosopher, scientist and bishop, the Dominican friar Albert was considered one of the greatest minds of his time. He is sometimes better known now as the teacher of St. Thomas Aquinas who studied under Albert both at Paris and at Cologne. Albert contributed greatly to the understanding and acceptance of Aristotle's metaphysics and natural philosophy (science). He commented on most of Aristotle's writing, as well as on the *Sentences* of Peter Lombard and on scripture. Albert served as bishop of Ratisbon for two years and performed several diplomatic missions for the papacy. He outlived Thomas Aquinas, and died as professor emeritus of Cologne in 1280.

Alexander of Hales. Born in Halestown, England, Alexander studied philosophy and theology at the University of Paris, where from around 1220 until his death he was a regent master of theology. Roger Bacon, a fellow theologian of the time, called him "a good and rich man . . . and also a great master of theology in his time." In 1236, to the wonder of everyone, he gave up his wealth and became a Franciscan. He kept his position as a theologian, however, and so the Franciscans now had their first chair of theology at Paris. Alexander was the first theologian in Paris to use the *Sentences* of Peter Lombard as the textbook for theology, and his teaching greatly influenced succeeding generations of scholars.

Aristotle. See entry in the glossary at the end of Chapter 4.

Bonaventure. Born Giovanni di Fidanza, this saint and scholar took the name of Bonaventure when he joined the Franciscans in 1244. By then he already had his master's degree in philosophy. He studied theology under Alexander of Hales, among others, and soon started teaching in Paris himself. Bonaventure was elected head of the Franciscan order in 1257, and appointed as a cardinal and bishop of Albano in 1273. He died the next year while attending the ecumenical council held in Lyons. Bonaverture is known not only as a great theologian, but also as a deeply mystical writer and perhaps the greatest of the biographers of St. Francis of Assisi.

Cathars. See Chapter 4.

Corpus Christi. A holy day celebrating the institution of the Lord's supper and especially the presence of the risen Lord in the sacrament. It is traditionally held on the Thursday following Trinity Sunday. Blessed Juliana of Liège had a vision c. 1230 in which the Lord asked that a special feast be established to celebrate his presence in the eucharist. When Juliana's confessor, Jacques Pantaleon, became Pope Urban IV, he extended the feast of Corpus Christi to the entire church. The feast was not an immediate success, and was only slowly adopted in the different European countries. By the middle of the fourteenth century, however, the feast had become very popular and was not only the occasion for a large procession with the consecrated host, but also the setting for a town festival.

Fourth Lateran Council. One of the great disciplinary and reforming councils in western Christianity, the Fourth Lateran Council was called by Pope Innocent III in 1215. Among other important issues, the council used the word "transubstantiation" for the first time in an official church document. The council also made annual confession and communion mandatory for all Christians and outlawed "simony," the practice of charging for spiritual services.

Gabriel Biel. A philosopher and theologian, Gabriel was born c. 1420 and educated in the universities of Germany. He was instrumental in founding the University of Tübingen, where he held the chair of theology. Among other works, he wrote a long and influential commentary explaining the mass.

John Hus. John received his master's degree from the University of Prague in 1396, and became dean of the Philosophical Faculty in 1401. He was also a well-known preacher, urging reforms based partly on the earlier work of the English theologian John Wyclif. John's theology provoked the clergy of Prague to denounce John's teachings at Rome in 1407, and the archbishop of Prague forbade John to preach. Even so, he received political support, and by 1409 was rector of the university. In 1411, however, Hus was condemned by the new pope in Avignon, John XXIII. In 1414 John appealed to the ecumenical Council of Constance. Having been granted a safe conduct of the Holy Roman Emperor Sigismund, he arrived at the council to find himself in grave danger. He defended his views, but was condemned to death. He was burned at the stake on July 6, 1415. He immediately became a hero to the Bohemians, who pushed forward his reforms, establishing a church which continues to this day.

John Duns Scotus. Franciscan friar, philosopher, and theologian, John was born in Duns, Scotland. He studied and taught at both Oxford and Paris, as well as Cologne. Known as the subtle doctor, he is best known for his insightful use of logic in philosophy. He strongly defended the free will of God against the belief that God could not do anything unreasonable. He died at the young age of forty-two.

John Peter Olivi. John entered the Franciscan order when he was only twelve. He studied at Paris, and then taught in southern France. Some of his teachings aroused the anger of other scholars, and finally in 1283 a committee of seven scholars was appointed to investigate his work. John's works were banned, but he managed to defend himself and in 1287 was allowed to teach again in Florence. He continued to teach until he died some years later. John was a Franciscan for almost forty years, and he strongly defended the ideal of poverty envisioned by St. Francis. Probably his views on poverty were the cause of his censure. After his death, John was venerated as a saint especially by those Franciscans who felt that he embodied the true Franciscan love of poverty. John also taught a controversial approach to the eucharist, suggesting that the bread and wine might be present along with the body and blood of the risen Lord.

John Wyclif. Born near Richmond in England around 1330, John Wyclif taught at Oxford from at least 1356 until 1382 when he retired to the parish church of Lutterworth after his teachings were condemned. Wyclif bitterly criticized the Christianity of his day. He urged that the Bible be translated into English, and thus be available to simple laypeople. Based on his study of scripture, he rejected the claims of the papacy to absolute authority. Wyclif urged the civil government to undertake the reform of the church, claiming that spiritual power was based on grace, and that immoral clergy could therefore be removed from office by civil authority. His greatest criticism came, however, from his attack on transubstantiation, which he held was philosophically unacceptable and led to superstitious practice. This attack on transubstantiation caused the condemnation of his teachings by the university in 1381 and by Archbishop Courtney in 1382. Wyclif spent the last two years of his life writing pamphlets defending his positions. After his death in 1384, his work was carried on by his followers, who gradually became known as the Lollards, a group that continued until the time of the reformation. Wyclif's works also became widely known and supported in Bohemia and were one influence on John Hus.

Plato. See entry in the glossary at the end of Chapter 3.

Thomas Aquinas. Thomas d'Aquino was born to a minor nobleman in the castle of Roccasecca, located in the northernmost reach of the kingdom of Sicily. At the tender age of five, he was presented to the monastery of Monte Cassino, where he remained for eight years. Thomas then went to the university in Naples, where he met members of the new Dominican order. Despite family opposition, he joined the order in 1245. He studied in Paris under Albert the Great, moving with Albert in 1248 to Cologne to continue his studies. Thomas returned to teach in Paris from 1252 to 1259. During the next nine years Thomas taught in Italy, mostly at newly established Dominican houses. In 1269 he returned to Paris, where he taught for three years before returning once again to Italy. He was on his way to the ecumenical Council of Lyons when he became ill and died at the Cistercian monastery of Fossanova south of Rome on March 7, 1274. Thomas is certainly the best known of all the medieval theologians, and at the Council of Trent his teaching was held up as a model of Roman Catholic orthodoxy. During his own lifetime, however, much of his teaching was controversial, especially his use of Aristotle. In fact, in 1277 some of Thomas' teachings were condemned at Paris. Thomas was canonized, however, in 1323, and the condemnations of Paris revoked in 1325.

William of Auvergne. William taught in Paris from at least 1223 until his death in 1249. He wrote continuously, and most of his writings are collected in a huge work known as the *Magisterium Divinale* (*Divine Teaching*). He also served as bishop of Paris from 1228 on. William used the newly discovered texts of Aristotle in his teachings and supported the new orders of Franciscans and Dominicans who were just coming to Paris at this time.

6

Diversity Denied: The Reformation: Luther and Zwingli

The story of the reformation of the sixteenth century is one of the most frequently told, and most complicated, in the history of western Christianity. There was not one but many separate reforms—almost, it sometimes seems, as many as there were reformers. Not a single Christian group in the west survived the reformation unchanged. Even the Roman church emerged a very different entity than that of the medieval church. The Council of Trent so thoroughly reformed those churches who remained loyal to the papacy that it can be justly said that the medieval church we have described in the last two chapters disappeared from the scene. Different churches retained different customs of the old medieval church, to be sure, and some of the churches, especially the Roman Catholic and Anglican churches, treasured their continuity with the medieval centuries. Yet it is important to remember that none of the churches which emerged from this great upheaval can claim the past as exclusively their own. The modern Roman Catholic Church started in the sixteenth century just as surely as the Lutheran and Calvinist churches. To repeat what was said in the first chapter, before the reformation there were no Protestants, no Anglicans, no Roman Catholics. Christians were simply Christians—eastern and western Christians sometimes, but mostly simply Christians.

During the sixteenth century, western Christianity splintered. The issues over which Christians differed, and the reasons why their differences led to centuries of division, are myriad. Politics, economics, and the recent technology of printing all played an important role. The subtle interweaving of these factors is important for understanding the complex phenomena of the different reformations of the sixteenth century, but this story is much too complicated to rehearse here. Our concern rests with the question of the Lord's supper, the eucharist: how ought Christians to celebrate this ancient ceremony, and what does that ceremony so celebrated achieve toward the salvation of the participant? As you might have guessed, this question touches the heart of the theology of the reformation, the question of how and why humans are saved.

Erasmus of Rotterdam and the New Scholarship

By the beginning of the sixteenth century, nothing was clearer to most educated Europeans than the necessity of reforming the church. The earlier revolts of Wyclif and Hus continued, and were joined by calls within the church for a council to cure the most blatant evils of the late medieval church. In Chapter 5 the misuse of indulgences was discussed and, as we will see, this remained a central target for the reformers. In order to understand why some of the reformers so strongly attacked the medieval hierarchy, two other issues need to be explained.

The first was the system by which clergy were paid in the late medieval ages (and indeed in some churches until much later). The "benefice system," as it was known, fit in well with the rest of the feudal system. In feudal society, land was wealth. Money only slowly came into its own as a form of payment. So, for each ecclesiastical position, a certain amount of land was allotted. For a parish there might be two or three small fields, a stream for fishing, and part of an orchard or forest. The priest didn't necessarily farm this land (although poorer priests did). A peasant family farmed the land and sent part of the produce to the priest for his support. Now this system existed on a much grander scale for bishops and abbots who owned extensive territories. The grandest territories of all, of course, were the papal states which made up most of central Italy.

This "payment" was considered separate from the actual position of bishop or abbot, and hence not subject to the strict rule against the buying and selling of spiritual benefits laid down by the Fourth Lateran Council held in 1215. Therefore a king or lord or bishop or pope could bestow or even sell benefices, while still maintaining the legal fiction that he had not sold the office. Imagine, for instance, that you are granted the job of mayor of your town or city. It's free; you are appointed or elected because of your virtue and good sense. However, there is one slight snag. You have to pay a substantial sum in order to get the salary that goes with the job. You can have the job, but you don't get paid until you pay off the local lord, or bishop, or the pope himself.

"Benefices" eventually became market commodities, as well as payment for a clerical position. The right to appoint benefices gave the pope and bishops tremendous financial power. By the late middle ages, some people greatly abused this system by collecing benefices just as they collected relics and masses for the dead. One of the worst examples of this sort of exploitation was Thomas Wynter. In the early sixteenth century, he was at the same time dean of Wells Cathedral, provost of Beverley Cathedral, archdeacon of York Cathedral, archdeacon of Richmond Cathedral, prebendary of Wells, York, Salisbury, Lincoln and Southwell, and rector of Rudby in Yorkshire and of St. Matthew's Church in Ipswich. A conservative estimate of his income in 1990 dollars would be some $150,000. Even more remarkably, Thomas Wynter was in the equivalent of grade school at the time.

To be fair, Thomas Wynter did none of these jobs. He was a child. His very powerful father arranged for someone else to be paid out of Thomas' vast income to actually do these jobs, for, of course, much less money. How did Thomas get these jobs? His father paid the papacy to "exempt" Thomas from the age requirements for the job; then dad just appointed Thomas to them. Oh yes, he also had to get little Tommy exempted from bastardy, for that was indeed Thomas' state. His father was not married. His father could not marry, since he was the most high cardinal Thomas Wolsey, cardinal legate and lord chancellor of England.

I suspect you are beginning to see the potential for evil in this system. Even if Wolsey and his son were an exception, and they most certainly were, a few outrageous examples of misuse such as this went a long way in undermining respect for the institutional church. The problem ranged from the poor parish priests who were paid by some distant figure who actually "owned" the parish benefice, to the papacy which allowed people like Wolsey exemptions from the rules established to protect the church from such abuse. Once again, the feeling one got was that the church, like heaven itself, was for sale. Even if many people agreed that the system needed reform, few were interested in giving up their vested interests to implement those reforms.

A second issue which greatly affected the desire for reform was a sweeping change in scholarship. In the twelfth and thirteenth centuries, the discovery of the texts of Aristotle changed scholarship, but the desire to recover ancient documents did not end with Aristotle. As part of the renaissance movement of art and music came a desire to imitate not only the art of Greece and Rome, but also the philosophy of the ancients. People continued to search for the most ancient Greek manuscripts, and the study of ancient languages became fashionable. In northern Europe particularly, this desire to get back to European roots extended to scripture study. Once again libraries were scoured to find the most ancient Greek and Hebrew versions of the Bible. Rather than trust St. Jerome's Latin translation of the Bible, scholars wished to read the original Hebrew and Greek for themselves. Rather than study scattered paragraphs of Augustine, Ambrose, or even Origen found in Peter the Lombard's *Sentences*, they wished to read the entire work in the original version.

When scholars actually got back to the sources, they made two great discoveries. First, the translation by Jerome, even with the corrections made by medieval scholars, had several important errors, and a new version of the Bible was badly needed. Even worse, church teaching was sometimes based on misreadings either of scripture or of the early church writers. But second and more important, by reading the original language of scripture, and the original language of the early church, scholars found that the whole elaborate structure of benefices and exemptions and indulgences and masses for the dead simply did not exist in the early church. Scholars called for a return to a simpler and purer church based not on the elaborate theology of Aquinas or Bonaventure, but on the original words of scripture and on the example of the early church.

The most respected voice of the new scholarship was the priest, linguist and satirist Erasmus of Rotterdam. Erasmus was an accomplished linguist, and not only edited several of the writings of the early church, but also one of the most famous editions of the

Bible, which compared the Hebrew, Greek and Latin texts on the same page. As famous as Erasmus was for these accomplishments, he was even more famous for his satire of sixteenth century life *In Praise of Folly*. In this hilarious parody, Erasmus argued that stupidity (folly) was the greatest of sixteenth century virtues, and the one thing necessary to succeed in the Europe of his time. The church came in for particularly hard treatment.

Because of the sarcasm of *In Praise of Folly*, and Erasmus' insistence that scholars return to the original language of scripture, he was considered suspect by many church officials and theologians. Indeed, Erasmus did sincerely wish reform. His idea of reform, however, was a return to the simplicity and purity of the gospel. A retiring man by nature, Erasmus rarely spelled out his own ideas of what Christianity should be like, but in the preface to Erasmus' edition of the New Testament, Erasmus wrote movingly of the "philosophy of Christ" found in the gospels:

> The journey is simple, and it is ready for anyone. Only bring a pious and open mind, possessed above all with a pure and simple faith. Only be docile, and you have advanced far in the philosophy. It itself supplies inspiration as a teacher which communicates itself to no one more gladly than to minds that are without guile. This doctrine in an equal degree accommodates itself to all, lowers itself to the little ones, adjusts itself to their measure, nourishing them with milk, bearing, fostering, sustaining them, doing everything until we grow in Christ. . . . It casts aside no age, no sex, no fortune or position in life. The sun itself is not as common and accessible to all as is Christ's teaching. It keeps no one at a distance, unless a person, begrudging himself, keeps himself away. Indeed, I disagree very much with those who are unwilling that Holy Scripture, translated into the vulgar tongue, be read by the uneducated, as if Christ taught such intricate doctrines that they could scarcely be understood by very few theologians, or as if the strength of the Christian religion consisted in men's ignorance of it. . . . I would that even the lowliest women read the Gospels and the Pauline Letters. And I would that they were translated into all lan-

guages so that they could be read and understood not only
by Scots and Irish but also by Turks and Saracens. Surely
the first step is to understand in one way or another. It
may be that many will ridicule, but some will be taken
captive. Would that, as a result, the farmer sing some
portion of them at the plow, the weaver hum some parts of
them to the movement of his shuttle, the traveler lighten
his weariness of his journey with stories of this kind! Let
all conversations of every Christian be drawn from this
source (*The Paraclesis*).[1]

As you might well imagine from these beautiful and powerful
words, Erasmus was a hero to many young scholars, including
Luther, Zwingli and Calvin. In the end, however, Erasmus did not
join them. He remained with Rome. Erasmus hated controversy,
and hoped always that reform could take place without rancor. He
died in 1536, suspected by many Romans as a secret supporter of
the reformers, and scorned by the reformers as a man too weak to
leave Rome and follow his convictions. In the beginning of the
sixteenth century, though, Erasmus was a powerful voice urging a
return to the simple teaching of Christ found in the scriptures. His
call would be heeded by all the reformers.

Among Erasmus' friends was another scholar, better known
for his very successful political career, Thomas More, later lord
chancellor of England under Henry VIII. In fact Erasmus wrote his
In Praise of Folly while staying at More's house. More, following in
Erasmus' footsteps, also wrote a satire on sixteenth century life, the
very popular *Utopia*. Now *Utopia* was a great joke from the very
beginning, since More convinced many people that this was a real
place, found by one of the explorers of the new world recently
discovered by Columbus. Even today, More's joke continues, since
most people think Utopia means "the perfect society." It doesn't.
It's a word More made up which means, in Greek, "no place."
When people speak of a "utopia," they are really saying "no place."
More, an incurable practical joker, would have loved the irony. In
any case, More, too, painted a picture of a purer form of devotion
and included many suggestions for reform in his "perfect society."
Some have a very modern ring:

Priests [in Utopia] are elected by the whole community. The election is by secret ballot, as it is for all public appointments, to prevent the formation of pressure groups, and the successful candidates are then ordained by their colleagues. . . . Male priests are allowed to marry—for there's nothing to stop a woman from becoming a priest, although women aren't often chosen for the job, and only elderly widows are eligible. As a matter of fact, clergymen's wives form the cream of Utopian society, for no public figure is respected more than a priest. So much so that, even if a priest commits a crime he's not liable to prosecution. They just leave him to God and his own conscience, since, no matter what he has done, they don't think it right for any human being to lay hands on a man who has been dedicated as a special offering to God. They find this rule quite easy to keep, because priests represent such a tiny minority, and because they're so carefully chosen. After all, it's not really very likely that a man who has come out top of a list of excellent candidates, and who owes his appointment entirely to his moral character, should suddenly become vicious and corrupt (*Utopia*).[2]

Especially when one compares this description of how priests are chosen with the despicable career of Thomas Wynter (whom More would have known), the impact of More's work in his time becomes clear. Some of his suggestions here are still controversial. Of course, scholars question whether More was just poking fun at his society or whether he really intended "Utopian" ideas to be adopted in Europe, especially since he later persecuted reformers in England and attacked Luther in print. Most importantly, More was to die rather than break with Rome when Henry VIII declared himself head of the church in England. Many things, too, had changed between the publication of *Utopia* in 1516 and More's death in 1536.

Erasmus published *In Praise of Folly* in 1509 and *Utopia* appeared a few years later. Both were best sellers, widely read and distributed by the newly-invented printing presses. These were only the most popular of a series of works that questioned whether the Christianity of the day was more of a human invention than a divine organization. Scholars were comparing the church of the apostles with that of the renaissance popes, and the comparison was shocking. Common people knew little of this, but they did know that their parish priest was poor, ignorant, and hired by someone far away. The common people also felt that something was wrong when the rich accumulated relics, indulgences, and ecclesiastical control, and when wealth seemed to determine one's position even in the afterworld.

Martin Luther

At least from the perspective of the twentieth century, it seemed only a matter of time before something happened that blew the lid off things. What happened was that a college professor, a teacher of scripture at the newly-established German university of Wittenberg, got very, very angry. The teacher was the Augustinian priest Martin Luther, and the reason he got angry was because, right outside town, a really sleazy indulgence salesman, Johannes Tetzel, was busy selling his wares.

The story is a classic and worth retelling. A twenty-four year old young man named Albrecht of Brandenburg was archbishop of Magdeburg and of Halberstadt at the time. He held several other posts as well. Albrecht was not the best of priests. In fact, the major interest in his life seemed to be his own pleasure. He traveled publicly with his mistresses, although he did dress them up as boys to keep the scandal down. Albrecht also wanted to be archbishop of Mainz, but in order to get this job and keep his other offices, Pope Leo X required payment of 31,000 ducats. Albrecht borrowed the money from the Banking House of the Fugger family. In order to pay off this debt, he received permission, again from Leo X, to sell indulgences. Half the money went directly to Rome to help pay, among other things, for the magnificent St. Peter's Basilica. The other half of the money went to the bankers whose representatives traveled with the indulgence salesman to make sure they got their take of the action.

The salesman that Albrecht hired was Johannes Tetzel. Tetzel was reputed to have made wild boasts about the power of the indulgences he sold. One person, Friedrich Myconius, claimed to have heard him and recorded the following:

> The claims of this uneducated and shameful monk were unbelievable. Thus he said that even if someone had slept with Christ's dear Mother, the Pope had power in heaven and on earth to forgive as long as money was put into the indulgence coffer. And if the Pope would forgive, God also had to forgive. He furthermore said if they would put money quickly into the coffer to obtain grace and indulgence, all the mountains near St. Annaberg (the mining town where he was preaching) would turn to pure silver. He claimed that in the very moment the coin rang in the coffer, the soul rose up to heaven. Such a marvelous thing was his indulgence (*History of the Reformation*).[3]

Now Friedrich was almost certainly exaggerating, since he disliked Tetzel, yet from what we know of his sermons, Tetzel did tend to play on the emotions of his audience and overstate the power of indulgences. In any case, there was enough there to infuriate the zealous young professor of scripture in nearby Wittenberg. In 1517, Martin Luther called for an academic debate on the power and usefulness of indulgences by posting a notice of this discussion on the door of the church in Wittenberg. Immediately the document was printed and reprinted all over Europe, and many people, including Erasmus, cheered on the young scholar in his challenge to the abuses to which indulgences were put.

From there, events moved rapidly. The discussion of indulgences led to a larger discussion about the reform of the church in general. Luther found himself more and more disillusioned with the leadership in Rome. In 1520 he wrote three pamphlets presenting his ideas for the reform of the church: *To the Christian Princes of the German Nation*, *The Babylonian Captivity of the Church*, and *On the Freedom of Christian Men*. In these he advocated that the German rulers take the power to reform the church into their own hands. Among other things, the celibacy of the clergy, masses for the dead, pilgrimages, and religious orders should be abolished. Luther also attacked transubstantiation, communion in one kind, and the doctrine of the sacrifice of the mass. Only baptism and the eucharist were held to be rituals clearly established by Jesus. These works made any compromise with Rome unlikely, if not impossible.

Luther's teachings were condemned in 1520, and he was excommunicated in 1521. Protected by his ruler, the elector of Saxony, he became the religious leader of the reformation in Germany. He continued to preach and teach and write as professor of scripture in Wittenberg until his death in 1546. A fiery writer, master of the German language, and gifted teacher, Luther was seen as the champion of the reformation. Students of a purer Christianity flocked to Wittenberg, and Luther's ideas spread throughout Europe. Again, it is not possible to tell the whole, amazing story of Luther's break with Rome, and how the fire of the reformed spirit spread throughout Europe. Luther had lit a match which, set to the tinder prepared by Wyclif and Hus, Erasmus and More, and others like them, would set Europe ablaze.

The fire came not, however, from these men alone, important as a personality like Luther might be. The true fire of the reformation came from the central theological tenets which Luther, Zwingli and Calvin espoused. The first of these, that all Christian truth must be based only on the scriptures, had found a champion already in Erasmus, although he would not apply this principle as assiduously as the reformers. More importantly for our study was the great insight advanced by Luther even before he posted his ninety-five theses on the church door in Wittenberg. What Luther discovered in his study of scripture changed his life and remains one of the central themes in reformed thought. The idea is simple and yet essential to understanding Luther's theology, especially his theology of the Lord's supper. Salvation is a freely given gift of God. Salvation can never be earned, and no human action contributes to salvation. Nothing we can do can ever deserve salvation. Righteousness in the eyes of God is a gift, earned for us by Christ on the cross, and not earned by any acts on our part.

Luther as a young man had been oppressed by the thought that he could never do enough to please God. Whatever fasting or mortifications or prayers he offered, he could not be certain that God loved him or that he would be saved. In this he was typical of many people in the late middle ages who were frightened by the thought that they had to be saints to be saved. Of course, the practice of indulgences and masses for the dead encouraged this insecurity.

What was enough? What kind of cruel God demanded more and more and more from people? Luther found the answer to this dilemma in Paul's letter to the Romans:

> At last, by the mercy of God, meditating day and night, I gave heed to the context of the words, namely, "In it the righteousness of God is revealed, as it is written, 'He who through faith is righteous shall live.' " There I began to understand that the righteousness of God is that by which the righteous live by a gift of God, namely by faith. And this is the meaning: the righteousness of God is revealed by the gospel, namely, the passive righteousness with which the merciful God justifies us by faith, as it is written, "He who through faith is righteous shall live." Here I felt that I was all together born again and had entered paradise through open gates (*Preface to the Complete Edition of Luther's Latin Writings*).[4]

What Luther discovered in scripture was the assurance that he was saved, not by indulgences or celibacy or masses or fasting or even charitable acts. Luther was saved by faith. Not faith as some sort of intellectual assent to certain beliefs, but faith as trust in God that God would save people despite their sins. God saves us not because we deserve it, but in spite of our unworthiness. For Luther, and for those who heard his message, this was tremendously liberating. No more did one have to pay for mass after mass for one's dead parents. No more did peasants, merchants, or miners have to worry that heaven was closed to those who married and lived in the world. Being a "spiritual athlete" who wore a hair shirt and lived in a cave would not win you heaven. Nothing won you heaven. Heaven, and faith itself, was a gift—a pure gift of love from God.

No wonder, then, that Luther left the Augustinian order and married the former nun Catherine Von Bora in 1524. No wonder that he attacked masses for the dead, indulgences, and many other practices as worse than useless. Luther was rightly afraid that all these devotions led people to believe that just because they performed them, they deserved heaven.

In *The Babylonian Captivity of the Church*, Luther laid out a comprehensive theology of the church and the sacraments. This

early work of Luther would set the stage for much of the reformation discussion of the Lord's supper. Based on the principle that
scripture was the only reliable guide to Christian faith and practice,
Luther also did away with all the sacraments except baptism and
the Lord's supper. Only these two were clearly part of the New
Testament church. Later Luther was also to allow confession as a
ritual justified by the New Testament.

Central to Luther's belief about the eucharist was his conviction that all the baptized were priests. "Ministers" or priests were
those designated from the community, and, more importantly, by
the community, to preach the word of God. There was no difference of status between clergy and laity, but merely one of function.
In fact, the separation of clergy and laity had become one of the
greatest causes of abuse in the church:

> In virtue of a physical anointing, when their hands are
> consecrated, and in virtue of their tonsure and vestments,
> the clergy claim to be superior to the Christian laity, who,
> nevertheless, have been baptized with the Holy Spirit.
> The clergy can almost be said also to regard the laity as
> lower animals, who have been included in the church
> along with themselves. Thus it arises that they make bold
> to command and demand, to threaten and urge and op-
> press, as they please. In sum, the sacrament of ordination
> is the prettiest of devices for giving a firm foundation to all
> the ominous things hitherto done in the church, or yet to
> be done. This is the point at which Christian fellowship
> perishes, where pastors become wolves, servants become
> tyrants, and men of the church become worse than men of
> the world. Now we, who have been baptized, are all uni-
> formly priests in virtue of that very fact. The only addi-
> tion received by the priests is the office of preaching, and
> even this with our consent (*The Babylonian Captivity of the
> Church*).[5]

The eucharist, then, was not a "work." Saying masses or having masses said for you did not in the least aid one's salvation. Only
one thing could save a person, and that was faith, faith in God's
promise that our sins were forgiven due to Jesus' sacrifice on the

cross. There was no sacrifice in the mass apart from this one sacrifice, and since one could only have faith for herself or himself, it
was utter nonsense to speak of offering a mass for someone else,
living or dead. To put this in Luther's own words, ". . . the Mass is
a divine promise which can benefit no one, be applied to no one,
intercede for no one, be communicated to no one, except only the
believer himself by the sole virtue of his own faith."[6]

The eucharist, for Luther, both signified the one great offer of
salvation from God, declared that offer, and sealed the offer by
giving us the true body and blood of Christ in communion. Yet,
once again, it was faith, and faith alone, that could accept the offer,
believe in God's promise, and so only in faith could the true eucharist be celebrated.

> Therefore the Mass, in essence, is solely and simply the
> words of Christ just quoted, viz., "Take and eat, etc.; as if
> He has said, "Lo! thou sinful and lost soul, out of the pure
> and free love with which I love thee, and in accordance
> with the will of the Father of mercies, I promise thee with
> these words, and apart from any deserts or undertakings
> of thine, to forgive all thy sins, and give thee eternal life.
> In order that thou mayest be most assured that this my
> promise is irrevocable, I will give my body and shed my
> blood to confirm it by my very death, and make both
> body and blood a sign and memorial of this promise. As
> often as thou partakest of them, remember me; praise and
> laud my love and bounty, and be thankful." From all of
> which you will see that nothing else than faith is needed
> for a worthy observance of the Mass, and the Mass is truly
> founded on this promise (*The Babylonian Captivity of the
> Church*).[7]

This, then, was the heart of Luther's teaching on the eucharist.
The Lord's supper was a sign and seal of the same offer of salvation
which was proclaimed in the preaching of the word. Anything that
detracted from this one central function of the sacrament was to be
discarded. Luther called for a return to a simple service, one resem-
bling as nearly as possible the last supper. "Now the closer our Mass
resembles that first Mass of all, which Christ celebrated at the Last

Supper." Luther insisted, "the more Christian it will be."[8] Luther knew that this would entail a complete renovation of the liturgy, as well as a radical change in the life of the clergy. Luther accepted that challenge:

> But, you will say: What is this? Surely your contentions will overturn the practices and purposes of all the churches and monasteries, and destroy those by which they have waxed rich for many centuries. . . . You will deprive them of their largest incomes. My answer is: That is the very thing which led me to write that the church had been taken prisoner. For this sacred testament of God has been forced into the service of impious greed for gain by the opinions and traditions of irreligious men (*The Babylonian Captivity of the Church*).[9]

In this one early writing of Luther, the most important of the themes embraced by all the later reformers were put forward. First, the Lord's supper was not a "work," not something that could be "offered" to God. Rather it was a gift offered by God to us. Second, the gift given in all the sacraments was the same gift given in the gospel message, the free offer of salvation in Christ, given out of love, and never earned. Third, everything taught about the eucharist had to conform to scripture, and therefore the purest form of celebration would be that which most perfectly conformed to the descriptions of the celebrations of the early church. By 1520 the basic framework for the theology of the reformers on the eucharist had been established, and remarkably, despite all the disagreements that would follow, the reformers would agree on these three points in solid opposition to Rome.

In other areas Luther was less adamant, and although he always gave his opinion, he regarded other questions as side issues. He felt that the followers of John Hus were right in asserting that the consecrated wine be offered to the believers, if they so insisted. Since Jesus clearly had commanded all to eat and all to drink, scripture was clear, and the church had no power to revoke Jesus' command.[10] Transubstantiation Luther felt to be "an unfortunate superstructure [built] on an unfortunate foundation."[11] Scripture, not Aristotle, should be the foundation for all Christian thinking on the eucharist, and Luther was well aware that the teaching of Aquinas on transubstantiation depended on a very shaky reading of Aristotle. In any case, all this metaphysics was completely unnecessary. Scripture seemed clear enough. Jesus promised us that we receive his body and blood when we received the bread and wine. We should therefore believe the word of God. The body and blood are present in the bread and wine, which are also present. If it seems impossible that both should be present, we should remember that all things are possible to God.

> The authority of the word of God goes beyond the capacity of our mind. Thus, in order that the true body and true blood should be in the sacrament, the bread and wine have no need to be transubstantiated, and Christ contained under the accidents; but, while both (bread and wine; body and blood) remain the same, it would be true to say: "This bread is my body, this wine is my blood," and conversely. That is how I would construe the words of divine Scripture and, at the same time, maintain due reverence for them. I cannot bear their being forced by human quibbles, and twisted into other meanings (*The Babylonian Captivity of the Church*).[12]

Luther would admit, however, that whoever wished to believe in transubstantiation was welcome to it, as long as that interpretation was not forced on either himself or anyone else. If a position must be taken, Luther preferred the teaching known as "ubiquity," that is, that the body of the risen Lord could be present anywhere, since the divine nature of the Lord was present everywhere (*ubique* in Latin). If the Lord were present at all in the eucharist, he must be present both as God and as human, since the two natures cannot be divided:

> Here you must take your stand and say, where Christ is according to His divinity, there He is a natural divine person and is present in a natural and personal way, as His conception in His mother's womb shows. For if He was to be the Son of God, He had to be naturally and personally in the womb of His mother and had to become man. If He

is present naturally and personally where He is now, He must be there also as a man. For there are not two separate persons, but one single person. Where this person is, there He is as one undivided person. And when you can say, Here is God, then you must also say, Christ, the man, is also here. If, however, you were to show me a place where the divine nature is and not the human nature, the person would be divided because then I could say in truth, Here is God who is not man and never has become man. That is not my God. For it would follow from this that space and place would separate the two natures and divide the person, though neither death nor all the devils could ever separate and divide them (*On Christ's Supper*).[13]

Luther knew full well that his views would invite heated reply from the Roman theologians, and he was surely right. Luther would continue to defend his views on the eucharist right up until the end of his life. What Luther did not expect were the bitter disputes concerning the sacrament that grew up among the reformers themselves. Within a few years after writing *The Babylonian Captivity of the Church*, Luther found it necessary to defend his views not only against the Roman theologians, but also against the great Swiss reformer, Ulrich Zwingli.

Ulrich Zwingli

In 1518, just a year after Luther had begun his battle over indulgences, the town council of Zurich in Switzerland appointed a new priest and preacher to a post at the central church, the Great Minster. Extremely well trained in the new humanism of Erasmus, Ulrich Zwingli had earned a reputation for both his learning and his fiery sermons. Inspired by both Erasmus, and later by Luther, Zwingli persuaded the town council to implement a series of drastic reforms of the church during the decade of the 1520s.

You may have noticed something interesting here. The town council, not the bishop or the local lord or the king, implemented the reforms, and even appointed priests to different town posts. This sounds pretty much like some kind of democracy and not much like sixteenth century Germany. Well, it was a sort of democracy. Switzerland had just emerged from a long and bitter battle for independence against the emperor, and, amazingly, had won. (The story of William Tell and the apple immortalizes that struggle.) The Swiss organized their newly independent areas called cantons into fairly democratic governments. The reformation in the Swiss cities of Zurich, Berne, Basle and Geneva (to mention only the most famous centers) took a completely different form from that of Germany or England. The reformers would present a plan for reform to the town council, and then it would be publicly debated, representatives of the bishop opposing the reformers. Finally, a vote was taken by the council, and the entire city would have to follow the majority decision. As you can imagine, the composition of the town council was very important in bringing about the reformation, and elections were often crucial for the cause of reform.

The Swiss were fiercely independent, famous for their mercenary armies, and ready to fight for their religious beliefs. The sixteenth century popes hired the Swiss to protect them, and to this day the Swiss Guards at the Vatican are really Swiss! In fact, Zwingli was only forty-seven years old when he died in battle against the Catholic cantons in 1531. Zwingli fought for his independence not only with his sword and pike, but also with his scholarship. Although he greatly admired Luther, he considered the reformation in Switzerland to be autonomous. He was not afraid to disagree, even violently, with the great German reformer, and the cause for such a disagreement arose because of Zwingli's very different understanding of the Lord's supper.

The linchpin of Zwingli's theology was his radical separation of spirit and matter. Only spirit, God, could save human beings, and nothing in the material realm could effect salvation. Zwingli praised Luther for his attack on religious orders, on the useless ceremonies of pilgrimages, indulgences, and masses for the dead. Zwingli, like Luther, was absolutely emphatic that no "thing," no "work," could save a person. Only faith could save, and faith was a gift unearned, freely given to us by God because of Christ's redemptive death.

Zwingli went further than Luther, however, in his rejection of any vestige of a material religion. In 1523 he convinced the town council to abolish the Roman mass and to remove all the statues, paintings, and stained glass windows from the churches of Zurich. In 1524 monasteries and nunneries were closed, the organs were taken out of the churches, and, more importantly for our story, a new form of liturgy was introduced to replace the mass. The altars were removed and replaced by simple wooden tables. Unleavened bread and wine were distributed by the congregation, and the central act of the service became the reading of scripture and the sermon, rather than the consecration and the communion. What remained of the raucous, earthy and often superstitious ceremonies of the late middle ages was replaced in Zurich (and in those cities that followed Zurich's lead) by a spare, intellectual and wholly spiritual service.

Zwingli's justification for this dramatic shift lay in his unwavering conviction that Christianity was founded upon and should concern itself only with the things of the Spirit. Even in speaking of the incarnation, Zwingli would regard only the divine nature of the God-person Jesus Christ as our true savior. "Christ gave life to the world," Zwingli insisted, "not because he is flesh, but because he is God and the Son of God."[14] ". . . we have put our trust in Christ, not because he put on human nature, but because he is the only true God."[15] This understanding of the very separate natures of Christ was similar to that of the "Nestorians" of the fourth century.[16] The effect that such a theology had on Zwingli's thought was to make it impossible for him to understand how anyone could really believe that the human nature of Christ was at all present in the Lord's supper, or indeed what possible use such a presence could serve. The whole idea repulsed him:

> That the symbolic bread is the flesh of Christ is so opposed to the sense of all the faithful that no one of us has ever really believed it, but rather we have either left it out of our thought through negligence or inertia, or have through folly kept ourselves from thinking about it. What better evidence could there be that this notion is not in accordance with the will of God? For if faith is there, the heart delights in things which are most strange to the flesh, as I said in regard to the birth from a virgin. Sweeter than honey is the word of the Lord taken into the mouth of the faithful soul. This word about the tearing of

the flesh is so repugnant to the mind that it does not venture to eat it but casts it out of the mouth (*Subsidiary Essay on the Eucharist*).[17]

Unfortunately, many people *did* believe just what Zwingli denied, and not all of those who did were followers of Rome. One of the firmest adherents to the real presence of the body and blood of the risen Lord in the supper was Martin Luther himself. These two strong-willed men were bound to clash, and sooner rather than later. By the end of the 1520s the debate between them was public and bitter. Fear spread that the hostility between Zwingli and Luther would split and weaken the reformation.

In many ways Zwingli had the harder argument to make, since hundreds of years of theology and devotion affirmed the real presence of the Lord in the sacrament. Zwingli, like Luther, however, claimed that scripture alone, not tradition, should be the guide for Christians, and for Zwingli, at least, scripture was clear. In the sixth chapter of the gospel of John, Jesus had clearly, once and for all, explained that eating his flesh meant believing in him and in his Father. "It is the spirit that gives life," Jesus had said. "The flesh is of no avail. The words that I have spoken to you are spirit and life" (Jn 6:63). Zwingli, following John, concluded:

For it is forever true: what is born of flesh is flesh, and on the other hand, what is born of spirit is spirit. Christ, therefore, means here a spiritual eating, but of what nature? Such that we are to say that Christ is eaten here physically? Are to eat spiritually and to eat physically one and the same thing then? Even the logician knows that is absurd. If it is spiritual eating why do you call it physical? If it is physical, what else can it do but comfort the body? Christ means, therefore, that unless we eat his flesh, that is, unless we believe that he underwent death and poured out his blood for us, we shall not attain life. Again, that if we eat his flesh, that is, believe he died for us, and drink his blood, that is firmly believe that his blood was poured out for us, then Christ is in us and we in him. But is Christ in anybody physically? By no means. Why, then, are we speaking about eating the body? His body is eaten

when it is believed that it was slain for us. It is faith,
therefore, not eating about which Christ is speaking here
(*Letter to Matthew Alber*).[18]

Zwingli's insistence on a spiritual presence of Christ in the sacrament might seem completely new in the sixteenth century, especially
considering the emphasis that the later middle ages had placed on
miracle hosts and the feast of Corpus Christi—all proofs of the real
physical presence of the risen Lord. Yet Zwingli's theology has a
certain medieval ring to it. Remember that the medieval theologians
(as discussed in Chapters 4 and 5) had argued that the real point of the
eucharist, the *res tantum*, was the participation in the life of the
church and in the life of the risen Lord. This union could be achieved
apart from actual sacramental communion through "spiritual communion."[19] Coupled with Zwingli's insistence that only Spirit mattered,
the teaching on "spiritual communion" as the most important aspect
of the sacrament could easily lead one to think that spiritual reception
was the *only* reception. To this form of reasoning, Zwingli added the
belief that the physical body of the risen Lord, as opposed to his
divine nature, could only be in one place, and that was heaven:

> It is characteristic of human nature to be limited, to be
> tied to one place (his sitting at the right hand of the Father
> does not alter the case) while it is characteristic of the
> divine to extend, permeate, be present everywhere, to
> hold, know and dispose all things (*Friendly Exegesis, that is,
> Exposition of the Matter of the Eucharist to Martin Luther*).[20]

To confuse the divine and human nature, as Luther did, was
gross ignorance. Perhaps the risen Lord could be present everywhere as God, but not as a human. This went against the very
meaning of "human." Furthermore, as Zwingli consistently pointed
out, there was no point in arguing about it, since physical things
were useless for salvation.

Faced with a growing threat from the empire and the papacy,
several reformed theologians and political leaders felt that a split in
their own ranks could be fatal to the reformation. Therefore, after
much negotiation, they managed to get Luther and Zwingli to agree
to meet in the city of Marburg to try to work out their differences

and come to a common understanding of the Lord's supper. The meeting commenced on October 1, 1529, and though the reformers reached agreement on many points, they could reach no compromise on their understanding of the eucharist. Luther left Marburg convinced that the words "This is my body" must be taken literally, while Zwingli left equally convinced that it was both unnecessary and absurd to claim that the body of Christ was present in the sacrament.

More importantly, both Zwingli and Luther refused to recognize each other as legitimate teachers of Christianity. No Christian fellowship could be reached between Zurich and Wittenberg. The Protestant churches themselves were now split. Zwingli died only two years later, but his teaching was developed and continued by theologians like Martin Bucer and John Calvin. Luther remained adamantly opposed to Zwingli's teaching, and shortly before his death again insisted:

> I rate as one concoction, namely as Sacramentarians and fanatics, which they also are, all who will not believe that the Lord's bread in the Supper is His true natural body, which the godless or Judases receive with the mouth, as did St. Peter and all other saints; he who will not believe this, I say, should leave me alone and hope for no fellowship with me.[21]

Lutherans, until fairly recently, have refused communion to those who accept the teaching of Zwingli, and this was certainly Luther's opinion. Writing to the church in Frankfort in 1533, Luther urged the parishioners to avoid pastors who adopted this heresy:

> Therefore it is my honest advice which before God I owe you who are at Frankfort and whoever else may be in need of it. If anyone knows that his pastor teaches the Zwinglian way publicly, he ought to avoid him. He should rather abstain from the sacrament all his life, than to receive it from him, and even die and suffer all things.[22]

Two great splits had already occurred in the Christian understanding of the eucharist, and so our story of the many centuries of its unity are drawing to a close. The reformers of both Switzerland and Germany had irrevocably declared their separation from Rome, and, in turn, Rome rejected both of them and their call for a reform of the church in head and members. Within the reformed movement itself, Zwingli and Luther had rejected each other's understanding of the Lord's supper, and with this rejection, Luther, at least, refused to accept the Swiss as fellow Christians.

These splits were a cause of deep concern to all parties, and many attempts were made to reach some sort of reconciliation. No one expected that western Christianity could long be divided. The reformed churches gradually gave up trying to compromise with Rome and aimed rather at conversion. Within the reformed churches, however, the attempts to reach a common understanding of the Lord's supper continued in earnest. Chief among the protagonists in this struggle were Luther's right hand man, the young biblical scholar, Philipp Melanchthon, and the friend and colleague of Zwingli, Martin Bucer, the reformer of the city of Strassburg. Both had been present at the Marburg meeting, Philipp supporting Luther and Bucer supporting Zwingli. Both devoutly hoped that some middle position between their mentors could be found. Philipp Melanchthon's attempts to find a middle group between Luther and Zwingli would only lead to a bitter dispute within early Lutheranism, finally settled in 1577 by rejecting Philipp's views in the Formula of Concord.

Martin Bucer's theology or, more accurately, theologies, since he tried many times to come to an understanding of the sacrament which would be acceptable to both Swiss and German reformers, met with much more success. Or perhaps it would be better to say that Bucer's students' theology met with success, since it was Bucer's students who systematized his ideas and continued them. The most famous of Bucer's students was the great reformer, John Calvin.

GLOSSARY OF PERSONS

Martin Bucer.   Born in 1491, Bucer became a Dominican priest. He heard one of Martin Luther's first disputes with the Roman theologians in 1518, and was immediately won over to the reformation. He left the Dominicans in 1521 and was married the next year. He became the leader of the reformation in the city of Strassburg, where he worked with and influenced the young John Calvin. In 1549 he moved to the University of Cambridge where he taught until his death in 1551. Under the reign of Mary, his body was dug up and publicly burned.

Desiderius Erasmus.   Probably born in 1469, Erasmus was the son of a priest. He studied under the Brethren of the Common Life at Deventer and was ordained to the priesthood as a member of the Augustinians in 1492. He visited England in 1499 where he met and became friends with Thomas More. Erasmus spend most of his life moving to wherever he could best pursue his scholarly activities. From 1509 to 1514 he lectured on Greek at the University of Cambridge. From 1521 to 1529 he lived in Basle, moving to Freiburg im Breisgau where he lived until 1535. He died in Basle, overseeing his new edition of the works of Origen. The greatest scholar of his age, Erasmus' two famous works are his critical edition of the Greek New Testament published in 1516, and his bitter satire of sixteenth century life, *In Praise of Folly*, published in 1509.

Leo X.   Giovanni de Medici was the son of Lorenzo the Magnificent, the powerful nobleman of Florence. Tonsured at seven, nominated archbishop of Aix at eight, a cardinal at thirteen, Giovanni became Pope Leo X in 1513 at the age of thirty-eight. Leo is reported to have said, "As God has given us the papacy, let us enjoy it." This he surely did. Pleasure loving, and a notorious nepotist, he left the Vatican bankrupt upon his death in 1521. He was responsible for the sale of indulgences in Germany that so infuriated Luther. He also excommunicated Luther in 1520.

Martin Luther.   Born 1483 in Saxony, son of a miner, Luther was educated at the Cathedral School at Magdeburg, at Eisenach, and at Erfurt University. In 1505 he entered the monastery of the Augustinian Hermits at Erfurt, in fulfillment of a vow made during a thunderstorm. He was ordained in 1507, and in 1508 he was sent as a lecturer to the newly founded university at Wittenberg. In 1511 Luther was appointed doctor of theology and professor of scripture at Wittenberg, a post which he held until his death in 1546. In 1517, furious with the sale of indulgences by Johannes Tetzel, he proposed for discussion ninety-five theses on indulgences by posting them on the church door at Wittenberg. Immediately his attack on the abuse of indulgences was hailed throughout Europe, and Luther was required to defend his views. Refusing to recant after being summoned before Cardinal Cajetan, he fled to Wittenberg under the protection of the elector Frederick of Saxony. In 1520 several of his teachings were condemned by the papal bull *Exsurge Domine*. Luther responded by burning the bull along with canon law books and theological tracts. On January 3, 1521 Luther was excommunicated by the bull *Decet Romanum Pontificem* and summoned by the emperor to appear before the Diet of Worms. Luther again refused to recant and was placed under the ban of the empire. Luther hid under the protection of the elector of Saxony in the castle at Wartburg near Eisenach for eight months, until he could return safely to Wittenberg. In 1524 he discarded his religious habit and married the former nun Catherine von Bora. Until his death he was the real leader of the reformation, particularly in Germany, translating the Bible into German and writing the catechisms and hymns which helped shape not only the Lutheran faith but also the German language.

Philipp Melanchthon.   Philipp Schwerzerd was born in 1497 and studied at the universities of Heidelberg and Tübingen, becoming professor of Greek at Wittenberg in 1518. Like other scholars of the period, he translated his last name, Schwerzerd, into Greek, "Melanchthon." (Both "Schwerzerd" and "Melanchthon" mean, roughly, "black earth.") Once at Wittenberg, he immediately became friends with Martin Luther, and became his close friend and right hand man in the reform movement. He was mainly responsible for the Augsburg Confession of 1530, an important statement of Lutheran beliefs even today. He was first and foremost a scholar in temperament, and sought to find a way of reconciling the differing opinions of Luther, Calvin and the theologians of Rome. Unfortunately, he found himself embroiled in controversy for much of his life. Melanchthon died in 1560.

Thomas More.   Born in 1478, More studied classics as a student, but due to the wishes of his father, Sir John More, he began to study law in 1494 and started his practice in 1505. More had a extremely successful political career, entering parliament as early as 1504. In 1515–16 More wrote his best known work, the satire *Utopia*, which was an instant best seller. The next year he entered the service of the king, rapidly rising in prominence. During this time More wrote several works attacking the teachings of the reformers, at least one of which was directed specifically against Martin Luther. In 1529 he was chosen to replace Cardinal Thomas Wolsey as lord chancellor. Three years later, in 1532, he resigned, being unable to agree with the king over the matter of his divorce. More was imprisoned in the Tower of London in 1534 for refusing to sign the Act of Succession and thus recognizing the independence from Rome of the Church of England. He was executed on July 6, 1535 for the same reason. In 1935 More was canonized by Pope Pius XI.

Friedrich Myconius.   Born in 1490, Myconius became a Franciscan in 1510 and was ordained in 1516. He was soon attracted to the teachings of Luther, however, and became a leading figure in the Lutheran reformation. Famous as a preacher during his own lifetime, Myconius is now best known for *History of the Reformation*, a valuable eyewitness account of events in Germany during this period. While he was still a student in 1510, Friedrich heard Johannes Tetzel preach.

Johannes Tetzel.   Johannes Tetzel entered the Dominican order sometime around the year 1490, and in 1517 he was appointed one of two deputies for the preaching of a special indulgence to finance the building of St. Peter's and to repay the losses incurred by Albrecht, archbishop of Magdeburg, Halberstadt and Mainz in attaining those posts. In January of 1518 Tetzel disputed the opinions of Luther, even defending the jingle which the indulgence salesmen used: "Before the money in the box rings, the soul to heaven springs." Tetzel died on August 11, 1519.

Thomas Wolsey.   Educated at Oxford, and elected a fellow of Magdalen College, Wolsey was ordained in 1498. Wolsey rose quickly in the royal service, becoming privy councilor to Henry VIII in 1511, bishop of Lincoln in 1514 and archbishop of York in the same year. In 1515 he was created cardinal and also appointed lord chancellor of England. Wolsey's fall was as rapid as his rise. He tried unsuccessfully to attain an annulment of Henry VIII's marriage to Catherine of Aragon, and because of this failure the king forced him to give up the chancellorship as well as forfeit all his property. He died in 1530 on his way to London to answer to charges of high treason.

Ulrich Zwingli.   Born in 1484, Zwingli was educated in Berne, Vienna and Basle, and ordained a priest in 1506. He was an avid admirer of Erasmus, and while pastor at Glarus in Switzerland, he spent much time in humanistic studies. In 1518 Zwingli was appointed people's preacher at the Old Minster in Zurich, a post he held for the rest of his life. He used his position to further reform in the church. In sermons of 1519 he attacked purgatory, the invocation of saints and monasticism. In 1522 he published a tract advocating liberation of believers from bishops and the papacy. Basing his theology solely on the gospel, Zwingli argued against the authority of the pope, the sacrifice of the mass, fasting, and clerical celibacy. By 1525 the mass was abolished, images and pictures were removed from churches, and Zurich became the model for the Swiss reformation. Zwingli died fighting against the Catholic Swiss in 1531.

7

Diversity Denied: The Reformation: Calvin, England and Trent

John Calvin

Just about the time that Calvin was undergoing his religious conversion to reformed Christianity, Zwingli, Luther, Melanchthon and Martin Bucer were meeting and disagreeing about the meaning of the Lord's supper at the Marburg Colloquy. The young preacher Calvin, his first attempts to convert the city of Geneva a disaster, moved to Strassburg, and there worked closely with Martin Bucer, learning from him, but also giving his ideas a rigor and consistency that Bucer's own attempts lacked.

Following Bucer, Calvin tried to steer a middle course between Zwingli and Luther in the firm belief that an agreement could be reached between the two reformed positions. In his "Short Treatise on the Holy Supper of our Lord and only Savior Jesus Christ," which he wrote in 1540, he praised both men and put forward a position which he hoped would be acceptable to all. Calvin failed in his attempts, and not all his works were so laudatory. His theology does show, however, that he learned from both theologians and wished to avoid any extravagant claims about the eucharist.

First and foremost in Calvin's theology was the insistence that the purpose of the Lord's supper was to strengthen and confirm the gift of faith given to us by God through Christ. "The principal object of the sacrament, therefore, is not to present to us the body of Christ, simply, but rather to seal and confirm that promise, where he declares that his 'flesh is meat indeed' and 'his blood drink indeed,' by which we are nourished to eternal life . . ."[1] or, even more clearly, ". . . the person who supposes that the sacraments confer any more upon him than that which is offered by the Word of God, and which he receives by a true faith, is greatly deceived. Hence also it may be concluded, that confidence of salvation does not depend on the participation of the sacraments, as though that constituted our justification. . . ."[2]

Following Luther, Calvin insisted that salvation was a freely given gift of God, and that nothing one did could possibly justify us before God. The liturgy could never earn any merit for us, nor could it provide anything further than the gift of faith already given to the saved. The eucharist is a confirmation of that active gift of the Spirit which is salvation, but it neither makes that gift possible nor adds anything to it. Consequently, Calvin's condemnation of the Roman understanding of the mass was thorough and harsh. According to Calvin, any thought that humans controlled salvation, or could order God to appear on the altar, was pure and simple idolatry and sorcery. A few samples of Calvin's language should suffice:

> Now this perverse opinion [transubstantiation], having been once accepted, has given rise to many other superstitions. And first, this carnal adoration, which is nothing but idolatry. For to prostrate oneself before the bread of the Supper, and to adore Jesus Christ in it as though he were there contained, is to make an idol displace the sacrament. We have no command to adore, but to take and eat ("Short Treatise on the Holy Supper of our Lord and only Savior Jesus Christ").[3]

And again:

> Now intelligible doctrine of the Mass is so lacking, that on the contrary the whole mystery is considered spoiled, if everything is not done by stealth, so that nothing is understood. Therefore their consecration is nothing but a piece of sorcery, seeing that, by murmuring and gesticulating in the manner of sorcerers, they think to constrain Jesus Christ to descend into their hands. We see, then, how the Mass being thus arranged, is an obvious profanation of the

Supper of Christ, rather than an observance of it ("Short Treatise on the Holy Supper of our Lord and only Savior Jesus Christ").[4]

And finally:

> Wherefore, I conclude that it is a most criminal insult, and intolerable blasphemy, both against Christ himself, and against the sacrifice which he completed on our behalf by his death upon the cross, for any man to repeat any oblation with a view to procure the pardon of sins, propitiate God, and obtain righteousness. . . . And that there might be no limits to [the Romans'] folly, they have not been satisfied with affirming it to be a common sacrifice offered equally for the whole Church without adding, that it was in their power to make a particular application to any individual they chose, or rather to every one who was willing to purchase such a commodity with ready money. Though they could not reach the price of Judas, yet, to exemplify some characteristic of their author, they have retained a semblance of number. Judas had sold Jesus for thirty pieces of silver; these men, as far as in them lies, sell him, in French money, for thirty pieces of copper; Judas sold him once; they sell him as often as they meet with a purchaser (*Institutes*, IV, 18, 14).[5]

Calvin not only agreed with Luther in his detestation of the Roman understanding of the mass, he also shared Luther's dislike of Zwingli's spiritualist theology. Calvin, like Luther and like the Roman theologians, insisted that the body and blood of the Lord were truly present in the supper:

> . . . we shall confess without doubt that to deny the true communication of Jesus Christ to be offered us in the Supper is to render this holy sacrament frivolous and useless—a blasphemy execrable and unworthy of attention. Moreover, if the reason for communicating with Jesus Christ is in order that we have part and portion in all the gifts which he has procured for us by his death, it is

not only a matter of being partakers of his Spirit; it is necessary also to partake of his humanity, in which he rendered complete obedience to God his Father, to satisfy our debts; though rightly speaking, the one cannot be without the other ("Short Treatise on the Holy Supper of our Lord and only Savior Jesus Christ").[6]

"He who perceives not that many miracles are comprehended in these few words," Calvin jeered, "are more than stupid."[7] But a real presence in the eucharist did not mean that the presence was there to be adored, as was the Roman custom. The liturgy was a supper, and therefore the bread and wine were meant to be eaten and they had no meaning outside of that action. Futhermore, both the bread and the wine were to be received by the faithful, not once a year, but every time the community gathered. "The observations which we have already made respecting the sacrament abundantly show that it was not instituted for the purpose of being received once in a year, and that in a careless and formal manner, as now is the general practice; but in order to be frequently celebrated by all Christians, that they might often call to mind the sufferings of Christ. . . ."[8]

For Calvin, then, participation in the Lord's supper was extremely important, as it confirmed the faithful in their trust that they were saved. The faithful had already been joined to Christ, body and soul, by the gift of faith; the eucharist merely affirmed that union. It did not, and indeed could not, bring that union about nor add anything to it. There was a real union and real presence in the sacrament, but it was not a different union than that of faith, nor even a different kind of union.

So far, Calvin's theology did not differ radically from that of Luther. However, when it came to explaining how the Lord was present in the supper, Calvin found that he simply could not accept Luther's teaching. Luther, as you remember, had explained that the body and blood of the risen Lord could be truly present in the liturgy through the power of Christ's divinity. Since God could be everywhere, the body and blood of Christ could also be everywhere, since they shared in the divinity of the God-person who was Christ. Further, Luther argued that the bread remained bread, and the wine remained wine. The body and blood of the

Lord were present along with the bread and wine, or, more exactly, the body and blood were present through, with, and in the
bread and wine.

As much as Calvin admired Luther, he could become furious at
this teaching. Following the lead of Zwingli, Calvin felt that Luther's theology hopelessly confused matter and spirit and, in fact,
led to a denial that Jesus had any real body. A real body must have
dimensions and be in one particular place; this is part of what makes
a body a body. Christ's body is in heaven and can only be in this one
place, or it ceases to be a body at all. To accept Luther's theology
would be to revive the old Gnostic teaching that Jesus was a pure
spirit with no real body. The argument is similar to that made by
Peter Olivi in the thirteenth century.

> It pleased [God] for Christ to become in all respects like
> his brethren, sin excepted. What is the nature of our
> body? Has it not its proper and certain dimensions? is it
> not contained in some particular place, and capable of
> being felt and seen? And why, say they, may not God
> cause the same flesh to occupy many different places, to
> be contained in no particular place, and to have no form or
> dimensions? But how can they be so senseless as to re-
> quire the power of God to cause a body to be a body, and
> not to be a body at the same time? It is like demanding of
> him to cause light to be at once both light and dark-
> ness. . . . Therefore body must be body, spirit must be
> spirit, every thing must be subject to that law, and retain
> the condition, which was fixed by God at its creation.
> And the condition of a body is such, that it must occupy
> one particular place, and have its proper form and dimen-
> sions (*Institutes*, IV, 17, 24).[9]

One can see here the old problem raised by William of
Ockham and his student Robert Holcott. If the body and blood
were locally and substantially present in each and every celebration
of the eucharist, and yet not seen or sensed in any way, then the
possibility was opened for us to doubt the reality and validity of
everything our senses presented to us. Calvin firmly drew the line.
Even God doesn't mess with our minds like that. Bodies are bodies

are bodies, and therefore it is very dangerous to start to "mystify" and "divinize" the body of the risen Lord.

Furthermore, such mental machinations were not necessary. It was quite possible for God to unite us to Christ body and soul, and yet for the body of Christ to remain in heaven. It was not Christ who descended to us in his body, but rather we who ascended to heaven in the spirit. The power of the Holy Spirit raised us up to heaven and united us to the living Christ, body and soul. Speaking against transubstantiation, and the form of presence that it entailed, Calvin explained:

> Nor is there any need of this [form of presence], in order to our enjoying the participation of it; since the Lord by his Spirit gives us the privilege of being united with himself in body, soul, and spirit. The bond of this union, therefore, is the Spirit of Christ, by whom we are conjoined, and who is, as it were, the channel by which all that Christ himself is and has is conveyed to us. For, if we behold the sun darting his rays and transmitting his substance, as it were, in them, to generate, nourish, and mature the roots of the earth, why should the irradiation of the Spirit of Christ be less effectual to convey to us the communication of his body and blood? Wherefore, the Scripture, when it speaks of our participation of Christ, attributes all the power of it to the Spirit (*Institutes*, IV, 17, 12).[10]

Calvin had a further disagreement with Luther, however, a disagreement that would become the major difference between Lutheran and Calvinist theologies of the eucharist. Luther had believed that both the worthy and the unworthy received the body and blood of the Lord in the communion service. This reception, of course, meant damnation for the unworthy and salvation for the faithful. This position was close to the Franciscan theology of the thirteenth and fourteenth centuries which disagreed with the teaching of Albert the Great and Thomas Aquinas when they argued that the body and blood were present even for unbelievers and animals.

Calvin agreed with Luther that it would detract from the honor of God to hold that the state of the recipient could determine the presence of the risen Lord in the supper, but disagreed that the unworthy actually received that presence. Actually, in Calvin's theology, it would be meaningless to say that the unworthy received. After all, the supper was a celebration of a union which already existed between the faithful and the risen Lord. What could it possibly mean for someone without that union and without faith in Christ to "receive" Christ? Further, if they did receive Christ, that must mean that they are saved, since reception is a sign of salvation. Calvin simply could not image why someone would want to argue that Christ was present, but not active and saving and alive. For Calvin, the Lord was a dynamic Lord whose presence saved. ". . . Christ, considered as the living bread and the victim immolated on the cross, cannot enter a human body devoid of his Spirit."[11] To speak of the Lord being present but that presence not being effective was to talk nonsense.

> And this is the perfection of the sacrament, which the whole world cannot violate, that the flesh and blood of Christ are as truly given to the unworthy, as to the elect and faithful people of God; but it is likewise true, that as rain, falling upon a hard rock, runs off from it without penetrating into the stone, thus the wicked, by their obduracy, repel the grace of God, so that it does not enter their hearts. Besides, a reception of Christ, without faith, is as great an absurdity, as for seed to germinate in the fire (*Institutes*, IV, 18, 33).[12]

One area where Calvin agreed with both Luther and Zwingli (and even with Rome, although I doubt he would admit it) was in regard to the effects of the eucharist. Calvin spoke often and movingly of the acts of charity and the regard for one's brothers and sisters that must flow from the union of Christ and the faithful. One of the many passages in which Calvin made this point will have to suffice:

> We have derived considerable benefit from the sacrament, if this thought be impressed and engraven upon our minds, that it is impossible for us to wound, despise,

reject, injure, or in any way to offend one of our brethren, but we, at the same time, wound, despise, reject, injure and offend Christ in him; that we have no discord with our brethren without being, at the same time, at variance with Christ; that we cannot love Christ without loving him in our brethren; that such care as we take of our own body, we ought to exercise the same care of our brethren, who are members of our body; that as no part of our body can be in any pain without every part feeling correspondent sensations, so we ought not to suffer our brother to be afflicted with any calamity without our sympathizing in the same (*Institutes*, IV, 18, 38).[13]

Calvin's theology is important because John Calvin would leave Strassburg in 1541 to return to Geneva. From then until his death in 1564, he became known as the most famous of the reformed theologians. Geneva was renowned as the best example of what a reformed community could be like, "a school for saints," as one of its admirers dubbed it. All city life was controlled by a close working relationship between church and state. Unrepentant sinners found themselves remanded to the city council for punishment. Banishment or excommunication could be and often was imposed. On the other hand, Geneva had no beggars; all the poor were given food and shelter, and even special hospitals were set up for them. To this city, and to the great teacher, John Calvin, flocked devout students of the reformation. Back streamed these fiery missionaries to their home countries, to France, to Scotland, to Holland. Especially in these three countries Calvinism flourished, and (after a long and bitter struggle) continues to flourish to this day.

Meanwhile, the other cities of Switzerland looked to Geneva for leadership as well. In May of 1549, an agreement of beliefs was signed between Geneva and Zurich, and from that point on, Calvin's theology of the Lord's supper joined Zwingli's as acceptable to the Swiss reformation and those churches descended from that reformation. So thoroughly has Calvin's theology become associated with the Swiss reformation that people refer to those churches which follow the teachings of Geneva or Zurich as "Calvinist."

The English Church

By the death of Calvin in 1564 there were at least three major theologies of the eucharist being proclaimed in western Christianity: that of the Swiss reformers ("Calvinists" or "Reformed"), that of the German reformers ("Lutherans"), and that of those loyal to the pope ("Roman Catholic"). The picture is not quite as simple as it might appear, however. The Calvinists had both the writings of Zwingli and Calvin to consider, and the two were not in agreement. Local churches would be free to choose between the theologies. Lutherans would emphatically reject both Zwingli's and Calvin's teaching in 1577, but in 1564 bitter debates still raged over how far Lutherans (following the lead of Philipp Melanchthon) should modify their views to reach a union with the Calvinists. Outside these larger communities, many smaller reformed communities existed. Several groups, known as "anabaptists" because they insisted on the baptism of adults exclusively, also adhered to the theology of Zwingli, although the Swiss (and German) communities rejected and persecuted them. Under the capable leadership of Jacob Hutter (d. 1536) and Menno Simmons (1496–1561), these groups continue to the present day under the names of their leaders (Hutterites and Mennonites). Still smaller and less organized groups also appeared, most short-lived, many with still more spiritualized ideas about the sacraments than Zwingli. European Christianity was breaking apart, it seemed, into smaller and smaller pieces.

Meanwhile in England, a long and bitter struggle was coming to a close, or, at the very least, entering a new phase. In 1558 a new queen of England, Elizabeth I, had ascended the throne, and in the following year she had appointed the wise, tolerant and scholarly Matthew Parker as the head of the English church. Tolerance and wisdom were certainly needed. Over the preceding quarter of a century, England had been torn by an intense political and spiritual struggle. In a series of laws passed between 1533 and 1535, Henry VIII of England had effectively declared that the church of England was free to manage its own affairs without any interference from Rome. The claim, in comparison with those being made in Wittenberg, Zurich, and Geneva, was hardly dramatic, but Rome's reaction was excommunication. Henry responded by seizing the monastic lands in England and by ordering that an English translation of the Bible be available to the faithful in every church in England. The reformers thought that another country would be added to the list of those converted to the new, purer Christianity. They were overly optimistic. Henry did not like control by Rome, but he did, for the most part, support the theology of the Romans.

England began, slowly and tentatively, to take a path quite different from any other nation. Official theology under Henry remained fundamentally that of the late middle ages. Church structure certainly remained that of earlier centuries. The king was not eager to turn over his prerogative to appoint bishops and priests to the local communities, as Luther and Calvin suggested. Henry was quite ready to persecute and even execute followers of either Geneva or Wittenberg. Yet he was equally willing to dole out similar punishments to those who maintained that Rome had any rights over the English church. In 1539 the Act of the Six Articles passed Parliament with the strong support of the king. The Act "insisted rigidly on transubstantiation, communion in one kind only as necessary, clerical celibacy, the inviolability of vows of chastity, private Masses and auricular confession."[14]

Yet, despite Henry's opposition, the influence of Luther and Calvin was beginning to be felt more and more strongly in England. In 1532 Henry appointed the Cambridge theologian Thomas Cranmer as archbishop of Canterbury. He would become, short of the king, the leading figure in the English church. Cranmer had spent most of the previous two years on the continent and had studied the teaching of the reformers. He had also married the daughter of the Lutheran reformer Andreas Osiander. (Since Henry did not approve of married clergy, Cranmer had to first keep his new wife in seclusion, and finally in 1539 to banish her.)

Cranmer was instrumental in the translation and distribution of English bibles, and when Henry died in 1547, Thomas Cranmer became the chief spiritual advisor to the young king Edward VI. Edward held little political power, which was based in a privy council, dominated first by the duke of Somerset, and later by the duke of Northumberland. Edward's markedly reformed tendencies, however, soon made themselves felt in important legislation. In 1547 the Act of the Six Articles was repealed; in 1548 images were abolished, clerical marriages were recognized, and, most importantly, the use of a new standard liturgical book, the Book of Common Prayer, was imposed. The Book went through two editions, that of 1549 and that of 1552. The major author for both books was Thomas Cranmer, who, in these compositions, proved himself to be one of the greatest liturgists in the English language.

In both the Book of Common Prayer and in his many writings on the eucharist, Cranmer showed a growing preference for the position of Martin Bucer. This is not surprising, as Cranmer helped arrange for Bucer to move from Strassburg to the University of Cambridge where Bucer taught from 1549 until his death in 1551. Just as Calvin had surpassed his teacher Bucer as a theologian, so Cranmer surpassed him as a liturgist. Under Cranmer's influence, two major documents of the English Church appeared, the Book of Common Prayer already mentioned, and the statement of beliefs contained in the Forty-two Articles of 1553. Whatever his own beliefs, Cranmer's purpose in both the Book of Common Prayer and the Forty-two Articles was to reach a compromise between the growing group of reform-minded clergy and the majority of the country which remained staunchly Roman in attitude.

In 1553 the hopes of the reformers in England were dashed by the death of Edward and the accession to the throne of his older sister Mary. Mary was a devout Catholic who had married Philip II, the king of Spain and the strongest political opponent of the reformation. Mary reversed the laws of Edward and began to persecute those who remained loyal to the reformation. On March 21, 1556, Thomas Cranmer was burned as a heretic; the following year, the body of Martin Bucer was exhumed from Great St. Mary's Church in Cambridge and also publicly burned.

When Mary died in 1558, the country was badly divided in religious beliefs. Opinions ranged from those who staunchly supported Rome under Mary (in fact the majority of the country was predominantly Catholic) to those who had fled to Geneva during her reign and were now returning determined to secure Calvinism as the religion of England. Elizabeth attempted, with the help of Matthew Parker and other like-minded scholars, to steer a middle path between Rome and Geneva. This "middle way" (*via media* in Latin) became the central approach of the Anglican Church, which sees itself as an independent church from Rome, but in continuity with the ancient and medieval church. Anglicans are not Protestants, unlike Lutherans and Calvinists. The central documents of this third way are the Book of Common Prayer, issued by Elizabeth in 1559, and the Thirty-nine Articles, an explanation of Anglican beliefs which was approved by the queen in 1563.

The 1559 Book of Common Prayer was fundamentally a reissuing of Thomas Cramner's book of 1542, just as the Thirty-nine Articles are based on the Forty-two Articles of 1553. In both cases the changes which did occur included modifications in the presentation of the understanding of the eucharist. In the 1552 Prayer Book, an explanation accompanying the communion service clarified that kneeling at the service did not imply any reverence for the presence of the body and blood of the risen Lord. This was dropped from the 1559 edition.[15] The words in which the priest offered the consecrated bread deliberately left room for a variety of beliefs:

The body of our Lord Jesus Christ which was given for thee, preserve thy body and soul into everlasting life: and take and eat this, in remembrance that Christ died for thee, and feed on in thy heart by faith, with thanksgiving.[16]

And similarly for the wine:

The blood of our Lord Jesus Christ which was shed for thee, preserve thy body and soul into everlasting life: and drink this in remembrance that Christ's blood was shed for thee, and be thankful.[17]

The liturgy was to be celebrated at a table covered with a white cloth. "And to take away the superstition, which any person hath or might have in the bread and wine, it shall suffice that the bread be such as is usual to be eaten at the table with other meats, but the best and purest wheat bread that conveniently may be gotten. And if any of the bread and wine remain, the curate shall have it for his own use."[18] Well, there was something here to both please and infuriate both those adhering to Rome and those following Geneva. Neither in the end would be satisfied, and the debate over the Prayer Book would continue. The purpose of the major author, Thomas Cranmer, and of those who modified his work, however, was not purely political. It was the same as that of scholars in

Rome, Geneva and Wittenberg: the pursuit of a true understanding of the Lord's supper. That theologians in England wished to pursue a middle ground between warring factions would seem to be wise given the history of reformation disputes about the eucharist which preceded Elizabeth's reign.

The Thirty-nine Articles, which became the most important statement of Anglican beliefs, also attempted to avoid the errors of extremes in the midst of controversy. Here, however, the tendency was to follow the teachings of Bucer, Calvin and, of course, Cranmer. The issue of the eucharist still proved troublesome, and an important modification of the Articles demonstrates this concern. Section Twenty-nine of the Articles was not part of the original Forty-two Articles, but added in 1563. Before publication the article was removed, presumably by the Queen herself, because it would offend both Catholics and Lutherans. When Elizabeth was excommunicated in 1570, the article reappeared in the first English edition of 1571. The text speaks for itself:

XXIX. OF THE WICKED WHICH EAT NOT THE BODY OF CHRIST IN THE USE OF THE LORD'S SUPPER

The Wicked, and such as be void of a lively faith, although they do carnally and visibly press with their teeth (as Saint Augustine saith) the Sacrament of the Body and Blood of Christ, yet in no wise are they partakers of Christ: but rather, to their condemnation, do eat and drink the sign or Sacrament of so great a thing.[19]

This teaching clearly agrees with that of Calvin over against both the Roman position and the Lutheran position. Article Twenty-eight, which describes the Lord's supper, also tends to side with Calvin, but could be acceptable to those sympathetic with Luther:

XXVIII. OF THE LORD'S SUPPER

The Supper of the Lord is not only a sign of the love that Christians ought to have among themselves one to another; but rather is a Sacrament of our Redemption by Christ's death: insomuch that to such as rightly, worthily, and with faith, receive the same, the Bread which we break is a partaking of the Body of Christ; and likewise the Cup of Blessing is a partaking of the Blood of Christ.

Transubstantiation (or the change of the substance of Bread and Wine) in the Supper of the Lord, cannot be proved by Holy Writ; but is repugnant to the plain words of Scripture, overthroweth the nature of a Sacrament, and hath given occasion to many superstitions.

The Body of Christ is given, taken and eaten, in the Supper, only after an heavenly and spiritual manner. And the mean whereby the Body of Christ is received and eaten in the Supper is Faith.

The Sacrament of the Lord's Supper was not by Christ's ordinance reserved, carried about, lifted up, or worshipped.[20]

The statement, despite its anti-Roman rejection of transubstantiation, is fairly moderate in its claims. It does not state, for instance, that the sacrament cannot be reserved, carried about, lifted up or worshiped, but only that this was not decreed by Christ himself. The attempt of the English reformers was to reject both Zurich and Rome, and Article Twenty-eight does just that. And if this statement were not clear enough, Article Twenty-five is directly specifically against the spiritualist teaching of Zwingli:

Sacraments ordained of Christ be not only badges or tokens of Christian men's profession, but rather they be certain sure witnesses, and effectual signs of grace, and God's good will towards us, by which he doth work invisibly in us, and doth not only quicken, but also strengthen and confirm our faith in him.[21]

If the teaching of the Thirty-nine Articles parallels that of Calvin and Bucer, the structure of the English church certainly did not. Anglicans retained the medieval structure of bishops, priests and deacons, along with the benefice systems. The national government, not the local communities, retained firm control of the ecclesiastical establishment. The English church, as it appeared under Queen Elizabeth, offered yet another alternative to European Christianity. Four major options now existed, along with many smaller groups. In Switzerland, Holland, Scotland and parts of France at least, the theology and church structure envisioned by Zwingli, Bucer and Calvin were becoming firmly entrenched. In Scandinavia and much of Germany, the teachings of Luther were followed and adapted to local circumstances. England went its own way, espousing a structure similar to that of Rome and a theology influenced by Calvin, but remaining independent of all its sources. In Spain, Italy and much of France, people remained loyal to Rome, but this was not the church of Rome which had existed in 1517. Reform had reached even into the Vatican palace.

The Reforms of Trent

The year 1564, the year Calvin died, also saw the promulgation of the decrees of the Council of Trent, which would define and direct the life of the Roman Catholic community until the middle of the twentieth century. While Protestant forms of Christianity seemed to be breaking apart, Trent pulled the Roman church into a greater unity and conformity. Strict discipline, along with a renewed spirituality and a sincere reform of the worst of the late medieval abuses, attracted back to the Roman fold a good many former converts to reform theology. The Roman church to which they returned, however, was definitely not the church they left.

The Council of Trent took forever, it seemed, to finally meet. Once assembled, the council seemed destined to never disband. For years the policy of the popes was to avoid calling a council. Cardinal Aleander summed up this approach in his advice to Pope Clement VII, "Never offer a council, never refuse it directly; on the contrary, show a readiness to comply with the request but at the same time stress the difficulties that stand in the way; by this means you will be able to ward it off."[22] In 1534 the oldest and most intellectual of the cardinals, Alessandro Farnese, was elected Pope Paul III. Not exactly a shining example of virtue, he often made political decisions based on the fortunes of his illegitimate children, Pierluigi and Costanda. He did, however, see the need for a council to reform the church and persisted against the opposition of the curia (the papal bureaucracy) in his intention. He appointed reform-minded cardinals and proceeded to negotiate the delicate political question of where the council should meet. The opening session on December 13, 1545 was not auspicious. Four cardinals, four archbishops, twenty-one bishops and five generals of religious orders were present. No representatives from either the Lutheran or Calvinist groups came. Even at the end of the council, the membership would be dominated by Spanish and Italian interests. Two hundred and fifty-five prelates signed the final acts of the council and of them, one hundred and eighty-nine were Italian.

The council met, on and off, for eighteen years, although for long periods the council was actually "on hold." Under Paul III the council met from its opening in 1545 until 1547 when a majority of the council moved to the city of Bologna to avoid a plague that had broken out in Trent. Discussions continued in Bologna, but the emperor was furious with the move and insisted that the council be moved out of Italy and back into imperial territory, that is, back to Trent. The council was reformulated in Trent under the new pope, Julius III, and business as usual resumed in 1551. Meanwhile, the military activity of the Lutheran princes caused the German archbishops to leave in haste. When even the emperor had to flee from the city of Innsbruck, the council began to fear for its safety, and in April 1552 it voted to adjourn indefinitely.

The council was not to reconvene until the middle of January 1562. First, political pressures, then the death of Julius III in 1555, and finally the one-month papacy of Marcellus II delayed the continuation of the council. When, however, Cardinal Gian Pietro Carafa was elected Pope Paul IV to replace Marcellus, the council was stopped dead in its tracks. Tall, ascetic, and passionate, the new pope intended to reform the church, but on his own terms, and with no help from a council. Only upon the death of Paul IV in 1559 did the council have a chance of reconvening.

The new pope, Pius IV, a member of the powerful Medici family of Florence, was slow in supporting the reform of the church. When his brother died in 1562, however, he appears to have undergone a kind of conversion. From that point on he began to seriously work to continue the council and the reforms. The council reconvened in 1562, and on January 26, 1564 the pope solemnly confirmed the council's work. One of the greatest of the reform councils in the history of the west finally closed.

Theologically, the council reiterated the medieval positions on the eucharist with little change. The true, real and substantial presence of the risen Lord in the sacrament was affirmed, although transubstantiation was merely described as "apt" rather than required for belief:

> But since Christ our Redeemer declared that to be truly His own body which He offered under the form of bread, it has, therefore, always been a firm belief in the Church of God, and this holy council now declares it anew, that by the consecration of the bread and wine a change is brought about of the whole substance of the bread into the substance of the body of Christ our Lord, and of the whole substance of the wine into the substance of His blood. This change the holy Catholic Church properly and appropriately called transubstantiation.[23]

The council also reaffirmed the teaching that the mass was a sacrifice and that its merits could be applied to the living and the dead:

> If anyone says that the sacrifice of the Mass is one only of praise and thanksgiving; or that it is a mere commemoration of the sacrifice consummated on the cross but not a propitiatory one; or that it profits him only who receives, and ought not to be offered for the living and the dead, for sins, punishments, satisfactions, and other necessities, let him be anathema.[24]

The council equally condemned those who taught that the risen Lord should not be worshiped in the consecrated bread, thus justifying the devotions of benediction and the feast of Corpus Christi. The use of the Latin mass was upheld, as well as the use of the single species of bread in communion. In summary, the council reaffirmed the teaching of the medieval theologians, and specifically and clearly rejected the teaching not only of Zwingli, but also of Luther and Calvin.

If the council saw no need to change the doctrinal stance of the medieval church, it was a far different matter when it came to liturgical and structural reform. No more would the liturgies of the Roman church be witness to the carnivals of the late middle ages:

> They shall also banish from the churches all such music which, whether by the organ or in the singing, contains things that are lascivious or impure; likewise all worldly conduct, vain and profane conversations, wandering about, noise and clamor, so that the house of God may be seen to be and be truly called a house of prayer.[25]

More importantly this same decree strongly condemned the sale of masses and the whole avaricious system of mass stipends that so offended the reformers:

> And that many things may be summed up in a few, they [the holy council] shall in the first place, as regards avarice, absolutely forbid conditions of compensations of whatever kind, bargains, and whatever is given for the celebration of new Masses; also those importunate and unbecoming demands, rather than requests, for alms and other things of this kind which border on simonical taint or certainly savor of filthy lucre.[26]

The nefarious post of indulgence salesman was completely abolished, not only in one, but in two different canons. Tetzel and company were to disappear from the European scene completely— never, one hopes, to be seen again.

The abuses of the benefice system were also attacked. Pluralism was condemned in two different sessions, just to make sure that the more corrupt clergy realized that the council wasn't kidding. Moreover, strict new standards were set for the life of the clergy, starting with the cardinals and bishops. In the twenty-fifth session of the council, the way of life to which such prelates were to aspire was described in some detail:

> It is to be desired that those who assume the episcopal office know what are their duties, and understand that

they have been called not for their own convenience, not for riches or luxury, but to labors and cares for the glory of God. For it is not to be doubted that the rest of the faithful will be more easily roused to religion and innocence, if they see those who are placed over them concentrate their thoughts not on things of this world but on the salvation of souls and on their heavenly country. . . . Wherefore, after the example of our Fathers in the Council of Carthage, it commands not only that bishops be content with modest furniture and a frugal table, but also that they take heed that in the rest of their manner of living and in their whole house, nothing appears that is at variance with this holy ordinance, or that does not manifest simplicity, zeal for God and a contempt for vanities.[27]

This may have been (and may remain) more of a hope than a reality, but at least it was clear that the old ways must change. The requirements for ordination, even to minor orders, became much stricter. All clergy were to be examined in the divine law before being ordained, no one could receive a benefice until he reached the age of fourteen, and every diocese was required to have a seminary for the training of the clergy. Moreover, the seminaries should seek to serve the poor rather than the wealthy:

Onto this college shall be received such as are at least twelve years of age, are born of lawful wedlock, who know how to read and write competently, and whose character and inclination justify the hope that they will dedicate themselves forever to the ecclesiastical ministry. It wishes, however, that in the selection the sons of the poor be given preference, though it does not exclude those of the wealthy class, provided they be maintained at their own expense and manifest a zeal to serve God and the Church.[28]

Not only was there to be a new class of well-trained and spiritual clergy to lead the church, but the older clergy were also to be reformed or removed:

Since illiterate and incompetent rectors of parochial churches are but little suited for sacred offices, and others by the depravity of their lives corrupt rather than edify, the bishops may, also as delegates of the Apostolic See, give temporarily to such illiterate and incompetent rectors, if otherwise blameless, assistants or vicars, with a portion of the fruits sufficient for their maintenance or provide for them in some other manner, every appeal and exemption being set aside. But those who live a disgraceful and scandalous life, they shall after admonishing them, restrain and punish; and if they should continue to be incorrigible in their wickedness, they shall have the authority to deprive them of their benefices in accordance with the prescriptions of the sacred canons, every exemption and appeal being rejected.[29]

Oh yes, exemptions from the law were still allowed, as the above passage implies, but only for the gravest of reasons, and, more importantly, exemptions were always to be given for free. The laxity of the renaissance and late medieval clergy was officially condemned. "Luxury, feastings, dances, gambling, sports, and all sorts of crime and secular pursuits" on the part of the clergy were now subject to severe punishment. The Roman church which emerged from the Council of Trent may have retained the theology of the late middle ages; it did not retain its depravity.

Along with much bad also went some good. The earthiness, the spontaneity and the variety of medieval liturgies also disappeared, not to surface among Roman Catholics until the twentieth century, and even then timidly. The new liturgy issued under Pope Pius V in 1570 allowed for no variation. Every Roman priest in every country bowed, knelt and prayed in lockstep, and every Catholic knew that wherever she or he traveled the same Latin prayers, the same gestures, the same vestments would make up the celebration of the mass. According to the German scholar, Erwin Iseloh:

A generation had sufficed to change the face of the Church. Following the close of the Council of Trent the Popes carried its decrees like a banner and had gathered and encouraged the religious forces at hand. . . . The new centralization, replacing the fiscally oriented late medieval centralization, was based on religious and spiritual foundations. The papacy had given the norms of Trent validity. One Bible, the Vulgate [Jerome's Latin translation], one liturgy, the Roman; one Law Code guaranteed unity and effected a far greater uniformity of church life than the pre-Tridentine Church had known.[30]

The Church of Trent would endure for centuries, unchanged in its unity. It was as stark and as uncompromising in its outlines and devotions as was its counterpart in Geneva. A generation had sufficed not only to change (or, more accurately, to create) the Roman church, but to transform the one western church into the churches, every one of which had a different understanding of what the church might be.

Conclusion

Within a period of fifty years, roughly 1517 to 1567, the entire religious picture of Europe had changed. In 1517 one could travel from the northernmost reaches of Scotland to the southern tip of the Italian peninsula, from Lisbon to Lodz, and be welcomed at what would be a fairly familiar liturgy. No more. The Calvinists refused to accept Catholics or Anabaptists at their communion tables; Lutherans excluded Calvinists as well as Catholics and Anabaptists, and Catholics excluded all others. Reginald, the young clerk from Oxford who attended the imaginary liturgy in York described in Chapter 5, would have lived to see the changes. Imagine how shocking and disturbing such an overwhelming change would have been. In 1472, there seemed little hope for the few heretical groups espousing change, but by 1530 all of Europe would be enveloped in a rapid and spreading reform, and by 1570 little of medieval Christianity would be left. If you were, say, twenty years old in 1517 when Luther nailed the ninety-five theses to the church door at Wittenberg, you would only be recently retired when Trent concluded its proceedings. And people think things change rapidly now!

So, what about our imaginary liturgy for this chapter? Well, there certainly isn't one liturgy to attend. From the basically medieval liturgies of England and Rome to the unstructured meeting of the Anabaptists, variety and intolerance would abound. There is no one liturgy to attend, nor would we be allowed to attend all of the liturgies in question. Our story of the unity of the communion of Christianity is at an end. Now the stories, the histories, of different communities and communions begins, and that is not our story. With the grace of God, and with time and good will and much prayer and hard work, those stories will all share a similar happy ending. Now, though, it is time to draw this story to a close, and perhaps offer a few reflections on how the story of our unity can help us bring the stories of our diversity into a continuous story of growth once again.

GLOSSARY OF PERSONS

John Calvin.   Born in 1509, Calvin was originally destined for a career in the church, receiving his first benefice at the age of twelve. From 1523 to 1528 he studied theology at the University of Paris. His father decided that law would be a better career, and so Calvin took up the study of law in 1528. Sometime before 1533 he underwent a religious conversion and undertook the cause of the reformation. While passing through Geneva in 1536, he was convinced to stay and help convert the city to reformed views. He worked there until 1538, when he was expelled from Geneva because of the harshness of his reform measures. From 1538 until 1541 he lived and worked in Strassburg with Martin Bucer. Supporters of Calvin came into power in Geneva in 1541, and he was invited back to the city. Calvin became the spiritual and moral leader not only for Geneva, but of the Swiss reformation until his death in 1564. The seminary at Geneva gave refuge to both the French and English religious exiles and trained hundreds of missionaries who carried his views to Scotland, Holland, England, and France and from there all over the world.

Clement VII.   Guilio de Medici was pope from 1523 until 1534. During the years that the reformation was spreading rapidly throughout Germany and Switzerland, Clement's policy was one of firm procrastination. He not only refused to call a council to deal with the reformation demands, he also continually put off making a decision in the annulment case of Henry VIII of England. A cousin of Pope Leo X, he was a true renaissance prince, supporting the artistic masterpieces of Michelangelo and Cellini.

Thomas Cranmer.   Born in 1489, Cranmer became a fellow of Jesus College at the University of Cambridge and was ordained a priest in 1523. Cranmer suggested that Henry VIII seek support in the universities of Europe for his annulment case, and so was appointed by the king to undertake this mission. Cranmer had spent two years in Europe when he was recalled by the king to be appointed archbishop of Canterbury. While in Europe Cranmer had studied the teachings of the reformers, and not only had accepted them, but had married Margaret Osiander, the niece of Andreas Osiander, the

Lutheran reformer. During the reign of Henry VIII, Cranmer supported the translation of the Bible into the vernacular and was responsible for the law requiring churches to provide this translation for their congregations. During the reign of Edward VI, Cranmer was the principal author of the Forty-two Articles of 1553 and the Book of Common Prayer of 1542. The statement of beliefs embodied in the Forty-two Articles became the basis for the Thirty-nine Articles of 1563, which, despite modifications over the years, is still the standard statement of Anglican belief. Cranmer's Book of Common Prayer is a masterpiece of both liturgy and of the English language, forming the basis for all later editions up until modern times. Cranmer was burned at the stake in 1556 during the attempted restoration of Roman Catholicism under Queen Mary.

Edward VI.   Born in 1537, Edward was the son of Henry VIII and Jane Seymour, Henry's third wife. Upon the death of his father in 1547 Edward ascended the throne. Political power actually lay in the privy council, which was controlled first by Jane Seymour's brother, Edward the duke of Somerset, and later by the duke of Northumberland. During his reign the church of England, newly separated from Rome, adopted a more reformed theology and liturgy, based mostly on the teachings of Bucer and Calvin. Under the direction of the archbishop of Canterbury, Thomas Cranmer, a statement of beliefs (the Forty-two Articles) and a new liturgy (the Book of Common Prayer) were issued. Never a healthy child, Edward died at the age of sixteen in 1553.

Elizabeth I.   Queen of England from 1558 until 1603, Elizabeth was the daughter of Henry VIII and Anne Boleyn, Henry's second wife. During Elizabeth's reign, especially under the direction of the archbishop of Canterbury, Matthew Parker, Anglicanism set out to deliberately steer a middle course between the religious positions of Rome on one hand and Geneva on the other. Two of the most important documents in the history of the church of England, the Thirty-nine Articles and the 1559 edition of the Book of Common Prayer were issued during her reign. In 1570 Pope Pius V excommunicated Elizabeth, thus removing any hope that the church of England might be reconciled in Rome. Elizabeth's reign was also important for her support of the exploration of the new world, leading to the establish-

ment of colonies in North America (Virginia was named for Elizabeth, "the virgin queen") and for the revival of English theater which
culminated in the plays of William Shakespeare (1564–1616).

Henry VIII.   In 1509 Henry VIII succeeded to the throne of England at the age of seventeen. In that same year he married his older
brother Arthur's former wife, Catherine of Aragon. Catherine, the
daughter of Ferdinand and Isabella of Spain and aunt of the future
emperor Charles V, had been married to the sickly Arthur for six
months before his death in 1502. For some eighteen years the marriage of Henry and Catherine lasted, but produced no male children to inherit an English throne recently torn by civil war. Henry,
under pressure as well as from his mistress, Anne Boleyn, appealed
to Pope Clement VII for an annulment. The pope, imprisoned by
Catherine's nephew, Emperor Charles V, was not in a political
position conducive to granting such an annulment. Even when released from the control of the emperor, Clement continued to stall.
Finally, with a series of acts passed in parliament between 1532 and
1534, England formally separated itself from Rome. As archbishop
of Canterbury, Thomas Cranmer granted Henry a divorce from
Catherine in 1533, and Henry married Anne Boleyn. Despite his
insistence that the English church constituted a separate church
from that of Rome, Henry remained conservative in his beliefs, and
this conservatism was expressed officially in the Six Articles passed
in 1539. Reformed theology made little headway until Henry's son
succeeded him upon his death in 1547.

Jacob Hutter.   Driven from Switzerland, the Anabaptists settled
near Austerlitz in Moravia (now modern Czechoslovakia). Under
the leadership of Jacob Hutter, over eighty Anabaptist settlements
were established in Moravia between 1533 until his death in 1536.
Hard-working and strictly moral, the "Hutterite" communities, as
they became known, believed in separation from the world and
common ownership of property. The Hutterian Brethren still exist
in communities in the United States.

Marcellus II.   Born Marcello Cervini near Siena in 1501, Marcellus
II served as pope for only twenty days, from his election on April
10 until his death on April 30 of 1555. As a cardinal, Cervini had

been one of the staunchest advocates of reform and very active at the Council of Trent. He is often thought of as the first pope of the Catholic reformation despite his untimely death.

Mary Tudor.　Queen of England from 1553 until her death in 1558, Mary was the daughter of Henry VIII and Catherine of Aragon. In 1554 she married Philip II of Spain, though the marriage proved very unpopular in England. Mary attempted to restore England to Roman Catholicism and to reverse the reform efforts made during the reign of her half-brother, Edward VI. Several of the leaders of the reformation were burned as heretics during Mary's reign, earning her the epithet, "Bloody Mary." Actually Mary was probably no more harsh than had been her father or other sixteenth century rulers. Mary died on November 17, 1558.

Matthew Parker.　Born in 1504, Parker became a fellow of Corpus Christi College at Cambridge in 1527. He steadily rose in church circles during the reigns of Henry VIII and Edward VI, but under Mary was deprived of his positions. Elizabeth I appointed Parker archbishop of Canterbury in 1559. His theological position supported a moderate reform and sought a middle ground between the position of Calvin and that of the Roman theologians. He took part in the writing of the Thirty-nine Articles, the most important statement of Anglican beliefs. A scholar by profession and inclination, he also edited several medieval histories of England. He died in 1575.

Paul III.　Alessandro Farnese was a typical renaissance nobleman. Born in 1468, he was educated in Rome and Florence, became a cardinal in 1493 and was unanimously elected Pope Paul III in 1534. His political interests were often determined by his support for his four illegitimate children, but he did much to prepare for a reform of the church by appointing reformers as cardinals, and by pushing for a universal council which finally met, despite great opposition, in 1545 in the city of Trent. Paul III also encouraged the new reform orders, including the Jesuits. Like other renaissance popes, he supported art and learning, appointing Michelangelo as the chief architect of St. Peter's. He died in 1549.

Paul IV. The most rigorous of the reform popes, Gian Pietro Carafa was elected Pope Paul IV in 1555 at the advanced age of seventy-nine. Despite his age Paul IV vigorously enforced reform decrees. His policy toward the Protestant movement consisted of stern measures of repression. To this end Paul IV considerably strengthened the inquisition and introduced the Index of Forbidden Books. He even had one of the cardinals cast into prison on suspicion of heresy. He refused to reconvene the Council of Trent which had been dissolved in 1552 on the grounds that the pope, not a council, should reform the church. Paul IV, despite his reforming zeal, was a notorious nepotist, which led to political blunders and a growing disappointment and even hatred for the pope and his family. Upon his death in 1559 the Roman people destroyed the headquarters of the inquisition and defaced the statue of the pope in angry reaction to both the pope's nepotism and harshness.

Philip II. One of the most powerful rulers of his age, Philip became king of Spain and Naples in 1556 at the age of twenty-nine, and later king of Portugal in 1580. His fleet defeated the Turks at the important battle of Lepanto in 1571, but Philip failed in his attempted invasion of England in 1588. Philip was married to Mary Tudor, the queen of England, from 1554 until her death in 1558. He strongly opposed the reformation whenever and wherever he could do so, supporting the inquisition throughout his realm for this purpose. Philip died in 1598.

Pius IV. Elected pope in 1559, Gian Angelo Medici studied law and medicine before joining the papal administration. He was raised to the cardinalate by Pope Paul III. He is best remembered for the overseeing, reconvening and successful conclusion of the Council of Trent. The council had been dissolved in 1552 due to political factors, and Pius IV's predecessor, Paul IV, had refused to reconvene it. Pius IV began to enforce the decrees of the council, but died only two years after the council had ended in 1557.

Pius V. Born in 1504, Michele Ghislieri joined the Dominican order in 1518. He lectured in both theology and philosophy for the order as well as serving as novice master and prior. Ghislieri was made commissary general of the inquisition in 1551, and a cardinal in 1557. Unanimously elected Pope Pius V in 1566, he worked ceaselessly for the reform of the church. He is best remembered, perhaps, for his reformation of the breviary and of the Roman missal, works that became standards in the Roman Catholic Church until the recent changes of the Second Vatican Council. Pius V died in 1572.

Menno Simmons.   A parish priest in Holland, Menno Simmons renounced his attachment to Rome and joined the Anabaptist movement in 1536. For twenty-five years he was leader of the persecuted Anabaptist communities of Holland. Known for their strict passivism and their refusal to take oaths, the "Mennonites," as Simmons' followers became known, grew to be a large and respected community in Holland in the seventeenth and eighteenth centuries. The seventeenth century founder of the modern Baptist movement, John Smyth, was influenced by the Mennonites while in exile in Holland. Over 500,000 Mennonites still exist in communities in Holland, Germany, the U.S.S.R., Canada and the United States. The best known of the Mennonite groups in the United States are the Amish.

8

So Now What?

The story of the loss of the unity of Christianity is not only a sad story; it is a frustrating story. All the more so, since we are not at the end of the story and it seems to have been going on an awfully long time without a satisfactory end in sight. When people are frustrated and sad, they look for a scapegoat. All of this must be *somebody's* fault.

The most obvious scapegoats are those with whom one doesn't agree. Roman Catholics blame the Protestants and Anglicans for leaving the one true church. The Protestants and Anglicans blame the Romans for corrupting the one true church. The Lutherans accuse the Calvinists of misinterpreting both scripture and tradition, and the Calvinists have made the same claim for the Lutherans. Recently (in the last twenty-five years) these two groups have become closer, but differences still exist.

Now it seems that you should be able to check these claims. Who really is truer to scripture and tradition—the Roman Catholics, the Anglicans, the Lutherans or the Calvinists (just to mention the larger groups)? Couldn't one just go back to scripture and to the early church writers and check which claims are correct?

This was just what Luther, Calvin and Zwingli (and modern scholars) all did (and do). Oecolampadius, one of the Swiss reformers who was a great scholar and colleague of Erasmus, actually compiled a book with all the quotes he could find from the early church writers on the eucharist. He felt that the majority of the writers supported Zwingli's teaching. Luther claimed that this was irrelevant, as the gospel writers supported him. Zwingli retorted that the passage in John, chapter 6, clearly proved his claims, and the battle was on, and still continues.

The problem remains that both the scriptures and the early church writers did not agree themselves on the issues that concerned the reformation, or, to put it more accurately, these writers never even thought of the problems confronting the reformers. Therefore, all the different parties could find some support in scripture and in the past for their views. The position of Origen, of Ratramnus and of Berengar would support the views of Zwingli and Calvin. The writings of Hilary, of Ambrose and of many of the medieval writers would support Luther and the Roman Catholics. The Franciscan theologians of the middle ages would tend to support Luther, the Dominican theologians to support the papal theologians. It would seem that after four hundred years, and much debate by the best theologians in Europe, the problem won't be solved by an appeal to the sources, for the sources themselves disagree.

Who is to blame? Everybody and nobody, it would seem. Each of the different parties involved wished to protect certain themes in the tradition. The tradition, as represented in scripture and the early church writings, had never really tried to reconcile these different themes, and so when one aspect or the other of the traditional teachings was stressed, other themes seemed under attack. Given the political and economic interests at stake in the reformation disputes, the chances of a peaceful settlement of these conflicts was slim. I suppose one could argue that if Rome were less corrupt, if Luther were less explosive, if Zwingli were less rigid, if . . . then maybe a single eucharistic theology would have emerged from the reformation, or, better, a mutual recognition of acceptable differences. But even if Erasmus, Melanchthon and Bucer would have prevailed, and some sort of agreement were reached, the problems would not really have been solved because underlying conflicts still remained (and remain).

The two major difficulties underlying the reformation disputes only slowly emerged in Christianity. The best description of this process has been put forward by Dr. Bernard Cooke in his excellent study *The Distancing of God*.[1] The first trend saw a growing clericalization of the sacrament. That is to say, that a certain group of *men* (and it was definitely men, and only men) in the community, starting as early perhaps as the second century, took over the practice of celebrating the sacraments for everybody else. The *episcopoi* and *prebyteroi* described in Chapter 2 became the only people who were thought to really worship God, or at least they were the only ones who could *truly* worship God in the liturgy. Everybody else just watched them do it, occasionally (ritually, of course) cheering them on from the sidelines. The process grew more and more elaborate in the middle ages, when the bishops and priests not only led the liturgy, but also received communion in the place of everybody else, and, finally, were even thought to direct the "grace" of the sacramants to different people, both living and dead. The priest, in this understanding, is the only one who can really worship, the only one who can make the risen Lord become present and the only one who can decide upon whom the benefits of the liturgy are bestowed. When people did "participate" in the liturgy, it took the form of private devotions, rather than the actual celebration of the rite.

The central debates in the reformation homed in on just this point. Did God freely bestow salvation on people, or did the church decide who was to be saved and then set the minimum requirements for salvation? If salvation was given by God directly, then the priests were superfluous. Someone might be needed to lead the worship, read the scriptures, and explain them, but this leader had no more power or authority than did the person in the pew. This was exactly the point put so strongly by Luther, Zwingli and Calvin.

The real question, then, becomes not "What is the eucharist?" but "Who is in charge?" Does God save individuals directly or did God give the power of dispensing salvation to a certain group of people in the church? This is probably the most divisive question in Christianity, and the major reason why the Eastern Orthodox Church and the Roman Catholics still do not celebrate the liturgy together (except under unusual circumstances). The same can be said of the relationship between the Church of England and the Roman Catholics as well.

Can this problem be solved? If the problem were purely a theoretical one of looking back at scripture and tradition, the answer would seem to be yes. Most scholars agree that the scriptures do not set up any particular structure for the early church. Later centuries tended to copy the patterns of government that happened to be operative at the moment. The early church copied Jewish and Greek organizations and the medieval church copied the feudal system of government. In the eighteenth and nineteenth centuries, some churches, especially the Roman Catholic and, at first, the Church of England, modeled themselves on the divine right monarchies of France and England and strongly opposed the new movements of democracy when they appeared. None of the existing ways of organizing Christian communities *seems* to be inevitable.

Could the churches follow the more recent trend toward democracy? Most churches already have, so this is certainly possible. The Calvinist and Lutheran traditions have centuries of experience with this form of governance. Most Americans and Europeans would next probably ask: What's the problem then? Democracy is great; let's do it for all the churches, not just the Lutherans and Calvinist churches!

Most Christians do not understand history as accidental however. No particular structure of authority may *seem* to be inevitable, but that does prove that it was not God's will. If something happened, then God wished it to happen, and therefore we should not change it. The Greek Orthodox churches would say that the system of patriarchs and councils used in the fourth century is the structure ordained by God for the church. Calvinists model themselves on the democracy of the Swiss cantons in the sixteenth century; Lutherans tend to follow the pattern of seventeenth century Scandinavia and Germany, which allowed a good deal of independence to communities, but still retained bishops as overseers. In these communities the governments had a major voice in religion, as they had had in the middle ages. (Clergy are still paid directly by the government in Germany, for instance.) The church of England, although it has changed in the last fifty years, had allowed even a larger scope for intervention by the government. (The queen of England remains the head of the Church of England.) Roman Catholics, strongly opposed to the democratic movements of the eighteenth and nineteenth centuries, cling tenaciously to a government based on the divine right monarchies of the seventeenth and eighteenth centuries.

The question which divides the churches here has more to do with authority than with the eucharist. The question is not only which of the different church structures is correct, but who, ultimately, has the authority to decide which structure is correct. Nor would each of the churches put the question the way I have put it here. Most would claim that the structure they have adopted is based directly upon scripture and would be furious at the suggestion that later models are what was actually used. In this way of thinking, what the church is presently doing is what the church has always done, or at least what the church should always have been doing.

Finally, the rule which applied at the reformation still applies today. There are groups of people with a financial and political interest in things staying the way they are and in refusing to admit any other way of doing things can be right. This should not be shocking. Human beings (even authors and readers!) are all subject to the temptation to understand what best suits them as not only good for them but good for everyone because it is right.

Where does that leave us? With a long way to go, it seems. A great deal of prayer, and an even larger dose of humility, would go a long way toward helping to solve this problem. Perhaps John Calvin had the best answer to the dilemma:

> First, I pray all the faithful, in the name of God, not to be too offended at the great difference which has arisen between those who ought to be leaders in bringing back truth to the light of day. For it is no new thing for the Lord to leave his servants in some ignorance, and to permit them to dispute against each other. And this, not to leave them forever, but only for a time, to humble them. In fact, had all turned out as desired up till now, without any disturbance, men might possibly have forgotten themselves, or the grace of God be less acknowledged than is proper. Thus our Lord was pleased to deprive men of all cause for glory in order that he alone be glorified.[2]

The second issue that Dr. Cooke addresses in his book is the problem of God becoming more and more distant from the ordinary person not only in practice but in theory. If one follows the philosophy of Plato or Aristotle, the things of earth and the things of heaven are very separate. Our everyday lives, which we are meant to celebrate in the eucharist, seem trivial. Spiritual things have to do with spirits, not bodies. A great gulf opens up between this world and the next world. According to Platonic and Aristotelian understandings of the universe, there is another more real world, and more important world, than this one. We can only reach that second world by renouncing this one, either by meditation and asceticism, or by death. What we do now is puny and insignificant and unreal. The practice of renouncing family and career to pursue the divine dates back well before Christianity in the Platonic tradition.

The extremes of this approach would be realized in gnostics of the early church and the dualists of the fourth century and the middle ages. Separation of body and spirit was essential, as well, to Zwingli and before him to Ratramnus and Berengar. The reception of Jesus' body was not only repulsive to them, it was useless. Only the spirit saved, or, at best, a very spiritualized kind of body. Of course this means that the rest of us mere mortals, or at least the part of us that gets the kids ready for school and goes to work and cuts the grass and does the laundry and gets sick and tired of it all, doesn't matter. The best we can to is "offer this up" and wait for the second and more real world to break into this one and save us. Makes most of us pretty marginal, doesn't it?

Yet, in the message of Jesus, and even in the eucharistic prayers themselves, it is the earthly and the everyday that is supposed to be celebrated. If the body, and the everyday, is not important, then why did Jesus become a human being, why did he take on the everyday problems of people, feeding them, curing them, encouraging them? It seems that the bodily and the everyday are not only real, but involved intimately in our salvation. This is what the incarnation is supposed to mean.

But if Jesus was a human being, then the risen Lord that Jesus is now must be a human being too, a real human being. So now we come to the crunch. What does it mean to say, and believe, and experience the risen Lord as *really* present to us in the celebration of the liturgy?

For any true follower of Plato and Aristotle, real would not have to include the bodily. The real was the world of the forms or the substance that underlay sense data. The real was the world of the spirit. This is the way that some of the early church writers would have preferred to have understood the risen Lord to be present, and, of course, the way in which Zwingli saw the issue. But if they are right, then the gnostics, Manichees and Cathars are also right, and Jesus didn't need to a have a body and be a real human being. That's OK, but it's *not* Christianity, which does believe that Jesus was really human and really divine. Zwingli (and Ratramnus and Berengar) had a point, however. If one argued that the body and blood of the risen Lord were present, what did *present* mean? Surely it could not mean that the body and blood were sensed (seen, tasted, heard, smelled) because they plainly weren't. If they weren't sensed, then maybe they weren't there at all.

Luther, Calvin, and the Roman theologians refused to give up the salvation of the soul *and* the body. When they said the risen Lord was present, they wanted to include an encounter with a real human being, including a real human body. Using the categories with which they had to work, this was really tough. Plato and Aristotle weren't much help. Platonism had the advantage that it at least said that there were real things beyond sense data, and these authors agreed that the body and blood of the risen Lord were not sensed here. Aristotelianism offered a makeshift solution with transubstantiation, since one could then say that the substance of the body and blood were present, but not the sense data (accidents) attached to those substances. There were problems here too, though. First of all, the theory was not very true to Aristotle, since, according to him, substances and accidents did not exist all alone. Secondly, wasn't the substance of a body without the accidents really a spirit and not a body at all? These are, of course, exactly the questions raised by the opponents of transubstantiation.

You will notice that all the theologians we have discussed were trying to say that they *really* experienced the risen Lord in the liturgy. The problem was describing what "*really*" meant. If one followed Plato, the forms were real, so the form of the risen Lord had to be present; if one followed Aristotle, substance was real, therefore the substance of the risen Lord must be present. Both these approaches, however, tended to denigrate the bodily and thus reinforce the belief that everyday earthly existence didn't matter. Forms definitely belonged to another world, and if our souls were substance, then substances also awaited a better and different life than this one.

The alternatives were limited though. If one relied simply on sense data as reality, as medieval devotion tended to do, one had to believe that somehow a body, just like our bodies, was hidden under the bread and wine. So, if someone bit the host, or spilled the wine, blood would appear. In the words of the 1059 oath, the body of Christ was "crushed by the teeth of the faithful." Now this not only seemed just plain silly, but led to some very superstitious practices. There was, for instance, the man in the thirteenth century who stole the consecrated bread to put it in with his bees so they would make more honey. (In case you are wondering, the bees made *less* honey, since they were busy making a church out of wax for the host.) If there were dangers in asserting that only the "spirit" of the risen Lord (as substance or form) was present in communion, there were even greater dangers in asserting that the risen Lord was present in a way that could be sensed physically.

Now, it just depends on which you feel is the greater danger: too great an insistence on a spiritual presence which denies the incarnation, or too great an insistence on a physical presence which is obviously not there. Origen, Ratramnus, Berengar, and Zwingli were more worried about the second problem, Luther and most of the medieval theologians about the first problem.

Unfortunately, the only tools they had to attack the problem were inadequate, and sometimes just made the problem worse. The tools were, of course, the philosophies of Plato and Aristotle. This would suggest, then, that this is a problem we can solve. We no longer use those philosophies, so now we can just apply modern insights of science and somehow magically we can all agree how the risen Lord is present in the liturgy. Actually, some of the insights, especially of psychology and anthropology, *have* been very helpful in defining more closely what it means to be present, and these insights have helped to bring the churches closer together. Most importantly, the division between spirit and body has been shown to be artificial and unnecessary. If we think of ourselves as a unity, rather than as a sort of schizophrenic combination of spirit and flesh, we can begin to experience all of life as part of our salvation, not just the afterlife.

Even so, the central problem remains, even if we now know how better to attack it. Modern people tend to count as real only those things that they can sense, and the risen Lord is not touched, or tasted, or smelled, or heard in the liturgy. If (some) modern philosophers, anthropologists and psychologists agree that reality consists of more than sense data, modern science has made most people suspicious of those claims. Either things are there to be sensed, or they are not there at all. Now the one thing Christians have always tried to say about the presence of the risen Lord is that he is present and really experienced, but not physically. We still haven't quite gotten a language for such a thing.

So there we are. Christians still experience the risen Lord, and still have trouble finding the right way to express that presence. Why not just give up? you might say. Why try to express it, just do it—isn't that enough? It would be, if there weren't people, like the gnostics, Manichees and Cathars, who were wrong about the presence. Theology is a constant attempt to explain that certain ideas that are called Christian just can't be. For example, there are people who claim that "true" Christianity is the pursuit of wealth. A few minutes of reading the gospels, and one realizes that this is rubbish. But someone has to *say* that it is rubbish, and, since these people can be pretty persistent, *demonstrate* that it is rubbish. So, too, with the eucharist; we may not know exactly how to describe the presence of the risen Lord, but we do know some of the ways that it *can't* be described (and still be called Christian understanding).

So, like the early church writers, and the medieval writers, and the great reformation figures, we keep trying to describe the experience we have of Christ being present to us, and, like them, we know that we keep falling short. The one thing we do know how to avoid, however, is the mistakes of the past, and there is hope that the Christian groups will be able to unite in their understandings of what *cannot* be said of the Lord's presence. In this sense, the picture is more hopeful than that of debate over authority.

What Can Be Learned?

For over fifteen hundred years, Christians were, for the most part, "in communion." The Christian people, as a whole, have a much longer history of unity than of disunity. What can we learn from history that will help us regain the unity we have lost? First and foremost, we can see what went wrong. Gradually, one part of the Christian community tried to control access to salvation for the rest of the community. This led to the most bitter and most obstinate of all the differences between Christians. No easy solution to this conflict exists, but surely the first step toward resolution will be to carefully and honestly separate theological and spiritual questions from those of power. One step in this direction would be to make sure, in all Christian communities, that the same people who are chosen by the community to lead the liturgy do not also administer the funds and make personnel decisions. The less vested interest there is in retaining a position of power, the more likely it will be that honest discussion will take place. Even the holiest of people are still people, and the more seriously we take the petition in the Lord's Prayer, "lead us not into temptation," the more likely the question of authority in the churches will be resolved. Very serious issues of the relative authority of scripture and tradition, of scholars and church leaders, and of the role of the Spirit and prophecy would still remain. The separation of financial control, administrative authority and spiritual guidance will not, on its own, solve the problem of authority in the churches, but it will be a start. The past should at least teach us the dangers of not doing so.

To make my point in another way, let me tell you an old joke that made the rounds after the Great Depression. It seems a man walked into the local Socialist Party headquarters in Chicago and asked to become a member. He was sure of the collapse of capitalism, had lost his job, and wished to help build a better world. The head of the party was very impressed. "Just a few questions," she said, "and we will sign you up. First, if you had two houses, would you give one to the party?" "Of course," the man said, somewhat taken aback. "Good," the leader continued, "and if you had two cars, would you give us one?" Exasperated, the man exclaimed, "I told you, I'm ready to do anything!" "I'm sure you are," she continued. "Please, just two more questions. If you had two suits, would you give one to us." "Heavens, yes," the man cried, now really insulted. "Sorry for the formalities," the lady continued, unruffled. "Our last question is, if you had two shirts, would you help us with one?" "Absolutely not," the man adamantly proclaimed. "I don't understand. You'll give us your house, your car, your suit; why not your shirt?" "You see," the man said, "I *have* two shirts." The state of the question is often determined by what you have to lose.

Finding a common way of speaking about the presence of the risen Lord in the eucharist seems more hopeful than solving the knotty questions of authority. Modern insights into the unity of body and spirit and new ways of speaking of presence are making it possible for Christians to find a middle ground between relegating the presence of the risen Lord to a phantom spirit world and expecting blood to come gushing out of the host if we bite into it. At meetings between the different traditions, theologians have agreed that these extremes are mistakes. Agreements about what is *not* acceptable go a long way toward common understanding. Further, a view of the world that understands the everyday world of ordinary folk as itself involved and indeed essential to salvation would greatly aid in resolving the different understandings of presence involved in the reformation debates. The question whether the risen Lord is present spiritually or bodily would become irrelevant, since both categories are inadequate descriptions of reality (remember what Christians have always tried to say about the experience of the Lord in the liturgy is that it is *real*). Irrelevant as well would be questions about when, where, and how long the Lord is present. These questions depend on an understanding of reality which stresses the material as the only real. In any case, the risen Lord is present in our whole lives; that is the point of the eucharistic celebration. It seems rather niggardly to begin to debate whether Christ is more or less present here or there, which actually brings us back to the issue of whether we (or a small group of us) can control where the Lord is present.

To give just one example of how one can speak of presence that is real, but not physical, I might simply point out this book. I am not physically present to you, but I certainly am present. I am directing the flow of the words and the presentation of the material (remember the first chapter). By using the first person, I am not even trying to hide my presence. There is an offer here to share part of my life, my ideas, my life work. You can accept it by reading the book (or by at least buying it), or reject it by heaving it across the room (or by at least setting it down). You could go further, and agree with the book (or parts of the book). We would then share at least a small portion of our lives. Now, would you say I was present in, under, or with the book, or present only where the book was, or present to a mouse who nibbled the book? Seem like pretty silly questions, don't they?

Now the presence of the risen Lord is inestimably more real than my presence to you in reading this book, of course, but there is at least a useful analogy here. People (persons) can be present to us when they are not physically present, and actually can be absent to us when their bodies are present. Say, for instance, you find out that a very good friend of yours was sitting at the table next to you at the restaurant last week, and you never noticed each other. You would be physically in the same place, but not present to each other. Worse yet, your friend could have seen you at the restaurant and you could have seen her, and you both could have snubbed the other. Presence was offered and presence was rejected. Presence, then, is a more complex issue than mere proximity. Now the earlier writers knew this, but lacked tools sufficient to explain different modes of presence without getting caught up in the distinction between spirit and matter, body and soul. What we can learn from their attempts to express presence is to avoid the extremes of speaking of presence as purely spiritual or purely material, and, again, the best way to do this seems to be to discard the distinction itself.

To return to where we started: the eucharist is first and foremost a ritual meal, a sharing in the life, death and resurrection of Jesus the Christ by the community founded in his name. It is something one does, not something about which one talks. No more important statement can be made about the Lord's supper. It is a celebration, a way of life; a celebration of a way of life. All the many writers we have discussed agreed on that. They were eloquent on the necessity of living the eucharist, however much they may have disagreed about how it should be explained. In the end, the best lesson to learn from the great Christians of the past, and the best tribute one can pay to them, and, indeed, the real importance of the Lord's supper, is the living out of promises contained in it. And this living out entails the whole unity that is a human being. It is the living out of the sometimes boring, exasperating, betraying, mundane existence that is a gift from God. The great German theologian Karl Rahner expressed this well:

> Come, Lord, enter my heart, you who are crucified, who
> have died, who love, who are faithful, truthful, patient
> and humble, you who have taken upon yourself a slow
> and toilsome life in a single corner of the world, denied by
> those who are your own, too little loved by your friends,
> betrayed by them, subject to the law, made the plaything
> of politics right from the very first, a refugee child, a

carpenter's son, a creature who found only barrenness and futility as a result of his labours, a man who loved and who found no love in response, you who were too exalted for those about you to understand, you who were left desolate, who were brought to the point of feeling yourself forsaken by God, you who sacrificed all, who commend yourself into the hands of your Father, you who cry: "My God, my Father, why have you forsaken me?", I will receive you as you are, make you my innermost law of my life, take you as at once the burden and the strength of my life. When I receive you I accept my everyday just as it is. I do not need to have any lofty feelings in my heart to recount to you. I can lay my everyday before you just as it is, for I receive it from you yourself, the everyday and its inward light, the everyday and its meaning, the everyday and the power to endure it, the familiarity of it which become the hiddenness of your eternal life.[3]

Notes

1. Whose History Is It?

1. *Die Eucharistielehre der Vorscholastik* (Paderborn, 1936), pp. 290–406.

2. *Ibid.*, pp. 176–218.

3. *Berengar and the Reform of Sacramental Doctrine* (London, 1935).

4. 2nd. ed. (London, 1974), p. 1390.

5. "Church History as a Branch of Theology," *Church History in Future Perspective*, ed. by Roger Aubert (Concilium 57) (New York, 1970), p. 87.

6. "Eucharistic Celebrations Without Priests In the Middle Ages," *Worship*, vol. 55 (1980), pp. 160–68.

7. "The History of Theology: Fortress or Launching Pad," *The Sources of Theology*, edited by John P. Boyle and George Kilcourse, The Catholic Theological Society of America Proceedings, vol. 43 (1988) (Mercer University Press: Macon, Georgia, 1988), pp. 19–40.

2. The Origins of Diversity: The Early Church

1. Daniel J. Sheerin, *The Eucharist* (The Message of the Fathers, vol. 7) (Michael Glazier: Wilmington, 1986), pp. 29–30.

2. *Ibid.*, pp. 27–28.

3. *Ibid.*, p. 34.

4. *Ibid.*, p. 29.

5. *Ibid.*, pp. 37–38.

6. *Ibid.*, p. 265.

7. *Ibid.*, p. 249.

8. *Ibid.*, p. 252.

9. *Ibid.*, p. 188.

10. *Ibid.*, p. 264.

11. *The Letters of St. Cyprian*, translated by Sister Rose Bernard Donna, C.S.J., The Fathers of the Church, vol. 51, The Catholic University of America Press: Washington, D.C., 1964, pp. 247–48.

12. *The Letters of St. Ignatius of Antioch*, translated by Gerald G. Walsh, The Fathers of the Church, vol. 1, CIMA Publishing Co.: New York, 1947, p. 109.

13. *Ibid.*, p. 104.

14. Sheerin, p. 35.

15. *The Apology of Aristides the Philosopher*, translated by D. M. Kay, The Ante-Nicene Fathers, vol. 9 (Charles Scribner's Sons: New York, 1925), pp. 276–77.

3. The Origins of Diversity: The Patristic Church

1. Using the word "fathers" to refer to the writers of this period is a very ancient custom, and unintentionally accurate, since the authors quoted here are all men. Women did play important roles in the early church, but their writings were not the ones which influenced later (and again mostly male) thought on the eucharist.

2. Saint Hilary of Poitier, *The Trinity*, translated by Stephen McKenna, C.S.S.R. (The Fathers of the Church, vol. 25), (The Fathers of the Church, Inc.: New York, 1954), p. 285.

3. St. Cyril, Archbishop of Alexandria, *Commentary on the Gospel According to St. John*, translated by P.E. Pusey, vol. 1 (Rivington: London, 1874), p. 418.

4. Sheerin, *The Eucharist*, pp. 276–77.

5. *Ibid.*, pp. 279–80.

6. *Ibid.*, p. 60.

7. *Ibid.*, p. 78.

8. *Ibid.*, p. 67.

9. *Ibid.*

10. *Ibid.*, p. 95.

11. *Ibid.*, p. 98.

12. *Ibid.*, p. 99.

13. *A Select Library of Nicene and Post-Nicene Fathers*, edited by Phillip Schaff, 1st series, 14 vols. (New York, 1886–1900), vol. 7, p. 168.

14. *Ibid.*, p. 175.

15. Sheerin, pp. 222–23.

16. *Ibid.*, pp. 291–92.

17. St. Gregory the Great, *Dialogues* translated by Odo John Zimmerman, O.S.B., The Fathers of the Church, vol. 39 (Fathers of the Church, Inc.: New York, 1959), pp. 272–73.

18. Sheerin, p. 73.

4. Diversity in Practice: The Early Middle Ages

1. Rosamund McKitterick, *The Frankish Church and the Carolingian Reforms: 789–895* (London, 1977), p. 154.

2. Gary Macy, *Theologies of the Eucharist in the Early Scholastic Period* (Cambridge University Press: Cambridge, 1984), p. 27.

3. *Ibid.*, p. 28.

4. *Ibid.*, p. 29.

5. *Ibid.*, p. 39.

6. *Ibid.*, p. 36.

7. *Ibid.*, p. 37.

8. *Ibid.*, p. 45.

9. *Ibid.*

10. *De sacramentis Christianae fidei*, book 2, part 8. Jacques Paul Migne (ed.), *Patrologiae cursus completus . . . Series latina* (Paris, 1878–90), vol. 176, col. 470. Translation by the author.

11. *De sacramentis altaris*. Edited by J. Morson, Sources chrétienne, vols. 93–94 (Paris, 1963), p. 364. Translation by the author.

12. Edited by the Collegium S. Bonaventurae, 4th ed. (Rome, 1981), p. 293. Translation by the author.

13. *Collectanea in Paulis epistolas*. Migne, *Patrologiae*, vol. 191, col. 1624. Translation by the author.

14. Macy, *Theologies of the Eucharist*, p. 120.

5. Diversity in Decline: The Later Middle Ages

1. Contained in H. Denzinger, *Enchiridion symbolorum*, ed. A. Schönmetzer, 32nd ed. (Freiburg, 1963), #802. Translation by the author.

2. William of Auvergne, *Magisterium Divinale, De sacramentis (Opera omnia*, Paris, 1674, reprinted Frankfurt, 1963), p. 434. Translation by the author.

3. St. Thomas Aquinas, *Summa theologiae*, edited and translated by the Dominican Order, vol. 38 (McGraw-Hill Book Company: New York, 1963), p. 117.

4. Jacques de Vitry, *Historia occidentalis*, c. 38 (edited by John F. Hinnebusch, Fribourg, 1972, p. 240). Translation by the author.

5. Alexander of Hales, *Quaestiones disputatae 'Antequam Esset Frater'* (edited by PP. Collegium S. Bonaventurae, Quaracchi, Florence, 1960), p. 700. Translated by the author.

6. *Commentaria in quatuor libros sententiarum* in *Opera Omnia*, vol. 4, Quaracchi: Florence, 1889, p. 307. Translated by the author.

7. *Ibid.*, p. 308. Translated by the author.

8. For a fuller discussion of the Franciscan critique of transubstantiation, see David Burr, *Eucharistic Presence and Conversion in Late Thirteenth-Century Franciscan Thought*. Transactions of the American Philosophical Society, vol. 74, part 3, Philadelphia, 1984.

9. Lyons, 1518, unpaginated. Translated by the author.

10. Edited by the Collegium S. Bonaventurae, 4th ed. (Rome, 1981), p. 308. Translation by the author.

11. I have copied the translation by Francis Clark in his *Eucharistic Sacrifice and the Reformation*, 2nd ed. (Basil Blackwell: Oxford, 1967), p. 89.

12. *Western Society and the Church in the Middle Ages* (Penguin Books: New York, 1970), pp. 140–41.

13. I have copied the translation by Francis Clark in his *Eucharistic Sacrifice and the Reformation*, pp. 546–47.

14. Quoted by Anthony Kenny, *Wyclif* (Oxford University Press: Oxford, 1985), p. 85.

15. Translation in *Great Voices of the Reformation*, edited by Harry E. Fosdick (The Modern Library: New York, 1954), p. 15.

16. *Ibid.*, pp. 49–50.

17. Quoted by Margaret Ashton, "Wyclif and the Vernacular," *From Ockham to Wyclif* (Basil Blackwell: Oxford, 1987), p. 313.

18. *The Imitation of Christ*, by Thomas à Kempis, translated by Ronald Knox and Michael Oakley (Sheed and Ward: New York, 1959), p. 196.

6. Diversity Denied: The Reformation: Luther and Zwingli

1. Quoted from *Christian Humanism and the Reformation: Selected Writings of Erasmus*, edited by John C. Olin, 3rd ed. (Fordham University Press: New York, 1987), pp. 100–101.

2. Translated by Paul Turner (Penguin Books: New York, 1965), pp. 123–24.

3. Quoted in *The Reformation*, edited by Hans Hillerbrand (Harper and Row: New York, 1964), p. 43.

4. Quoted from *Martin Luther, Selections from His Writings*, edited by John Dillenberger (Doubleday and Company, Inc.: Garden City, New York, 1961), p. 11.

5. *Ibid.*, p. 345.

6. *Ibid.*, p. 283.

7. *Ibid.*, p. 275.

8. *Ibid.*, p. 286.

9. *Ibid.*, p. 284.

10. *Ibid.*, pp. 257–64.

11. "This opinion of Thomas's, being without a basis in Scripture or reason, is so uncertain that it seemed to me as if he understood neither his philosophy nor his logic. Aristotle speaks of accidents and their subject very differently from St. Thomas. I feel we ought to be sorry for so great a man, not only for drawing his views from Aristotle in matters of faith, but also for attempting to found them upon a man whom he did not understand, thus building an unfortunate superstructure on an unfortunate foundation." *Ibid.*, p. 266.

12. *Ibid.*, p. 270.

13. *Vom Abendmahl Christi* (1528), quoted by Herman Sasse, *This Is My Body: Luther's Contention for the Real Presence in the Sacrament of the Altar*, Augsburg Publishing House: Minneapolis, 1959, pp. 151–52.

14. *Letter to Matthew Alber Concerning the Lord's Supper,* in *Huldrych Zwingli, Writings,* vol. 2, translated by H. Wayne Pipkin, Pickwick Publications: Allison Park, Pennsylvania, 1984, p. 135.

15. *Friendly Exegesis, that is, Exposition of the Matter of the Eucharist to Martin Luther,* in *ibid.,* p. 330.

16. See Chapter 3.

17. *Writings,* p. 218.

18. *Ibid.,* p. 134.

19. See Chapter 4.

20. *Writings,* p. 303.

21. Quoted by Herman Sasse, *This is My Body,* p. 293.

22. *Ibid.,* p. 284.

7. Diversity Denied: The Reformation: Calvin, England and Trent

1. *Institutes of the Christian Religion,* Book IV, section 17, paragraph 4, translated by John Allen, Presbyterian Board of Publication: Philadelphia, 1909, vol. 2, p. 528. The version quoted here is the final version of 1559.

2. *Institutes,* IV, 14, 14; Allen, p. 465.

3. Translated by J. K. Reid, *Calvin: Theological Treatises,* The Westminster Press, Philadelphia, 1954, p. 159.

4. "Short Treatise on the Holy Supper," *Theological Treatises,* p. 161.

5. Allen, pp. 596–97.

6. *Theological Treatises,* p. 146.

7. *Institutes,* IV, 17, 24; Allen, p. 550.

8. *Ibid.,* p. 579.

9. *Ibid.,* pp. 550–51.

10. *Ibid.,* pp. 535–36.

11. "The Clear Explanation of Sound Doctrine Concerning the True Partaking of the Flesh and Blood of Christ," translated by J.K. Reid, *Calvin: Theological Treatises,* The Westminster Press: Philadelphia, 1954, p. 285.

12. Allen, p. 565.

13. *Ibid.,* p. 573.

14. Bernard M.G. Reardon, *Religious Thought in the Reformation,* Longman: London and New York, 1981, p. 244.

15. The instructions, slightly modified, were added again in 1662 under pressure from the Puritans.

16. *The Book of Common Prayer, 1559, The Elizabethan Prayer Book*, edited by John E. Booty, The University Press of Virginia: Charlottesville, Virginia, 1976, p. 264.

17. *Ibid.*

18. *Ibid.*, p. 267.

19. Quoted from *The Faith of Christendom: A Source book of Creeds and Confessions*, edited by B.A. Gerrish, The World Publishing Company, Cleveland and New York, 1963, p. 195.

20. *Ibid.*

21. *Ibid.*, p. 193.

22. Quoted by Reardon, *Religious Thought in the Reformation*, p. 302.

23. Session 13, chapter 4, *Canons and Decrees of the Council of Trent*, translated by H. Schroeder, B. Herder Book Co.: St. Louis, 1941, p. 75.

24. Session 22, canon 3, *Canons and Decrees*, p. 149.

25. Session 22, Decree Concerning the Things to be Observed and Avoided in the Celebration of the Mass, *Canons and Decrees*, p. 151.

26. *Ibid.*

27. Session 25, chapter 1, *Canons and Decrees*, pp. 232–23.

28. Session 23, chapter 18, *Canons and Decrees*, p. 175.

29. Session 21, chapter 6, *Canons and Decrees*, pp. 139–40.

30. *Reformation and Counter Reformation*, vol. 5 of the *History of the Church* edited by Hubert Jedin and John Dolan, The Seabury Press: New York, 1980, p. 510.

8. So Now What?

1. Bernard Cooke, *The Distancing of God: The Ambiguity of Symbol in History and Theology*, Augsburg Press: Philadelphia, 1990.

2. "Short Treatise on the Holy Supper" *Calvin: Theological Treatises*, The Westminster Press, Philadelphia, 1954, p. 164.

3. "The Eucharist and Our Daily Lives," *Theological Investigations*, vol. 7, translated by David Bourke, Herder and Herder: New York, 1971, p. 224.

Suggestions for Further Reading

(The following books may be useful for those particularly interested in the history of the eucharist. There are many other fine books on the present theology of the Lord's supper which are not listed here.)

Baptism and Eucharist: Ecumenical Convergence in Celebration, edited by Max Thurian and Geoffrey Wainwright, Wm. B. Eerdmans: Grand Rapids, 1983.

Alexander Barclay, *The Protestant Doctrine of the Lord's Supper*, Jackson, Wylies and Co.: Glascow, 1927.

Ynge Brilioth, *Eucharistic Faith and Practice: Evangelical and Catholic*, S.P.C.K.: London, 1961.

David Burr, *Eucharistic Presence and Conversion in Late Thirteenth-Century Franciscan Thought*, Transactions of the American Philosophical Society, vol. 74: Philadelphia, 1984.

Robert Cabié, *The Eucharist*, vol. 2 of *The Church at Prayer*, The Liturgical Press: Collegeville, 1983.

Francis Clarke, *Eucharist Sacrifice and the Reformation*, Augustine Publishing Company: Devon, 1981.

Bernard Cooke, *Ministry to Word and Sacraments: History and Theology*, Fortress Press: Philadelphia, 1976.

Bernard Cooke, *The Distancing of God: The Ambiguity of Symbol in History and Theology*, Fortress Press: Philadelphia, 1990.

Robert Daly, *The Origins of the Christian Doctrine of Sacrifice*, Fortress Press: Philadelphia, 1978.

Joseph Jungmann, *The Mass of the Roman Rite: Its Origins and Development*, 2 vols., Benziger Brothers, Inc.: New York, 1951–55.

Living Bread, Saving Cup: Readings on the Eucharist, edited by R. Kevin Seaholtz, The Liturgical Press: Collegeville, 1982.

Gary Macy, *Theologies of the Eucharist in the Early Scholastic Period*, Clarendon Press: Oxford, 1984.

Joseph Martos, *Doors to the Sacred: A Historical Introduction to Sacraments in the Catholic Church*, Doubleday and Company, Inc.: Garden City, 1981.

Kilian McDonnell, *John Calvin, the Church, and the Eucharist*, Princeton University Press: Princeton, 1967.

Nathan Mitchell, *Cult and Controversy: The Worship of the Eucharist Outside the Mass*, Pueblo Publishing Co.: New York, 1982.

Joseph Powers, *Eucharist Theology*, The Seabury Press: New York, 1967.

Joseph Powers, *Spirit and Sacrament: The Humanizing Experience*, The Seabury Press: New York, 1973.

Willy Rordorf *et al.*, *The Eucharist of the Early Christians*, Pueblo Publishing Co.: New York, 1978.

Herman Sasse, *This is My Body: Luther's Contention for the Real Presence in the Sacrament of the Altar*, Augsburg Publishing House: Minneapolis, 1959.

Edward Schillebeeckx, *The Eucharist*, Sheed and Ward, Inc.: New York, 1968.

Daniel J. Sheerin, *The Eucharist*, (The Message of the Fathers, vol. 7) Michael Glazier: Wilmington, 1986.

Geoffrey Wainwright, *Eucharist and Eschatology*, Oxford University Press: New York, 1981.

George Worgul, Jr., *From Magic to Metaphor: A Validation of the Christian Sacraments*, Paulist Press: New York, 1980.

Index

Page numbers in *italic print* refer to glossary entries.

180, 181, 184, 186, 188, 189, 190, 191, 192, 195

Roman Empire, 17, 18, 37, 39, 44, 60, 64, 65, 67, 68, 97, 132

Rome, city of, 27, 35, 36, 37, 38, 39, 42, 58, 60, 62, 63, 64, 66, 67, 68, 77, 96, 103, 131, 133, 138, 142, 143, 173, 186, 204, 205

Rupert of Deutz, 79, *100*

Sacramentum, 57, 79, 80, 85, 86, 87, 90, 111

Sacrifice, 16, 17, 20, 21–22, 27, 29, 33, 46, 57, 93, 104, 114–116, 118, 126, 129, 143, 146–147, 160, 163, 177, 201, 205, 209, 210

Salvation, 15, 16, 20, 23, 24, 25, 29, 48, 49, 57, 71, 73, 76, 78, 79, 80, 81, 82, 83, 85, 87, 91, 116, 120, 136, 144, 146, 147, 148, 151, 154, 162, 166, 167, 179, 191, 194, 195, 196, 197, 199

Scotus, John Duns, 112–113, 114, 128, *132*

Seminary, 179, 183

Seymour, Jane, 184

Simmons, Menno and the Mennonites, 169, *188*

Sixtus IV, Pope, 118

Somerset, Duke of, 170, 184

Southern, Richard, 118

Strassburg, 115, 156, 157, 161, 168, 171, 183

Substance, 24, 41, 77, 78–80, 81, 105–110, 111, 113, 120, 166, 174, 177, 194, 195, 196

Syria, 35, 65, 66

Syrian Jacobites, 65

Taborites, 124

Tertullian, 19, *36*, 39

Tetzel, Johann, 142–143, 158, *159*, 178

Theodoret of Cyrrhus, 47, 49, 65, *66*

Thirty-nine Articles, 9, 12, 172, 173, 174, 184, 186

Thomas Aquinas, 9, 75, 101, 103, 104, 105–109, 110, 111, 112, 113, 128, 130, *133*, 138, 149, 166, 205, 206

Transubstantiation, 11, 81, 84, 104–108, 110, 112, 113, 114, 120, 121, 125, 128, 131, 133, 143, 149, 162, 166, 170, 174, 177, 195, 205

Trent, Council of (1545–1563), 9, 12, 106, 114, 133, 135, 161, 175–180, 181, 186, 187, 207, 208

Tübingen, University of, 115, 131, 158

Urban IV, Pope, 126, 131

Utraquists, 120, 124

Vandals, 60, 62, 68

Vatican, 151, 157, 175

Vatican, Second Council of (1962–1965), 9, 188

Vikings, 73, 74, 92

Von Bora, Catherine, 145, 158

William the Conqueror, 99

William of Auvergne, 104, *134*, 205

William of Ockham, 165, 206